For Mary Carras
   with fond regards
         Jagdish Kapur

July 25, 1982
Washington D.C.

INDIA—AN UNCOMMITTED SOCIETY

...Kapur speaks with force and authority. Whether or not one agrees with his powerful thesis, his is a voice that should be heard on both sides of the North-South line.

—*Alvin Toffler*

India
An Uncommitted Society

J C Kapur

VIKAS PUBLISHING HOUSE PVT LTD

VIKAS PUBLISHING HOUSE PVT LTD
Regd. Office: 5 Ansari Road, New Delhi 110002
H.O. Vikas House, 20/4 Industrial Area, Sahibabad 201010
Distt. Ghaziabad, U.P. (India)

COPYRIGHT © J. C. KAPUR, 1982

ISBN 0-7069-1878-9

1V2K6412

Printed at Roopak Printers, K-17, Navin Shahdara, Delhi 110032 (India)

Author's Note

Writing this book for me has been a process of self-realisation and many persons have contributed to this process, either through their writings or through personal contact, or both. But behind all this has been the invisible but towering presence of contemporary leaders, dreamers, and thinkers like Gandhi, Nehru, Aurobindo, Vivekananda and Ananda Coomaraswamy, who inspired me to sustain some of the idealism and hope. This presence has continuously reminded me of the realities of the world and of India with its roots in the distant past, concern for eternal values and a strong sense of continuity manifested in its arts, mythology, culture, social institutions and its needs for modernity.

I have had the unique opportunity and privilege of exchanging my thoughts with many persons representing a variety of disciplines and areas of concern and widely differing viewpoints. Some of these friends have been quoted in this book. I would particularly like to express my gratitude to Alvin Toffler, Buckminster Fuller, Yona Friedman, Patrizia Norelli-Bachelet, Sham Lal, Amaury de Riencourt, Ivan Illich, Edward Goldsmith and Orville Freeman.

The assistance of Trevor Drieberg in reading the manuscript and making valuable suggestions and Vinod Chugh in typing and arranging it with meticulous care is gratefully acknowledged.

My wife Urmilla made a significant contribution in putting up with long periods of withdrawals and frequently cutting my dreams down to size.

New Delhi   J. C. KAPUR

Contents

INTRODUCTION 3

PART ONE
1. *The Future of Humanity* 13

PART TWO
2. *Crafts to Consumerism* 65
3. *Energy* 114
4. *Power Centres* 152
5. *Uncommitted Societies: Pace-setters of Tomorrow* 166

PART THREE
6. *India—An Uncommitted Society* 197
7. *Three-Tiered Development* 217

*Dedicated
to the
Children of India
with the hope that they will create
the twenty-first century of their dreams*

INTRODUCTION

Introduction

The past, the present and the future are one continuous chain, the Upanishads say. Individual actions may seem important or significant, but the forces of history and continuity determine the shape of events. Individuals or nations may appear to take correct turns at the crossroads of history and become great, or take a wrong turn and enter blind alleys.

But in reality it is the accumulated compulsions of the past which push nations towards their future, preordained not because of the stars but in terms of continuity and the interconnectedness of events and phenomena. Whether we look at the frontiers of new sciences or seek images of the future through enhancing human awareness, the message of human physical limitations and supremacy of human consciousness come loud and clear.

We are the cause of our own misfortunes, and our pessimism is born out of our own excesses. The world around us is an image of our own minds. Insecurities, born out of injustices of which we are the instruments, are amplified thousandfold through the communication networks and are sending negative vibrations in all directions. This has numbed our faculty to reason. Every one of our actions is directed towards the fulfilment of a death wish, and every world event its manifestation.

The human cycle does not stop. The human race is condemned to perpetual change. And all change is the continuation of and evolution from human suffering and excesses. It will come with the pace that we have set ourselves and its dimensions will be determined by the extent to which we have drifted away from the cosmic phenomenon in all its physical, mental and conscious manifestations. Those who are not aware of the total reality are in a state of declared and continuous war against one or another aspect of reality and are thus unable to comprehend their past, present and future.

This is not an exercise in futurology or prophecy but an attempt to analyse the forces which have made our world what it is today. As few ever learn the lessons of history, it is easier to discern and draw conclusions from the processes of discontinuity, and the way nations mortgage their abilities for corrective intervention and continue on the path of illusion that prosperity will come through excesses and peace through war.

Consequently, it is an assurance that problems will seek their own unpleasant solutions and processes of evolution their own direction. More and more nations and people are led into the consumerist wilderness, burning the bridges behind every step they take and closing their options for escape into sanity. The message to friend and foe alike is: Follow us, abide with us, we shall not perish alone.

But due to the relentless historical processes, the arriving new age will belong to those whose options for the future are still open, whose retreat to the crossroads and search for new directions is only a short distance, whose commitments to the much-trodden path to consumerist utopias are relatively limited. The signs of regression of the high consumption civilisation are too obvious to be missed. If the emerging nations choose to project the processes of age-old continuity and within that frame strive for a new sustainable human order, the 21st Century will belong to them.

Technology is only an initiator of change and contributor of multipliers to economic processes. Continuous technological change has been one of the basic foundations of consumerism, but when this does not keep pace with productive processes even minor innovations or product face-lifts are ruthlessly projected as technological change through communication networks so as to preempt a larger share of market from competitors.

Such promotion invariably has consequences far beyond the market place. It continuously prompts a psychology of consumerism and waste. The cumulative effect of such techniques on a broad spectrum of the social system often creates disturbances of considerable magnitude, leading up to a call to arms in the world system, with the loudest call from those in a state of greatest crisis.

Exercises in futurology lead into blind alleys, and the art of prophecy, like that of Nostradamus of the Middle Ages, takes over to cajole and frighten believers and non-believers alike into new images of make-believe.

Through continuous manipulation, the economic phenomena have developed hardened arteries and immunity to known remedies. While changes in technology are bringing about widespread changes in the organisation of production, distribution, communication and transport, a change of the dominant energy source is rendering obsolete entire techno-economic infrastructures and introducing profound structural changes in the organisation of societies and the balances of power.

We are seeing the spectacle of a retreating industrial, technological, consumerist civilisation. The seeds of all this were sown centuries ago, when human consciousness was separated from man the creator. Man the innovator is thus unable to comprehend the consequence of his unidimensional creativity and the exploding foundations on which he built the edifice of his future. He cannot find solutions to problems outside his frame of vision and comprehension.

Creativity is therefore irreversibly launched on the destructive path of the fourth stage of consumerism under the illusion of a protective umbrella of nuclear weapons. Those who have such instruments are feeling insecure from their ability to inflict multideaths on every living organism. And for those who lack such instruments no cost is high enough to acquire them to increase the order of magnitude of their disorderly and destructive, but otherwise minuscule, power.

The greater the strength of a power centre and its commitment to the present, the greater the fossilisation of the awareness and intellectual capacities of its leaderships, and consequently the lower their manoeuvrability to retreat from the suicidal path. Not only are they destroying themselves but they are threatening others into submission, corrupting their leaderships into accepting the status of front-line suicide squads for the protection of their own interests. But they know not what they are doing.

We have already crossed the threshold into a new world. The history of the last two decades of the 20th Century has already taken birth, and this adolescent monster is on the loose. No wonder everybody is running for cover, friends, enemies and wayside spectators all alike. Every action, technological, socio-economic, warlike, has world-wide repercussions, and as the quality of these actions decline and the speed of communication accelerates the more responsive and sensitive observers can see and feel what is beyond the horizon.

Those with a lower level of emotional or infrastructural commitment and involvement with the ultimate, consumerist imperatives have a better hope of escaping the consequences of this colossal drift into oblivion. Such countries may have more to do with the contours of this new world. For them it is not a matter of retreat but of reorientation, not first to destroy and then build but to plan and build differently.

The conclusions are obvious for developing societies. They must either establish techno-economic complementarity with systems of high consumption and high waste and thus hold on to the illusion that the super-prosperity of the rich will lead to their own affluence, or to chart a new course which is not wasteful, less destructive of the environment, which will relate to the real human needs and to the times and not subvert the innovative capabilities of the large mass of the people.

The 20th Century techno-economic and human techniques of exploitation are far more sinister than 18th and 19th Century colonialism. The contours of colonial exploitation are being retained through unfair conditions of trade and generation of surpluses. As the abilities of the powers to do so within the existing environment is receding, violence and covert action are becoming the instruments of techno-economic policies.

The institutional framework which determines the condition of the affluent technological societies has developed serious cracks and is unable to contain the disorderly movement of the techno-economic processes. The high-energy, high-technology infrastructures are falling apart, because as energy costs cross the threshold of economic viability the economic system shrinks.

The need for new energy sources would mean the design of new infrastructures and obsolescence and replacement of the existing ones. This means vast social upheavals and the shift of initiative to societies with lower levels of infrastructural commitments to the existing sources of energy. It is not just the energy source that is changing, a way of life is facing extinction.

With high-energy, high-technology converters in fields and factories, increasingly large proportions of the working population are shifted to the service of socially less useful sectors of society. In some countries this sector has reached up to 60 percent of the social system and is heavily subsidised by the sector indispensable for human survival. And when systems get into techno-economic retreat the hundreds of the less useful sectors further accelerate this disintegrative process. In fact, in periods of prosperity the service sector gets the maximum benefits of the system while the advantages to the essential sector are marginal. First, in periods of decline the burdens on the socially useful sector accumulate, and thereafter, when these burdens become unbearable, the entire system retreats.

A relentless search for consumerist utopias, and equally relentless promotion of such utopias for two-third of the world's have-nots has made the institutional, resource and psychic commitment to these processes so complete that any rearrangement outside the existing framework is neither thinkable nor possible. On the other hand, to stem the continuity and decelerate these processes is being increasingly accepted as the minimum prerequisite in reordering more stable arrangements for the future.

But an unplanned deceleration has already started because of the counterproductivity of many economic processes and the socio-techno-economic costs of new technologies outstripping the multiplier effects of such technologies. These phenomena have already effected a broad spectrum of techno-economic processes, thus limiting their further expansion. The consequent search for order within the micro and macro systems through known socio-economic devices and through the acceleration of the very same processes, or through the search for viable new technologies is not bearing fruit.

We are therefore condemned to a perpetual state of crisis in one micro system after another, and this is aggregating itself into grave uncertainty within the national and world systems while we unsuccessfully struggle towards new economic, environmental energy, defence, technology or foreign policies. Experts and micro-level specialists are ceaselessly struggling to devise rational policy structures to be integrated into meaningful courses of action at the policy level.

But there are so many contradictions within one or other policy frame that we end up further aggravating the very same problem we set out to resolve. Most of these policies in reality are the one and the same policy in different manifestations, and these are so closely intertwined that no meaningful change may be introduced in any of them without serious repercussions in the rest.

High-energy and high-technology converters are one and the same thing and we cannot effect changes in one without serious changes in the other, and the ecological consequences of such policies cannot be isolated, as also their economic or military consequence. The educational and employment policies within a system in turn support the imperatives of the consumerist orientation of the techno-economic system. The demand for energy, resources and markets in turn influence the developmental, trade, and consequently foreign policies, of nations or groups of nations.

The manoeuvrability of nations to bring about radical changes in any of the politico-socio-techno-economic parameters of the subsystem thereof without bringing the entire system tumbling down is highly restricted. Therefore, to talk of peaceful transformation of systems, unless this is brought about as a part of long-term perspectives within a rational framework, is moonshine. Every major escape route from these blind alleys is checkmated by visions of disaster.

In the midst of these compulsions, the United Nations is in no position to decelerate the arms race. Nor can the United States alter its energy use pattern or evolve a relational energy policy. It cannot cut back on the arms race or learn a lesson from its recent foreign policy orientation, or contain the military-industrial complex. Even a Labour government in Britain could not bring order into its industrial policies or soften the aggressive posture of its constituents in wage demands.

While there are frequent pullbacks from the precipice through ad hoc crises actions, there is no integrated long-term policy to bring order into a disjointed situation of drift. Over-reliance on crisis management through a show of force or overkill defence preparation are all wasteful, counterproductive and ecological hazards.

You cannot encourage mass action and support dictatorships, propagate consumerism and advocate intermediate technologies. You cannot create high-prestige nuclear clubs and prevent nuclear proliferation, accelerate consumerism and resolve resource crises or contain environmental misuse, or project socialism through consumerist techniques of production, or expect the state to wither away in centralised societies. These and hundreds of other contradictions span the entire world horizon from the smallest micro-system to the international organisations casting their shadow on the entire spectrum of human activities.

Plagued by a multiplicity of choices in the midst of consumerist urges, resources, inadequacies, and an uncertain vision of the future, the developing two-thirds of the world is in an equally great crisis. Its inhabitants are learning the realities of a resource-hungry, directionless humankind the hard way. The post-colonial visions of rapid graduation to prosperity are vanishing as the prices of the diminishing energy and other resources skyrocket to a point hardly within the reach of even the most affluent. With per capita income way below $100, what percentage of the population can live with a price of $30 a barrel of oil or spend over 30 percent of GNP on energy. They cannot reconcile employment-oriented production policies with high-technology consumerist techniques of production.

In the present international evironment very few societies remain immune from such compulsions. Nobody can help anybody else when the potentials of complementarity between different techno-economic systems are diffused in the midst of resource crises, big-power confrontation, national interests, economies of waste and chronic unemployment. Without such complementary relationships, most economies are reaching points of saturation. Through such relationships, with the rising technological level of low-cost economies the high wage, high-cost economies become vulnerable with respect to employment and markets. They also create compulsions in the developing societies to seek employment-limiting technological parity. Therefore, even complementarity has its own problems.

With highly developed societies eating into each other's markets and employment potential, with developing societies seeking to enlarge their employment base and industrial potential, with the visible end of the road with regards to energy and other resources, every desirable move is checkmated or option restrictive. And these disabilities are further compounded by an armament race, power balances and intervention in the affairs of other countries and internal unrest.

The inability of the leaderships of these countries to synthesise the innumerable mutually neutralising variables in a rapidly changing situation has added a dangerous dimension to the world in turmoil. There is hardly a doubt about the declining power centres, nor is there any about the emerging centres. What could be in doubt is the speed at which some of the major power centres will fade away. The world of today is dying fast of its own contradictions.

Any attempt to preserve it through overt or covert action or destroy the integrity and break the resolve of uncommitted societies to seek new ways of life will be an attack on the potential for complementarity of economies and peaceful transformation. The way to the future will be shown by the victims of such aggression and not its beneficiaries.

PART ONE

1. The Future of Humanity

As the earth shrinks, with communication networks interconnecting a village at the foot of the Himalays with another in the Arctic Circle or the Gobi Desert, it tends to unify the thought processes, living habits, consumerist passions, hopes, dreams and concerns of otherwise entirely dissimilar peoples.

Through all the technological advances, whether in the realm of space, energy, communication or biological sciences, man is continuously committing himself to a future through decisions made in the present. Many scientists and innovators accept as certainty man's power within the next century to eliminate famine and disease to stabilise population and control his genetic development. And as this kind of future moves rapidly into the present the desire for an accurate assessment of what is coming, and how this can be controlled in a responsible manner, also grows.

Past Projecting into the Future

The quality of life the present generation enjoys or suffers from is the legacy of earlier generations. So when we talk of the human future today we are in fact commenting on our present abilities to design an adequate future for the generations to come.

Fear of the future is largely due to our lack of confidence in the justice of our cause, the institutions we uphold, the symbols and values we have to offer and, above all, our subconscious awareness of the gross injustice of the order these institutions tend to support and perpetuate. The relative instability of the system—national and international—we live in adds a new dimension to the fear psychosis.

The excessive use of resources and the abuse of environment to maintain indigestive consumer societies at some points and famine conditions at others, both within the national and international system, is another unbalancing factor.

While on one side threats of diminishing resources have introduced exploitative factors and pressures to sustain a consumerist status quo, on the other audiovisual communication networks are prompting economic systems and quick-fix solutions for the urge to produce and consume.

In many ways this is far more dangerous because it is far more pleasant, desirable and habit-forming. It is a symbol of acceptance in the high-consumer clubs. It gives a feeling of power, equality and parity. For the affluent, to retain their superiority and the validity of the system, it results in a much greater effort on the same path. It also means the containment of many more variables, calling for much greater complexity of the system to be operated, and results in much greater vulnerability, and hence much greater commitment to purely protective effort.

The immediate consequence of this is the emergence of an uncertain, insecure, unfair world leading in turn to the emergence of power centres representing identical interests and viewpoints and poised to subvert every international dissent to serve the larger group interest. All regional confrontations, all the aggregating violence, much of the human suffering and waste, owe their excesses to the protection of individual and group as against human interest.

The sacrifices and sufferings of one part of the human race to assure higher material rewards in another part, the price paid in human terms to assure continuity of an existing order of things and the perpetuation of the injustices of the past, are all of no consideration in the one-dimensional approach to man's future.

It is not so much the needs of development and growth and the useful purpose it serves in man's physical well-being that are the source of our present problems, but the conversion and subordination of most human attributes and gifts, including higher consciousness, to the new religion of consumerism with its own philosophy, mythology and rituals that cause our greatest concern. While the gods of religion still adorn the sanctuaries of churches the gods of consumerism have captivated the hearts of men.

The economic system in a consumerist society is premised on the proposition that man's desire for material goods is unlimited and that the demand for these can be self-stimulated. Continued belief and action on such a premise can be ensured only by fostering appropriate social and human values. The relevant value here is material success as a measure of human worth, which sustains and is sustained by an economy geared to the production of goods designed for obsolescence.

The desirability of raising the issue of consumerism in relation to societies where even the most basic needs for survival of most people are not satisfied is often questioned by the elite. What is not realised is that consumerism goes beyond the mere satisfaction of such urgent needs; rather it is essentially directed towards increasing the ability and desire of man to consume. It determines an entire system of values, techniques of production and distribution, educational philosophy and content, strategy for science and technology—in fact, the entire political, social and economic organisation of society.

Three Stages of Consumerism[1]

Consumerism evolves in three stages. In the first it helps accelerate the processes of production and expand the scope of welfare distribution. But it does not stop there. Firstly, the rapid proliferation of capital-intensive techniques of production takes over. Employment becomes less important as the basic consideration all along is to increase production irrespective of its effects on employment. These processes then work like a self-perpetuating positive feedback mechanism, assuring their continuity and the further accumulation of capital-intensive technologies. Demand continues to move ahead of supply, thus assuring a relatively stable milieu—for a time. There are no doubt many periods of adjustment up and down, but the basic thrust is towards higher production irrespective of its effect on capital intensity or employment.

When the stability and continuity of productive processes, and often of the economic system itself, are threatened at short intervals, the second stage of consumerism is ushered in—with a built-in-system of obsolescence of technologies, materials, machines and men. These self-accelerating processes have many inherent limitations—human, technological and social—including static employment, increased disparities and concentration of economic and political power.

The third stage in the development of consumerism begins when the upward spiral begins to destabilise under rapidly increasing production, decreasing employment and the exponential rise in the use of energy resources and the accompanying pollution. As in-

---

[1] J.C. Kapur, *India in the Year 2000*, New Delhi, India International Centre, 1975, p. 4.

creasing unemployment builds up pressure within the system non-consumer elements become the symbols of success in a fast-eroding value system. These elements include massive defence expenditure, new technologies, moon shots, space exploration, three-home, three-car families, and yachts rarely used.

In such a situation consumption of goods becomes the sole function and preoccupation of man. In other words, for the system to survive it becomes imperative to resort to unlimited waste and maintenance of pollution, all of which lead to high inflation, social unrest and the rapid dissipation of resources. This in turn leads to a stage of technological saturation where all the processes become self-defeating and self-neutralising. Further, for the system to survive nations are forced into certain types of corrective actions at frequeut intervals, and the largest rewards go to those who destroy and pollute the environment and squander resources most rapidly. These throw-away cultures have now stretched themselves to the outer limits of endurance.

Corrective actions manifest themselves in many ways, though they are most frequently to be found in the economy. Here one encounters regulated currency flow and income ceilings, all controlled by powerful interests which control the economic sub-systems within societies. Such societies rest on the foundations of many sub-spirals—social, political, economic or technological—where regulation or control of one sub-system causes disequilibrium in others. Economists by themselves are therefore unable to remedy the situation created by high waste, high consumption, high acceleration and multipower-centre societies without bringing the entire system crashing down. For by then the system has developed total immunity to all known remedies.

It is often argued that such a situation cannot arise in controlled societies and these failures are due to the political and economic arrangements within different social systems. Where greed is restrained, anti-social habits curbed and production regulated, it is possible, according to such arguments, to maintain a stable milieu in the process of accelerated economic growth.

This is perhaps true to an extent, so long as societies are in the first stage of consumerism. Once they cross over into the second or third stages and the value system is altered, other imperatives far more powerful than those of political, economic or social regulation, take over. It is then that such controlled societies embark upon the same disastrous course built into the second or third stages of consumerism.

For example, regulated societies, in an effort to build a protective shell while remaining in the first stage of consumerism, have to erect a massive superstructure of waste in defence production. This in turn lets loose within the system the same upward spiral of multiple technologies, production apparatus geared to obsolescence, pollution and waste, all of which are at least of the same magnitude as at the third stage of consumerism in the so-called market economies. Thus at some point in time the controlled system often develop imbalances similar to those of societies in the third stage of consumerism.

Massive pressures build up, necessitating more rigid control of the structure, and the system starts broadening the base of consumer production in a pattern which parallels that of relatively uncontrolled societies. The ultimate orientation of consumer societies, irrespective of the nature of social, political and economic control, irrespective of the priorities in a particular system, therefore tends to approach a similar state vis-a-vis employment, energy and resource utilisation, environmental limitations and, above all, the physical and psychic condition of humankind.

It will soon become evident that difference among societies which have accepted consumerism as their goal will be more of speed rather than direction, more because of the element in time than the content of welfare or the quality of life. An industrial technological society creates its own milieu to succeed. It makes no difference who sends a man to the moon, the organisation and planning that goes into it are identical, and the shock waves which such successes or failures send through such a society at large are also identical.

It makes no difference whether automobiles are mass-produced in Detroit or Moscow, the production techniques are different only to a degree and the differences in social attitudes, if any, also start getting blurred as the penetration of the consumer society increases. The question is not therefore whether we want a consumer society through the socialist planning or through the capitalist system or through a combination of both (as in India). The question is whether we wish to aim for a consumer society at all.

As you accelerate the processes of growth in a consumer society, the ability of a country to meet the challenge of unemployment recedes at the same time. Through thoughtless choice, through the compulsive urges of the elite to succumb to the symbols and values of another era and an age in decline, more and more of the developmental processes are pushed in the direction of the ultimate in consumerism.

It should thus be obvious that so long as accelerated consumerism is the ultimate goal of those who control the vantage points of the island republics of the elites,[2] they have also simultaneously to accept the only road that is open to them, namely the first stage of consumerism with all the limitations, risks, injustices and incentives. If they reject consumerism as the present goal but accept it as the ultimate, they must accept the rigidities of a controlled society to curb the mechanics of the strong consumer elites.

In other words, steps must be taken to curb the broadening spectrum of elitist needs till the minimum needs of the large bulk of the population are satisfied. No moral or ethical rules, no yearning for old cultures and traditions can be sustained in the midst of the forward motion of such processes, and we shall ultimately be catapulted into the rapidly ascending stages of consumerism.

This is the environment in which our images of the human future are taking shape.

Western View

It is not the intention to apply geographical limitations to such views or to state the differences in viewpoints of people east or west of Suez. Nor can such analysis be confined to a Marxian or non-Marxian approach for the reason that there are wide differences within one approach or the other that often in the process of moving away they come closer to their own antithesis.

These differences can no longer be expressed in terms of religion. Firstly, because most religions have had their origin in the East, and in the ultimate analysis (if the conceptual, linguistic and environmental limitations are ignored), we arrive at a common objective —that the only future towards which man can direct his thoughts and actions is one in harmony with ultimate reality. All intermediate or transitory futures are inadequate because of "suffering and death." Most of them accept this future as the divine mode of being.

[2]*Ibid.*, p. 4.

When we talk of differences between the Eastern and the Western view we do not mean racial or regional differences, differences in the scriptures people profess or do not profess, or differences in the gross national product. What we really mean is the urges, motivation, patterns of concern and driving force, which spur individuals, groups or nations to action or inaction.

If this was the only criterion it would be fair to say that all the so-called advanced, affluent and rest of communication-networked humankind is affected by consumerist passion and is at various stages of the disease—from highly contagious to dormant or in the incubation period or at best highly susceptible condition—and only a contact is awaited.

The differences in their condition are largely in terms of the intensity of directed communication, the individual and the societal predisposition, and of course a matter of time. Once nations or people accept one-dimensional development and launch on the road to consumerism, and when such development becomes the driving force in their lives, the differences between such nations are largely in terms of the time they have travelled on the consumerist road. Dissimilarities, if any, are only superficial and usually ritualistic.

Many scientists, technologists, leaders, teachers, saints and seers have for centuries endeavoured to project human fate, dreams, aspirations, hopes and fears into the future. And the value of these assessments depended largely on the perception level of those making such projections.

From Hindu and Arab astrology, the practice of Tarot, and I Ching to the teachings of great religions—all have been oriented towards the future. Present human actions were conditioned on the basis of rewards and punishments in the future, of heaven and hell. Some offered material rewards, others eternal bliss.

Limitations of One-Dimensional Approach

While the perception level of a few in search of the ever-receding Absolute is reaching out beyond the fourth dimension of space-time relations, the consumerist straitjacket is chaining the perception level of an increasingly large number of people to the lower dimensional world. For instance, Ouspensky writes that in the one-dimensional world there is a single line. There will only exist two points, ahead and behind, or just a point ahead. The one-dimensional being would call any change in state of these points as phenomenon, but will be unable to understand the constancy and variability, the duration or brevity, the periodicity or unperiodicity of the phenomenon. The being will not be able to imagine anything outside of this plane. Similarly, for a two-dimensional being, a cube will not exist, but only the square face of the cube in contact with the plane will exist for him. The being will have no idea of the phenomenon outside of the plane.[3]

Ouspensky elaborated this further through the example of a candle and coin.

Let us imagine that a coin and a candle—the diameter of which is equal to that of the coin—are on the plane on which a two-dimensional being lives. To the plane being they will appear as two equal circles, i.e. two moving and absolutely identical lines; he will never discover the differences between them. The functions of the coin and the candle in our world—these are for him absolutely *terra incognita*. If we try to imagine what an enormous evolution the plane being must pass through in order to understand the functions of the coin and of the candle and the difference between these functions, we shall understand the nature of the division between the plane world and the world of three dimensions and the complete impossibility of even imagining on the plane anything at all like the three-dimensional world, with its manifoldness of function.[4]

One-dimensional development satisfies the sensory needs and is largely material development, and all human intellectual and psychic attributes are made subservient to such development. That is why this development is highly unstable and vulnerable. While subject to the laws of the four-dimensional universe it stands on a one-dimensional foundation.

Three-dimensional beings, humans, possess sensation, perception

---

[3]P.D. Ouspensky, *Tertium Organum—A Key to the Enigmas of the World*, Vintage Books, 1970, pp. 51-62.
[4]*Ibid.*, pp. 51-52.

and concepts. The higher animals are two-dimensional and possess sensation and perception, while lower animals like snails possess only sensation and are one-dimensional. To understand the world of three dimensions and develop stable institutions human beings must cease to be two-dimensional.

This is not a recent phenomenon. Human beings were launched on the path of one-dimensional development over half a millennium ago, when the Copernican revolution changed the scale of thought and understanding and the way humans are seen in relation to the universe. That our conception of man's place in the world—its unique observer from a non-central moving platform—was bequeathed to us as an imperishable legacy by Copernicus.[5]

Man thus became the subject and the entire universe, of which he was an infinitesimal part, the object. The social purpose of science primarily became a search for knowledge for the sake of power and control, and that of social science to control human beings themselves.

Descartes, regarded as the father of modern Western philosophy, who influenced the course of modern biology greatly, regarded animals (in Christian tradition) as "engines without will" and asserted that only human beings had "souls." He urged man to abandon his "childlike" dependence on tradition, authority and revelation as basic truth and to assume for himself (as free and autonomous) the responsibility for determining reality and truth.[6] And thus the "reality of the real is determined henceforth as objectivity, as that which is conceived through the subject and for it as something thrown and held over against it."[7]

Now the entire cosmos is disclosed as a kind of picture or image or object for the human subject. Thus Western man assumes divine prerogatives. He tries to make himself God.[8]

The universe is revealed as a mathematically quantifiable field of energy present as an object for the subject. Thus Descartes projected man as the "master and possessor of nature." Anything which

[5]Nicholas H. Stenecked, *Science and Society: Past, Present and Future*, Ann Arbor, Michigan, University of Michigan Press, 1975, p. 69.
[6]Paul T. Durbin (ed.), *Research in Philosophy and Technology*, Greenwich, Connecticut, Jai Press Inc., 1979, vol. 2, pp. 245-49.
[7]Martin Heidegger, *Nietzsche II*, Gunther Neske, Pfallingen, 1957, p. 129.
[8]Robert Tuckers, *Philosophy and Myth in Karl Marx*, Cambridge, Cambridge University Press, 1972, pp. 1-105.

could not be measured with mathematical precision was considered unreal. And thus began the age of technology—the descent of man and the ascent of material man.

And once man makes himself "the determining ground of all reality, i.e. once he denies the existence of anything transcendent, then what will be the stand of his own component within the world?"[9] Thus modern man, "instead of trying to find his place within the magnificent and awesome cosmos, demands that the rest of nature find its place around the distates of man."[10] And as these processes accelerated man continued to lose contact with the essential feature of his existence, and in the words of Marcuse brought about a state of "happy consciousness."

Man thus becomes insensitive to the crumbling socio-techno-economic structure and

> reflects the belief that the real is rational and the established system, in spite of everything, delivers the goods. The people are led to find the productive apparatus, the effective agent of thought and action to which their personal thoughts and actions can and must be surrendered. And in the transfer the apparatus also assumes the role of moral agent. Conscience is absolved by reification, by the general necessity of things.[11]

This brings us to our present unfortunate state.

> Science has now become a means to strengthen the existing politico-economic situation. Science, by virtue of its own method and concept, has projected and promoted a universe in which the domination of nature has remained linked to the domination of man, the link which tends to be fatal to the universe as a whole.[12]

Now this attitude is permeating modern scientific medicine and human beings are regarded as physio-chemical machines whose different components or organs can be replaced with components with similar functions from elsewhere. But none of these attitudes,

---

[9] Paul T. Durbin, *op. cit.*
[10] *Ibid.*
[11] Herbert Marcuse, *One-Dimensional Man*, Boston, Beacon Press, 1964, p. 79.
[12] Paul T. Durbin, *op. cit.*, p. 166.

whether relating to the physical or biological sciences, which do not relate to the larger universal reality have any permanence. At best, they reach maximum growth and then disintegrate like a biological organism.

As these attitudes draw their sustenance from the socio-economic environment, the apotheosis and broad dispersal of such socio-economic frameworks becomes the key to the prolongation of this disastrous drift in to oblivion. The structure of interests and incentives which held such a system together has stretched beyond the point of resilience and nothing now converges, everything disintegrates. "At the present rate of progression since 1600," Henry Adams wrote in 1905 to Henry Osborne Taylor, "it will not need another century or half century to tip thought upside down. Law in that case would disappear as theory or a priori principle and give place to force. Morality would become police. Explosives would reach cosmic violence. Disintegration would overcome integration."[13]

For centuries the backwash of this development was transferred into a sink—the colonies and the so-called backward countries—and hence it was of no consequence in the larger scheme of things. But now it is moving dangerously close to its fountainhead. By the late 20th Century, through a process of uncontrolled forward drive, this development has been moving towards four-dimensional humans straitjacketed into unidimensional, rapid consumers of goods. Four dimensions of space-time relations have been transformed into a single-dimensional line with points in the past rapidly moving into the future, and human awareness of the other dimensions and perception of themselves in relation to their environments are all merged into their desire for material advancement.

Aftermath of Industrial Revolution

Thus from the industrial revolution till the recent decades of the 20th Century science and technology were concerned more with present conquests than future deliverance, more with the games of power and prosperity than order and direction, more with the game than the rules of the game. The complicating and intensification of the processes of science and technology have brought order and organisation to those small segments of a system which serve the

---

[13]Lewis Mumford, *Art and Technics*, New York, Columbia University Press, 1960, p. 144.

group interest and are essential to the efficient organisation and realisation of the scientific and technological, power, prosperity and prestige objectives of organisations, groups or nations. Classic examples are the efficient organisation behind space shots, the economic prosperity objectives of the Japanese state, nuclear development in China, organisation of the war effort in Vietnam. As Ellul says, "Order and organisation are imposed when a system becomes technical."[14] Without such order and organisation high technology objectives cannot be achieved. But as the system becomes more and more complex it becomes increasingly vulnerable. Dislocation through internal weakness or external intervention of any of the many variables within a complex system results in the breakdown of the entire system or sub-systems.

The breakdown of the American military machine in the Vietnam War, the collapse of the politico-economic and defence system in Iran, the breakdown of the urban metropolis system in the United States of America when their astronauts were landing on the moon, the dislocation of the world economic system with the increases in oil prices and aggravation of a world population explosion through the introduction of new drugs are just a few examples of how complex systems behave when one or more variables get out of control. This will also show that complex systems usually have side effects in other interrelated systems totally out of proportion to the benefits that a sub-system or a group interest may realise through their organisation and control.

Most one-dimensional studies by fraternities of scientists and technologists, planners and economists, mathematicians and town and urban planners and others suffer from this disorientation. Group interests, inherent contradictions within the sub-system, relative state of development of the component within the subsystem, and other interrelating systems and, above all, absence of long-term human perspectives towards which all sub-systems and systems should project, have helped to orient such exercises towards the intensification of the processes of preservation and promotion of group rather than human interests.

Science, technology, material development and the extension of the machines and their allied sub-systems of terror and supporting sub-systems constitute the bulk of the effort in this direction. He

---

[14] Jacques Ellul, *Technological Society*, New York, Alfred A. Knopf, 1965.

who pays the piper calls the tune. But mercifully these studies have suffered from the vulnerability of the very same processes, segments of sub-systems and systems which they seek to project into the future. If all else is under control the human element becomes the constraint. These one-dimensional studies representing specific aspects of human knowledge, often interact and interrelate within limits, but they continue merrily on their parallel, upward, downward or forward march to serve the ends of material development which all else is expected or designed to subserve.

The Finger and the Moon

Says a Buddhist proverb:

When a finger points towards the moon
Only a fool looks at the finger.

Humankind's exclusive commitment to consumerism has thus proved one of the principal causes of our problems. Our compulsive march towards acquisition of everything on earth, and now in space, and what its accumulated capital of resources and energy can provide at the fastest possible speed, to prop up each one of our muscles to feed as many cells of our body as we can reach and to cure each one of our maladies has been the human search and endeavour for many centuries. Each one has been contributing towards accelerating this process, whether through acquisition, example, promotion or invention of newer techniques.

Now that material man has captured the centre of the stage, all other human attributes have become subservient to the satisfaction of proliferating human needs. In this process human society is caught in a triple straitjacket of rising expectations, a broad spectrum of inadequacy of resources, and a Chinese wall of offensive and defensive weapons to control the floodgates of poverty from inundating the islands of prosperity both within nation states and the international system.

All the prognoses of the future are being made in this environment. As material man is in command his future is threatened and the subject of inquiry. Through the various stages of civilised life human beings have chosen their avenues of salvation in accordance with their needs and attributes, social environment and compulsions. Material man has occupied a place of power but has also inherited responsibilities and duties. Many societies were aware of the distinctively superior place of the human psyche and creativity. Thus the milieu remained in balance and distortions were corrected without undue suffering or sacrifice. With the subservience of all non-material attributes, balancing wheels give the appearance of being loaded in favour of material man.

Dream World of Continuous Growth

Undeterred by the discontinuities of the world, the alienation of man from his environment and God, the limitations of resources and the biosphere, Herman Kahn and others continue to build pathways to dream worlds of the 21st Century—of secular humanism, institutionalisation of scientific innovation and continuous economic growth.

These scenarios built around unstable assumptions and one-dimensional extrapolation of the present into the future lose their relevance as rapidly as they are constructed. They do not recognise the vulnerability of the technologies that they project into the future nor the ultimate meaning or goals of the social systems and the *Homo sapiens* behind them and the consequences of alternative courses of action. Obviously, qualitative changes in the social system or biopsycho changes in human beings and their altered relationship with other humans and society do not enter the vast array of growing quantitative or numerical assessments.

Kahn and William Brown state that

> In this dawning phase of a new era, a new plateau of relative material abundance can be predicted as the common lot of mankind. Within the next century current US and European standards of living could almost become a world norm in underdeveloped countries, give or take a factor or two.
>
> Our analysis leads the projections which tend to focus upon a world population levelling out near the end of the 21st century at about 10-28 billion with an average per capita income from $10,000 to $20,000 derived from a GNP of $100 to $300 billion.
>
> Contrary to what the others may say, for all the above $300 trillion of world productivity there will be no shortage of energy resources, food.[15]

[15]"And a Better Prospect for the Future," *Futurist*, December 1975.

Those who have set their sights on continued material growth are undeterred by the prognosis of the prophets of doom. They see man riding the next 500[16] to 10,000[17] years towards his destiny at a speed approaching that of light and on material resources stripped from the moon, Mercury and Mars. They believe that humans will populate space colonies and their life-support system can be built around a controlled atmosphere extracted from iron ore and bauxite.

Space colonists will construct and operate solar energy plants which would pay the cost of operating such colonies and supply cheap and perennial sources of power to the earth. All the materials will of course come from the other plants. Many believe that by the second half of the 22nd Century more people will be living in space than on earth. This and other projections are presented to stem the tide of growing disenchantment with the inherent capacity of science and technology to solve all problems. They assert that the course of natural events is determined by natural science. Russian Communists believe that the course of social events is determined by the laws of social science enunciated by Karl Marx. It is believed that as the natural sciences move on the course set by man, the social sciences will cast aside the hurdles of human limitations. All social events are caused by human actions and they are inevitable for the same reason. They are predictable because social events are determined by the known laws of social science.

More with Less

Through his well-known dictum More with Less, Buckminster Fuller projects a continued and rising crescendo of human material welfare. But there is seldom more with less. It may appear to be so, but never is. Even when in material terms we appear to be getting more with less the real cost may be elsewhere, in synergetic terms. It may be in material, in energy or in transformations of one to the other, some known and others unknown.

The conservation law of mass-energy says in effect that we cannot get something for nothing. According to the quantum field

---

[16] Burrham Putnam Beckwith, *The Next 500 Years—Scientific Prediction of Major Social Trends*, New York, Exposition Press, 1967.
[17] Adrian Berry, *The Next Ten Thousand Years*, London, Jonathan Cape, 1974.

theory we get something for nothing, but only for about a thousand trillionth of a second. Before we can really establish costs in a social system we have to evaluate the elements which are being traded off to achieve one-dimensional goals in a multidimensional environment. Then of course, there are forces even beyond intellect which provide the physical mechanisms with the insights to raise these to the level of understanding, which in reality is the vital force and not just the physical process of juxtaposition of information or facts which a computer could provide better.

Is this "third eye" the unseen human gaze, the price we pay in getting more with less? Is this the price which takes humankind from the grand vistas of true understanding onto the path of unidirectional inbreeding or straitjacketing of human intellect so as to limit its achievement exclusively to the narrow path of getting more material gains with less effort.

This search for more with less applies only to a very narrow spectrum of human endeavour, and is tantamount to directing all human effort or genius to the single unidimensional task of giving humankind a wide profusion of goods and services, or in other words launching everybody on the path of consumerism. Not only has this process its own inbuilt limitations but in reality we do not get more with less but more with still more.

If the meaning of more with less is that there is no need to change our objectives or our direction and all that we need is to further extend our intellectual search and our strategy, then along with getting more material welfare with less effort we shall also get more alienation, more strife, more terrorism with less effort. Indeed, the path will be open for getting more with less of everything and not just human consumption.

The very instruments of knowledge, understanding and techniques to achieve more with less also become increasingly more vulnerable in the process of satisfying our passion for consumerism. And when the obvious cost appears to be less than the satisfaction we achieve, the lust for greater satisfaction increases in synergetic terms. This is not just a matter of outer pollution but a clear case of inner devastation.

The last half-century witnessed the rapid acceleration of techno-economic processes through large mutiplier effects of new technologies. These knowledge inputs created the synergetic effects in providing more with less. The same processes of acceleration have altered the energy use pattern, substituted human labour with machines and human mental processes with cybernetics. But that little something which sparks great inventions also sparks social revolutions and provides new social frameworks to contain the excesses of technological and post-industrial societies.

The question is whether the continuing race to achieve more with less brightens and intensifies this spark or makes it dull and unidirectional. In our search for more and more with less and less increasingly large sections of the human race are deprived and often made totally unaware of this spark which distinguishes them from the other species. Even patterns of human concern are being metamorphosed into a blindfolded acquiescence with the symbols and values of a consumerist age.

The battle for more with less is also being lost on the unidimensional material plane where it belongs. Many techno-economic processes, on which the foundations of affluence rest, are rapidly becoming counterproductive. Not only are the multiplier effects of new technologies being neutralised in economic terms but in many instances a new phenomenon of technological reversal is causing the aggregation of mounting socioeconomic costs of the very same processes.

The physical and material being is limited by space and time. The vast dimension of knowledge imposes its own limitation on human capabilities. It is the limitlessness of the human psyche, or human spirit or spark or vital force, that has determined the outer limits of human achievement and awareness. Through a strange process we have set the human race on a course of making the limited into the limitless and directed the vast ocean of knowledge to serve the unidimensional purpose of consumerism. We cannot make the limited limitless, but we have placed our limitless self in a small unidimensional mould.

As our confidence in the institution that we uphold recedes further the promotion of material man, limited man, consumerist man is assuming vicious proportions. All other human attributes are eclipsed under the shadow of the consumerist machine.

And now the dispossessed are also launching on the same path in search of the same illusion towards the same end. All consumerist institutions, irrespective of the path, socialist or capitalist, ultimately end up with the same preeminence of machines over men, of concentration of political or economic power—usually both—and of the devaluation of the human consumer and the apotheosis of the system of consumerism.

Limited Overwhelming the Unlimited

The fundamental challenge facing us today is not how to get more and more with less and less but how to contain the limited from overwhelming the unlimited human attribute and thus keep the lights of the future from dimming. How can we evolve human institutions which can contain the greed of a few in the interest of the many and at the same time to enlarge human awareness to seek ever higher stages of evolution? When human hunger is satisfied and material burdens contained human consciousness enlarges and the search for new direction comes within human reach.

But when all the human attributes, physical, intellectual, aesthetic and spiritual, are made subservient to a single objective, increasing human consumerability beyond need and beyond reason, and there is an unending search of unidirectional techniques to get more with less, the evolutionary processes are barred or limited to the very few. This would lead to the moronic reversal of the human psyche. Only those who do not carry a material burden can aspire to be complete human beings. They alone can attain intuitional unity, the levels of awareness which illuminate all human thought, emotions and imagination.

We human beings are trustees or bearers of cosmic intentions, a creative ascending spirit. But we have been pushed into the blind alleys of so-called human progress. It is not my intention to exalt mysticism or denigrate the search for systematic knowledge, because that would reduce the rich variety of human experience.

> All search for knowledge is a form of prayer. Breaking through manmade social barriers, congregational prayer serves a better end than the self-absorbed ecstasies of the lonely hearts ready for the journey of "the alone to the Alone."[18]

Unfortunately, modern scientists send their benedictions from their ivory towers of science in the form of new knowledge, often not caring for the ends this knowledge serves. As the intermediary

[18] The poet Mohammed Iqbal.

processes of greed load the human spirit with burdens leading to a reversal of the evolutionary processes we are far removed from the Omega Point of Teilhard de Chardin.[19]

What we need to seek is change of attitude to experience. The chance of creative unfoldment never ceases, but we are bringing it to a halt through our servitude to the objects of our own creation. We have just taken to heart our machine-made children but allowed our state of mind to be transformed to serve the plans of others. If only we could open our hearts to the winds of change, discriminate between appearance and reality, clear the cobwebs which are holding us as they would a spider, we would then see that there is no permanence in this fast-changing world. To seek the truth we shall have to seek in deeper waters.

The tragedy of science and of our search for more with less has been that it has robbed us of faith in the future. We have been alienated from the depth of our being, our inner energy, our spark, our awareness are all being transformed into an energy which just produces goods, and such symbols and values as will make these acceptable, beyond our needs and as crutches for our ego. We need loyalty to higher values, to the higher nature of man, not to centres of political and economic power, loyalty to our true restless creative selves, our own ideal nature, and not to the drifting, impermanent, transitory, illusionary shadows of baser self that is human greed.

We have to seek self-renewal, to build new beings, and in this search we shall witness the rise of a new colossus, a profoundly new human state and not delinquent children or the different manifestations of the same consumerist machine which both the beneficiaries and the rabble-rousers of the world wish to promote.

The Club of Rome's *Limits to Growth*[20] and Alvin Toffler's *Future Shock*[21] and scores of similar works gave well-deserved shock treatment to victims of the consumerist hypnosis. Through a devastating attack on human greed, carelessness and sense of irresponsibility towards the environment, Rachel Carson crossed the line

---

[19] Teilhard de Chardin, *Future of Man*, London, Collins, 1964, p. 122.
[20] Denis Meadows and others, *Limits to Growth* (A Report to the Club of Rome), New York, Universe Books, 1972.
[21] Alvin Toffler, *Future Shock*, New York, Random House, 1970.

of single-dimensional development in *The Silent Spring*[22] and added one more dimension to the blindfolded reach of humans for an illusion they call the future.

The 1970s have been a period of reassessment, of soul-searching, a reappraisal of interests and strategies. The affluent and the starving are both bewildered by the intensity of promotion of consumerist utopias and space colonies at one end and of the fear of an uncontrolled drift towards a human holocaust at the other. Perhaps this intensity is the outcome of a protective urge for a dying utopia, or it is the need for loud shouting to be heard above the sound levels of the consumerist machine.

Club of Rome Reports

The reports to the Club of Rome on the predicament of mankind opened with *The Limits to Growth* by Dennis Meadows in 1972. This was a warning to man's compulsive drive in search of more and more material goods. With all its limitations the report sounded highly provocative to the promoters of consumerist utopias in the affluent and developing countries and created a sobering effect all around. It has in effect set in motion alignments of interest groups to acquire control of and protect available and potential resources. At the same time, a protective veneer has begun to appear so as to stretch their use and benefits to the national states to the maximum extent possible. Many in the developing world considered *The Limits to Growth* as a plot to decelerate the process of economic growth of the poor, while extending the acquisition or use of the resources by the affluent.

The second report to the Club of Rome, *Mankind at the Turning Point* by Mihajlo Mesarovic and Eduard Pestel,[23] was a computerised invitation to reason. The computer models make many assumptions based on experience, past and present. But the most chronic and dangerous maladies in the complex world system such as unemployment, alienation, system vulnerability and human limitation do not and possibly cannot find a place in them.

If mathematical precision could determine human actions and

---

[22]Rachel Carson, *The Silent Spring*, Greenwich, Connecticut, Fawcett Publication, 1962.

[23]Mihajlo Mesarovic and Eduard Pestel, *Mankind at the Turning Point* (the Second Report to the Club of Rome), New York, E.P. Dutton, 1974.

feelings, the second report will be an important contribution, but its scope and value are limited largely to what material man in search of a mirage should not, rather than should, do. Apart from this negative approach, the underlying assumption that mankind has accepted, and with some modifications and limitations can achieve, goals on the path already traversed by affluent societies must be considered both presumptuous and unreal.

The report spotlights the consequences and hazards of uncontrolled growth and many international relationships, but the basic issues which plague mankind, the crying need for social reforms and the hundreds of millions of unemployed who will roam the world in search of work and food, and whose thoughts and actions as in the past will condition the world of tomorrow, are fringe issues in the mathematical models. Problems have been posed in terms of material man in the crisis of affluence and not man in terms of his needs. The emergent forces in a fast-moving world receive scant attention.

The third report to the Club entitled *Reshaping the International Order* by Jan Tinbergen and his associates[24] makes attempt, in their own words, to translate into politically feasible first steps the courses of action which the international community might choose to take in the direction of a more human and equitable international order on the basis of knowledge currently available. There is a welcome realisation that exclusive pre-occupation with the economic question in the past had contributed towards accelerating many of today's problems. The authors have endeavoured to evolve the various stages through which the relations between the rich and the poor could be transformed in an increasingly interdependent world. There is indeed a refreshing tilt towards the needs of the poor.

The report is largely a reformist document, and its most obvious underlying assumption is that as a result of the shock treatment the world has received in recent years through various reports, and the politico-socio-economic crisis facing most of mankind, the time is now ripe to rearrange the existing institutional framework of the national states, of the instruments of regional coope-

---

[24] Jan Tinbergen and associates, *Reshaping the International Order* (a report to the Club of Rome), London, Hutchinson, 1977.

ration and world organisation such as the United Nations and many agencies.

The beginning of social justice will have to arise in the mind of man, in the smallest of social units within national states, before its logic will permeate the international community. Where the corrective thrust for such a development will originate is difficult to predict, but it certainly will not begin in an environment where the prosperity of increasingly large sections of communities within national states is being linked with the proliferation of more and more sophisticated weapons of destruction.

In a rapidly changing situation, the problems and perspectives are also undergoing change. A time frame for change therefore becomes equally important if it has to be achieved within an organisational structure or the modifications in such a framework are to have any relevance. A major theme of this report is that "the existing international system requires fundamental structural changes, not marginal reforms."

This is precisely where the international system failed to react in the postwar period, thus leading to the aggravation and accumulation of many problems we face. The power blocs have been trying to shape the world in their image, not to build it in that process but to transform it in such a manner as to support the pillars on which their own world rests. All they have been able to hold is the tail of the elephant, while it ambles, runs or sprawls in its own pattern, but much more restless, much less under control. Equity and reason have very little to do with the international system, and to expect to transform it in a period of world-wide political conflict, grave economic crisis and social unrest is just not practical politics, especially when those who are expected to take the initiative are themselves in the gravest of predicaments in recent times.

The most recent of the reports to the Club is on the *Goals for Mankind* by Ervin Laszlo and others.[25] A large group of world-wide collaborators have endeavoured to chart the course of human concerns in different parts of the world. A detailed examination of the goals of different countries, regions, groups that emerge out of this presentation spotlights the fact that as you raise the goals

---

[25] Ervin Lazlo and others, *Goals for Mankind* (a report to the Club of Rome), New York, E.P. Dutton, 1977.

to a philosophical, human or abstract level a unity of purpose and a commonness of approach become obvious. But then we have already lived through the eras of religious crusade, forced conversions and hundred-year wars. It is the economic man who dominates and is in a crisis. The economic goals are in conflict, and are becoming increasingly more so.

If there was confidence that the economic goals are even partially attainable, that the affluent can retain their economic viability and stability within the socio-economic systems they profess and the resources capital of mankind and the deprived can meet their minimum basic needs, through transfer of resources or through their own effort within an acceptable time frame, *Goals for Mankind* would be a very valuable contribution to reaching a wide consensus and establishing a common base for world-wide development. There are many more conflicting elements in the economic goals than are obvious.

Even more than goals, the techniques that go into the realisation of national, regional and group goals have been our greatest problem. For every protective effort to maintain the status quo within a national or international system there has been an opposite reaction to change it. For every interest group there has been a counter grouping to make it redundant. The ultimate consequence all along has been terrorism, disruption and organised force.

In the long-term perspective nothing seems to have worked. Everybody pontificates to everybody else on nuclear proliferation, on human rights, on civil liberties, on removal of social disparities, but they do nothing about these vital issues in their own national states. The credibility concerning the economic viability or social justice of a politico-socio-economic system should reduce in almost inverse proportion to the extent of force required to protect such a system from within and without. Otherwise, the unpleasant processes of attrition will proceed simultaneously with the processes of harmony and constructive effort.

In such a situation only those will lose who have something to lose. Many have the power to inflict injury, but no one has the power to reverse the processes which began at the conclusion of the Second World War of liberating the human mind from fear of those who possess greater authority, superior force or live in greater affluence.

To profess the goal that equality should be strengthened when disparities are increasing, that democracy should be strengthened in the midst of racial discrimination, that economic growth should be maximised in the midst of resources crisis, to build a peaceful world in the midst of arms proliferation are all beautiful sentiments to express, but nobody takes them seriously. If there is perhaps a logic of time behind all these contradictions we should say so rather than subvert all our efforts through a widening credibility gap.

No sophistry, no jugglery of figures, no amount of regulation of the means of communication can explain away the mounting evidence of a grave crisis within the politico-social systems built on foundations of waste and force. If behind the smoke screen of a "new world order" we are planning only to perpetuate the injustices of the past, if the racial discrimination and an island of prosperity in a sea of poverty is all that we have to offer for a new world order, if the language of force is to be the only instrument to determine the realisation of our goals, then all our efforts are a wasteful tragedy, and the sooner the innovators of the new world order realise this the better for mankind.

"In their haste to milch technology for immediate economic advantages, environment is being turned into a physical and social tinder." And as a consequence of this "our sense of continuity and discontinuity is being inextricably embedded in a throwaway culture with its barbie dolls, the paper wedding gowns, plastic containers and paper clothing . . . . the economics of permanence are being replaced by economics of transience."[26] Thus society is heading for an ecologically polluted, spiritually disabling synthetic mirage and is in a state of endless, continuously accelerating mobility. And to citizens this gives a sense of rootlessness, friendlessness, scattered as they are like leaves in a technological storm.

According to Toffler

> Future shock is the distress, both physical and psychological, that arises from an overload of the human organism, physical adaptive system and its decision-making processes or in other words human response to over-stimulations.
>
> In this disease brought about by rapid change man remains in the end what he started off in the beginning, a biosystem with

---

[26]Alvin Toffler, *op. cit.*, pp. 51-73.

a limited capacity for change. Where the capacity is overwhelmed, the consequence is future shock.[27]

Symptoms of this disease have already surfaced in many affluent societies and according to Toffler are "the outcome of continuously accelerating rate of change, largely brought about by fast proliferating new technologies."[28] But what Toffler fails to emphasise is the value system of a society which permits, nay encourages, the colossal misuse of this powerful weapon for not entirely social ends.

The process of rapid change carries within itself the possibilities of quick social readjustment. But when powerful sections of a society develop a nostalgia for the status quo, where technological change is prized but social change is considered taboo, corrective tensions within the system become inoperative or destructive and future shock becomes inevitable.

Unchanging Bureaucracy and the Superindustrial Revolution

Failure of the bureaucracy to meet the needs of rapid change is not just confined to developing societies like India but is becoming an even more serious threat to much faster moving societies like the United States. An imaginative and well-planned forward motion will not therefore be possible unless more rapidly responsive, continuously innovative forms of organisations replace the existing structure. This alone would be an assurance for an even and accelerated development against "the dizzying disorientation brought on by the premature arrival of the future."[29] And for humanising distant tomorrows, Toffler calls for shifting the emphasis from economic activity:

One reason for the lack of imagination of the bureaucracy is that when they think of technological advance they concentrate solely on economic activity. Yet the superindustrial revolution challenges the ends as well. It threatens to alter not merely the how of production but the why. It will, in short, transform the

[27] *Ibid.*, pp. 326, 342, 344.
[28] *Ibid.*, pp. 340-42.
[29] *Ibid.*, p. 11.

very purpose of economic activity. Before such an upheaval, even most sophisticated tools of today's economists are helpless.[30]

With the accelerating rate of change there is no time for decisions to take their leisurely way up and down the organisational hierarchies. This increasingly blurs the distinction between the leaders and the led and downgrades another characteristic of bureaucracy, namely hierarchy. The eclipse of bureaucracy is therefore inherent in any process involving rapid change. Attempts at perpetuating hierarchies can in the long run be disastrous for both developed and developing societies.

Even if Toffler's advice were to be partially successful the very politico-economic basis of the society will change. An urgent need for change and organised resistance to such change are indeed the causes of conflict in many systems.

An integrated systems approach to the problems of societies, an assessment of the social consequence of technological change, and the desirability of taming technologies call for a new design for living which will be dedicated to human welfare in the broadest sense and not just to the maximisation of material needs.

A responsible citizenry which places social needs above personal gain is an essential prerequisite for the success of such an effort. It also requires the commitment and the power of the state to assure the success of these processes of reorientation. This miracle is nowhere in sight. And as Toffler says today increasingly "less and less control over the forces of change are ever greater danger of cataclysmic, man-destroying upheavals."[31]

He therefore advocates a dramatic reassessment of the direction of change and a continuing plebiscite on the type of world people would like to have. But he does not consider the fact that even the democratic processes function through human-controlled mechanisms. Who will control the institutions? Who will formulate the questions for the continuing plebiscite? If popularly accepted institutions need to be discarded, will it be possible through this process? Toffler does not answer many of these questions. Can people at large be expected to make rational and at the same time identical choices? There may be millions of alternatives to choose from.

[30] *Ibid.*, pp. 219-20.
[31] *Ibid.*

Dogmatic adulation and promotion of different socio-politico-economic systems is a major stumbling block in taming technological change. Unfortunately, the overriding considerations of superiority in offensive and defensive weapons has had more to do with the proliferation and application of technologies than the welfare of man. Even if change and technology are guided by a sense of social futurism, the future will remain unpredictable forever. Thoughtless exploitation of new technologies for selfish and ill-considered economic goals will continue to contribute to the chaos.

World Order Models[32]

But before intellectuals can sit together and meditate on world order models they must first endeavour to influence structural changes within their own national states. In the affluent countries it would involve the containment of hyperconsumerism, reckless waste, aggression and intervention in the affairs of others, and of course the armaments race. Developing societies will have to understand that the era of consumerism is fast ending and will have to discard elitist development and institutions which make such development possible. Acceptance of acquisitive and consumerist values by the elites of developing societies, and direct and indirect support to these elites by the affluent nations, has contributed greatly to the emergence of antidemocratic forces and unhealthy developmental trends in these societies. This is also the reason for the development of politico-economic relations which have worked almost entirely to the detriment of capital-poor but resources-rich and energy-rich nations.

All regional or world-wide arrangements in the ultimate analysis reflect the interests of their constituent members, particularly those who are dominant. When such group or national interests take precedence over regional or human interests collaboration or integration in the larger context invariably leads to domination, exploitation and political unrest. And the emergence of satisfactory and stable relations is at best a distant dream.

In any process of restructuring international relations or making

---

[32]Series sponsored by the Institute of World Order, New York:
  (i) Rajni Kothari, *Footsteps into the Future.*
  (ii) Richard Falk, *Study of Future Worlds.*
  (iii) John Galtung, *The True Worlds: A Transnational Perspective.*
  (iv) Ali Mazrin, *A World Federation of Culture.*

world order models the affluent and the dominant bear much greater responsibility. And in dealing with the weaker countries perhaps the most important of these responsibilities is to bring about an atmosphere of confidence and credibility. But unfortunately confidence and credibility have been the most significant casualties in international relations in recent times.

The more recent decades have unveiled so much duplicity that nobody, friend or foe, trusts anybody else any more. The efforts of well-meaning visionaries often get lost behind the smoke screen of inspired and directed propaganda, and footsteps into the future lead into blind alleys.

Disparities and Discontinuities

For over two-thirds of the world's inhabitants life is a ruthless and unceasing struggle for survival, and the main concern of the nation states to which they belong is to develop and stabilise social orders which will provide the shortest route to satisfy their minimum basic needs.

In stark contrast to this, the political, social and economic structures in most affluent nations are built around consumerism, and the main concern of most of these societies is to sustain or assure the continuity of their high-obsolescence, high-waste productive processes. Their interest in the needs of the developing societies, or for that matter in the other affluent nations, is at best incidental to their own main concern. For them, the consequences of altering their present course are far too disagreeable to face.

As the economic crisis mounts and resources become increasingly less abundant, subconscious fears among the people of the affluent nations result in conscious indifference to the basic maladies in their own societies. Even warnings of ecological disaster, economic collapse and the risks of confrontation and war are all ignored to escape somehow the downward spin of the economic spiral.

In this process, their strategies in relation to the poorer two-thirds of the world—whether concerning aid, trade or defence are directed more towards strengthening the bulwarks of consumer elites than participating in the processes of alleviating mass poverty, more towards carving out spheres of influence in the world power game than joining hands in a common endeavour to serve a human purpose, more towards acquiring the resources of the developing nations rather than sharing sorrows.

For developing societies, which are passing through an era of discontinuities and where the age-old institutions are crumbling and new ones have yet to be established, there are many shocks in store. These will not be shocks of abundance but of abject poverty, and also of great disparities which new technologies enlarge and accentuate.

The growing disenchantment with material goals in affluent societies therefore has no relevance in countries where hundreds of millions of people are engaged in a touch-and-go daily struggle for survival. Nor are the many ills that come with prosperity an invitation to developing societies to adopt poverty as their goal and show contempt for economic growth. But all plans for development must look beyond prosperity and work towards human welfare in the universal sense. In this process the poor must avoid the narrow roads to catastrophe of some affluent societies and develop a new social framework which will enable them to contain the discontinuities of today's world from drifting into the nightmares of tomorrow.

To the elite, the major beneficiaries in all processes of economic development, who often become committed to age-old institutions or material goals alone, the present world crisis should be a warning. But such warnings have not so far encouraged processes for equitable distribution and restraint but have in fact set in motion processes for the preemption and control of world-wide resources so that the chill winds of poverty do not extinguish the consumerist passions of the affluent. No wonder therefore that while opting for the lowest plane of existence man has also chosen the most elaborate instruments of self-destruction to prevent himself and his fellow beings from evolving to the next higher plane.

The attempted effort towards organic growth, that is multidimensional growth in which the eventual size of the biological organism is predetermined by the genetic code that governs it, could be applied to the different regions of the world. Global cooperation would offer much better conditions than conflict for all concerned. But unfortunately most visions and intellectual effort of the community, and almost all the debate, concerns the invention, evolution and organisation of techniques to initiate or further accelerate the processes towards higher levels of consumerism.

Reason has been displaced by euphoria or despair or fear, and in this environment the only logic which seems to impress is the logic of force, and a substantial extent of this force is directed towards maintaining the status quo between the strong and the weak, the affluent and the dispossessed. The apotheosis of the beneficiaries of the system, their lifestyle, their love stories have become the mythology of this religion and are projected indiscriminately to encourage and satisfy the craze for a sweet life. Rituals are performed on golf courses and at country clubs, night clubs, late night shows.

A message has gone home to millions of the dispossessed and their leaders that to survive is to possess new technologies and new instruments of power, to develop is to control resources, and to succeed is to subvert. Therefore, it is not the logic or needs of development or the appropriateness of technique desirable in different situations but the game of power, the need for survival and the compulsion of the prevalent value system that determines developmental strategies.

It is a matter of honour which is pushing hundreds of millions of havenots into accepting transplantations of techniques alien to their culture, education and resources and finally putting everyone in a straitjacket of uniformity and placing the imperatives of consumerism above human future. Therefore, all knowledge, instincts, purpose and resources are compressed into a single objective—to serve and expand the social greed for goods. In this task, all the instruments of science and techniques are employed to accelerate the speed of this one-dimensional motion to its ultimate conclusion.

With the addition of the second dimension, which presents the negative or the opposite aspects of one-dimensional development, a state of realisation is beginning to emerge. But even with the inclusion of the second dimension, while human beings will see the consequence of some of their actions, it will be very difficult to understand the complexity of the phenomenon of our world as it appears to us.

Convergence of Consciousness—A Western Solution

A French Jesuit, Pierre Teilhard de Chardin, refused to accept that reflective consciousness—man's greatest gift—was a mere accident thrown up by nature, totally unrelated to the structure of our universe. He endeavoured to integrate this human capacity with the phenomenon of evolution. He detected symptoms in the great scientific, technological and social advances pointing to a rebound of evolution and deep undertow which was to carry us to the full development of a supermankind. Underlying all events, he discerned the same basic trend:

> Progressive unification of mankind, intensification of collective consciousness, birth of socialised mankind, and finally, movement towards the convergent structure of evolution as it seeks out its cosmic centre.[33]

Teilhard's approach thus transcends ordinary technological approaches, placing in human hands a key to the next stage of the cosmic process. He said:

> The sense of man believes in the magnificent future of the tangible world and the Gospel seems to despise it. . .And between the gospels of many orders and the sense of man there is at present a deep rift.[34]

Teilhard believed that although through centuries the East stood for spirit and the West for matter, a new saviour would not arise in the East.

> It was in the refined pessimist solution of the world that the soul of Asia was born and found its expression. In India, with its metaphysical sense of the divine, the invisible is more real than the visible. Realisation of the divine is only possible through relaxation of tension and not its intensification.
>
> The East has not solved the problem of the spirit taken in its complete totality. We would look in vain in that quarter for the dawn to illuminate it. History and experience both insist that it is in the Western direction that we must guide the progress of life. We must know more and must be the masters of more. Individual nations, races and religions, everything will disappear tomorrow which has not today hazarded its soul on the road to the West.[35]

It was not only the dreamer, the visionary and missionary in Teilhard but also many in Asia who believed that the road to the

---

[33] Teilhard de Chardin, *Towards the Future* (translated by Rene Hague), London, Collins, 1975, p. 9.
[34] *Ibid.*, p. 26.
[35] *Ibid.*, pp. 44-45, 141.

material West was the road to progress. All his hopes and aspirations and those of others started to disintegrate within a decade of the end of the Second World War. He had hoped in vain that

> every step in the material organisation on the earth will also mean a simultaneous step in the psychic and spiritual domain to balance, humanise and complete it.[36]

Maybe another Jesuit, Jacques Ellul, was right when he questioned "the vanity to pretend that the monolithic technical world that is coming to be can be checked or guided."[37]

It is hard to predict how Teilhard would have reacted to the dilemma of the West and the resurgence of the East at the threshold of the last two decades of the 20th Century, a few decades after his death. His highways to the future convergence of human consciousness and the tangible material world are littered with the decaying bodies of the victims of polymorphous violence, and where not the rule of law or individual or social mysticism of the East or West but soul of *Homo sapiens* reigns supreme.

Teilhard accepted all knowledge, its proliferation and its products as an essential and inevitable outcome of the evolutionary processes. Western life has instinctively adopted this road, to which it has irrevocably committed itself. The human vision must comprehend the essential features of these processes if the ultimate convergence with superconsciousness is to take place.

But the tragedy is that the continuously disintegrating and fragmenting processes in the tangible world have set in motion similar processes in the human mind. This does not give hope that the energy of the tangible universe and the intensified spiritual energy will reach out towards convergence. And unless there is a miracle—and miracles do happen—every step forward on the material plane today appears to be alienating human beings from their environment, their fellow humans and their God. This phenomenon is being manifested in a hundred different ways between one human being and another, between societies and between nation states. Teilhard however kept his faith

---

[36]*Ibid.*, p. 144.
[37]Jacques Ellul, *op. cit.*

that collective man through self-imposed unification can survive this increasing compression from which there is no escape, only by a higher degree of self-arrangement in his own structure...It would be easier to halt the revolution of the earth than it would be to prevent the totalisation of man.[38]

Through development of a common vision, centralisation or intensification of consciousness can be achieved. The next stage in development would be the spiritualisation of mankind. By this he meant the increasing predominance in the human layer of the reflective (or thought) over automatic reaction. Therefore, to Teilhard, the intensification, the complication and centralisation of scientific and development processes is one of the ultimate stages in the advancement of man and is a natural prelude to spiritualisation before his arrival at the ultimate and self-subsistence pole of consciousness, which would perhaps also be the Buddhist Nirvana or the Hindu Brahman.

The Upanishads remind us that "one comes to be of just such stuff as that on which the mind is set." And if works of art are any index we are not approaching an era of material reintegration through the imitation of divine forms but are merely exhibiting our own disturbed modes of thought. The inaudible sound that art is making audible, the perceptible truths that are peeping through the works of art present images not of spiritualisation but of brutalisation, not of centralisation but of specialisation and disintegration. They do not appear to be converging but drifting into a new kind of synthetic wilderness which corrupts the intellect and deadens the spirit. Everything around is deflating our illusions of progress.

An Eastern View—Branches and Roots

All animate and inanimate objects are subject to the laws of change. The Upanishadic question naturally arises: "Is change itself the ultimate reality or is there an unchanging essence?" The search for this essence has been the permanent foundation of Indian society from the growth of the Indo-Aryan culture. At the lower stages of evolution the appetite for material things could not be ignored. But as a result of experience and evolution people became disillusioned

---

[38] Teilhard de Chardin, *op. cit.*, p. 182.

with the glitter of the outer world and long for an inner calm.

In Hindu thought the desire for material things is not ignored in the lower stages of evolution. As the senses seek material enjoyment their total suppression is not considered desirable. Instead, Hindu thought provides the basis to transform gradually the inclination of the senses, will and mind so as to help in attaining what it calls man's spiritual ends.

Youth had to go through a process of learning and austerity in quest of truth. It was the time to build the foundation of man, a far cry from today's permissiveness and excesses to which youth is subjected. Instead of bringing young people face to face with reality they are led onto the path of operating the instruments of consumerism, alienation, hallucinations and extreme forms of sensual experience.

In the course of his life as a householder and citizen the individual performed his duties within the system. As a result of this experience and observations through life, he moved into the next stage of gradual retreat from the sensate environment and prepared himself for the final renunciation in search of ultimate truth graphically described as the "flight of the alone to the Alone." In this climb to the next step in the evolutionary process he had to leave behind the burdens of a material and sensate world, and he also stripped himself of the ego and desire.

> ...that man as we know him is not a completed being, that nature develops him only upto a certain point and then leaves him, either to develop further, by his own effort or devices, or to live or die such as he was born or to degenerate and lose capacity for development. We must start with the idea that without effort evolution is impossible; without help it is also impossible.[39]

The frequent appearance of such souls as the acme of Indian society demonstrated the health of the societal organism. There were many who chose the process of all four stages of human existence—Brahmacharya, Grihasta, Vanaprastha and Sanyasa. There were some who bypassed the second and third stages and went straight into the life of a recluse. Thus, the evolutionary

---

[39] P.D. Ouspensky, *The Psychology of Man's Possible Evolution*, London, Routledge and Kegan Paul, pp. 10-11.

processes within the individual and society continued while the individual marched along the path of learning and progress towards the attainment of what society considered its ultimate objective.

Whenever society reached a state of imbalance individuals who synthesised within themselves the Indian concept, the Indian way of life, appeared on the scene and provided the corrective thrust to the historical processes. Such individuals, sages and seers, emperors and kings, teachers, innovators, poets and scholars emerged on the Indian scene in a continuous stream and shone like a beacon many times in their immediate environment, often throughout the East and the world.

Buddha, Ashoka, Patanjali, Kalidasa, Shankaracharya, Akbar, Ramakrishna, Vivekananda, Aurobindo, Gandhi emphasised one or other aspect of the Indian personality according to the state of society and the needs of the times. But such emergence always commenced the processes of regeneration and reorientation, not through an aggressive communication system but through human contact, through word of mouth straight to the hearts of the people.

They integrated within themselves the age they wished to project. Their presence also demonstrated that social life was functioning smoothly and the processes of harmony with man's spiritual evolution were ascendant. There were specific norms for the acquisition of wealth according to Dharma. Devoid of spiritual purpose, wealth degenerated into lust for power and consumerist greed, and ultimately became the cause of all misery.

As the community understood that happiness and enjoyment from the material world were illusory, and that everlasting bliss could only be attained in the realm of the spirit, it helped keep social excesses in check. This Indian concept proved the cohesion and vitality of Indian society for many thousands of years.

We know that cause determines effect, yet we seek to establish peace through armament and war. We rob our fellow men and then give away our wealth in philanthropy, expecting eternal happiness thereafter. We accelerate the acquisition of wealth through every means, and then end up in utter ruin. We conquer nature through material resources, and in the end become slaves of matter and destroy nature. These illusions make the present-day world.

The Bhagawad Gita, which enshrines Indian wisdom, states that "those who take shelter in Me ultimately go beyond illusion."

But they must shake off their fetters first to be fit for the higher freedom. And the burdens they may carry in their upward progress must represent the highest inner law of their nature and its aspirations.

Many centuries later Shankaracharya elaborated this path:

> That which is free from duality which is infinite and indestructible, which is supreme, eternal and undying, meditate on this in thy mind. It is directly and immediately experienced without the instrumentality of the senses and the mind. It is consciousness in man that experiences universal consciousness. Ultimate values must be judged by the standard of eternity and not of time.[40]

Moving upward from matter to spirit will always be an arduous task. While individuals can leapfrog, societies must go through the processes of mass transformation. If this process is burdened with consumerist passions, if to sustain this in a higher gear becomes necessary for the very survival of social organisations and an obsession with individuals within society, the human evolutionary processes are barred to serve the imperatives of the consumerist machine.

Overfed consumerist societies cannot be launched on the road to evolution through communication networks on supersonic jets or flashy cars. This is precisely what has been the destructive aspect of one-dimensional development, to blur the vision of the other dimensions and bar the processes of human evolution by sustaining to death only one urge, desire for self-gratification. The sense perceptions fade with time, but compulsive desires for a sensate culture hold on till death and are projected even after death.

The Upanishadic[41] philosophy projects the concept of unbroken consecutiveness of phenomenon, and associate higher knowledge with religious awareness and lower knowledge with various sciences. Buddhists talk about relative and absolute knowledge or about conditional truth and transcendental truth.

According to the Chinese, Tao is the process in which all things are involved and the world is seen as a continuous flow and change.

---

[40]Sri Shankaracharya, *Self Knowledge* (translated by Swami Nikhilanand), Madras, Sri Ramakrishna Math, p. 119.
[41]Fritjof Capra, *The Tao of Physics*, Boulder, Colorado, Shambhala Publications Inc., 1975, p. 27.

In its original cosmic sense it is the ultimate undefinable reality. As such it is the equivalent of Hindu Brahman and Buddhist Dharmakaya.[42]

There is a Chinese saying: "The mystics understood the roots of Tao and not its branches, the scientists understand the branches and not its roots."[43] Through the direct psychic experience of the ultimate reality the mystic bypassed an entire range of intellectual experience and knowledge. Scientific experiences on the other hand only skirted the fringes of Tao, but every branch of knowledge and experience so gained has been exploited to create the infrastructure of welfare in the so-called technological societies of the West. While the search for Tao continues for a few scientists, to the dispossessed East—without even the minimum base for welfare—the roots of knowledge, with all their limitations, are becoming increasingly important.

The language of science has developed many concepts, symbols, mathematics, and experimentation to qualify, classify, measure and analyse rational knowledge. The inadequacy of these techniques in expressing or communicating absolute knowledge or reality is becoming increasingly obvious because such knowledge establishes a correlation between only visible or scientifically observable phenomena.

This narrows our view of life and the infinite universe around us hopelessly. And even with the massive proliferation of rational or scientific knowledge and the emergence of thousands of interrelationships mankind is no wiser today than it was many centuries ago. These limitations cannot be expressed better than through an aphorism of Einstein that "as far as the laws of mathematics refer to reality, they are not certain, as far as they are certain, they do not represent reality."[44]

Physicist and Mystic—Convergence of Concept

Modern physics, beginning with Einstein's theory of relativity, quantum mechanics, particle physics and now quarks, have opened up new vistas in our perceptions of reality. But as our representation of reality is so much easier to grasp than reality itself we tend

[42] *Ibid.*, p. 104.
[43] *Ibid.*, p. 306.
[44] *Ibid.*, p. 41.

to confuse the two and take our concepts and symbols for reality. To get any closer to such a reality the scientist has to become a participant in, rather than a mere observer of, these phenomena.

In this process atomic physics provided the scientists with glimpses of the essential nature of things. Like mystics, physicists were now dealing with the nonsensory experiences of reality and, like the mystics, they had to face the paradoxical aspects of this experience. From then on the models and images of modern physics became akin to those of Eastern philosophy.

> The further we penetrate into the submicroscopic world of subatomic particles, the more we realise how the modern physicist, like the Eastern mystic, has come to see the world as a system of inseparable, interacting and ever-moving component with man being an integral part of the system. Absolute knowledge or transcendental truth is thus an entirely nonintellectual experience of reality, an experience arising in a non-ordinary state of consciousness which may be called a meditative or mystical state.[45]

New and beautiful pathways are being carved through the intricacies of concepts and symbolism in the latest advances in the physical science and the mystical traditions of the East. Many intellectuals are weaving together the relatively less understood unity behind the linguistic, ritualistic and environmental diversity and the wide divergencies in the patterns of concern in the Hindu, Buddhist, Taoist and Zen Buddhist systems and many of their offshoots which in their totality are termed Eastern thought. This eastern thought may make a significant contribution, establishing cross-currents in hitherto parallel streams of thought and may well provide new perspectives in unfolding the deeper mysteries of the physical sciences and our comprehension of the universe.

> Science at the level of subatomic events is no longer exact, the distinction between objective and subjective has vanished, and the portals through which the universe manifests itself are, as we once knew a long time ago, those impotent, passive witnesses to its unfolding, the Is of which we, insignificant we, are examples.

[45] *Ibid.*, pp. 25, 29.

The cogs in the machine have become the creators of the universe.

If the new physics has led us anywhere, it is back to ourselves, which of course is the only place that we could go.[46]

Yet from the experience of many centuries it is hard to predict whether even in the time scale of eternity it will be possible to unfold the ultimate reality through dualism in Western thought and scientific conceptual approximation, experimentation and observations. Indeed, the use of the rapidly proliferating knowledge unveiled in this process for desirable as well as undesirable ends has created an element of grave uncertainty concerning the future of humanity on this planet.

In contradistinction, the central theme of Avatamska (the core of Mahayana Buddhism) is the unity and interrelation of things and events. This is a concept which is the very essence of the Eastern world view and represents one of the most important revelations of modern physics, an energy dance of pulsating process of creation and destruction. As in the *Dance of Shiva*[47] the manifestation of primal rhythmic energy unifies ancient mythology, religious art and poetry. It is indeed as Coomaraswamy has said: "poetry, but nonetheless science."

New Images of Duality

The objective view of society reigned supreme in the most fruitful periods of the history of the West. And in the course of its development, religions and churches were almost entirely related to the objective aspects of life. As Aurobindo says

> The modern age has been a time especially when humanity got rid of much that was cruel, evil, ignorant, dark and odious, not by the power of religion but by the power of awakened intelligence and of human idealism and sympathy. In fact, philosophy and science had in self-defence to turn upon religion and rend it to pieces to get a free field for their legitimate development.[48]

---

[46]Gary Zukav, *The Dancing Wuli Masters*, New York, William Morrow and Company Inc., 1979, p. 136.

[47]Ananda Coomaraswamy, *Dance of Shiva*, New York, the Noonday Press, 1957, p. 66.

[48]Sri Aurobindo, *Human Cycle*, Pondicherry, Sri Aurobindo Ashram, 1971, pp. 163-64.

This process has continued till recent times, Bertrand Russell says:

> Every step towards the better treatment of coloured races, or every mitigation of slavery, every moral progress there has been in the world, has been consistently opposed by the organised churches of the world.[49]

To stem the tide of disenchantment with faith in man's higher dimension, many like Teilhard and others in many parts of the world raised the flag of revolt against the tenets of the organised church to bring them in line with the needs of the evolutionary processes and new knowledge which were bringing about irreversible changes in the thoughts and lives of human beings. Every system of symbols and values was crumbling and a wide schism was developing between the sense of man and the orientation of the church. Teilhard was prevented and thwarted, as he believed, from "bringing forth tangible fruits."

He felt called upon to serve liberated man, a new type he saw emerging from the womb of modern civilisation in the vanguard of the evolution of the world, a man at once ambitious and delicate, now intoxicated by his power and now overwhelmed by it.

The sense of man and the religions of God, as we know them today, have not yet been cleansed of their commitments to the past, nor have they seen the vision of the future. The desire to hold on to the past and the present is stronger than the urge to seek an uncertain future. Their visions of the tangible world are crumbling and the territory of superconsciousness is not only beyond their reach, it is perhaps beyond their comprehension. Could the cause of this be that material man, under the weight of the tangible world, cannot rise above his immediate environment? Or is the tangible world the antithesis of the attainment of superconsciousness? Or is the human frame in which man reacts with his tangible environment contrary to the universal reality, where the minute atom and the smallest source of energy come into being, change their form and perish in accordance with the incontestable laws of harmony of attraction and repulsion and motion?

---

[49]Bertrand Russell, *Why I Am Not a Christian*, London, George Allen and Unwin, 1967, pp. 24-25.

Indian Approach—Dynamic and Static Balance

Over the centuries India has endeavoured to provide an answer to some of these questions. To develop a social framework to keep human society in balance has been one of India's important contributions. There have been periods in Indian history of dynamic balance punctuated by centuries of static balance. In periods of dynamic balance there was four-dimensional human advance, a golden age of material prosperity, intellectual enlargement and spiritual regeneration.

It was the morning of time when a warrior-king turned a Buddha and brought enlightenment and knowledge to the world. Earlier, a galaxy of seers, saints and sages had given voice to a civilisation and culture which has survived to this day despite the erosions caused by the seemingly superior weapons of conquest and oppression.

All through history down to the present day, India has adopted a multidimensional approach to life. She could deal with all kinds of eventualities with an understanding which rose above the mundane plane of material success and muscle power. She had glimpsed the mysteries of life in periods of static as much as dynamic balance. In periods of static balance, while society in general did not contribute much to material prosperity and thus suffered from famines, disease and pestilence, this did not dim the light of her teachers, sages and seers. They tried to correct the imbalances in the social environment through a new psychology of introspection, meditation and understanding, and projection of the human future to the highest possible attainment of the fourth dimension.

Humans did not carry a disproportionately heavy burden of material development, and this helped the process of keener realisation of the spirit freed from the coils of material advancement. The process triggered off new social arrangements, material growth and intellectual enlargement. And a new state of dynamic balance was reached. This has been a continuous stop-go process, in which the periods of balance—dynamic or static—were much longer than those of imbalance and uncertainty. The ultimate understanding of man and his environment, his objectives, directions and goals remained unblurred. They shone sometimes with intensity, but always clearly.

Reality of Man

The goals pertained to the ultimate reality, the reality of man, his infinite vision, his place in the universe and the limited role of his material needs. It was an evolutionary process, each aspect of human development contributing to the ultimate objective. What could not be achieved at an individual level was realised at the societal level. The objective was not to create a society of saints but one which honoured saints. There was an important place for material and intellectual advancement, and even for the call of the flesh (pleasure of the senses). But all these were ultimately transformed through various techniques, from the sublime to the bizarre, into the realisation of the ultimate human goal—to attain Nirvana. This state was reached by only a few, but society remained largely in balance.

> That according to the degree of expansion and elevation of the consciousness and the forms of its receptivity, the indices of space are augmented and the indices of time are diminished.
> The Hindu philosophy of Karma embodies the idea of the unbroken consecutiveness of phenomena. Each phenomenon, no matter how insignificant, is a link of an infinite and unbroken chain extending from the past into the future, passing from one sphere into another, sometimes manifesting as physical phenomenon, sometimes hiding in the phenomenon of consciousness.
> We know all this, yet nevertheless our positive science obstinately seeks to establish correlation between visible phenomena only, i.e. to regard each visible or physical phenomenon as the effort of some other physical phenomenon only, which is also visible. This tendency to regard everything upon one plane, the unwillingness to regard anything outside of that plane, horribly narrows our view of life.[50]

The technological society has driven all human attributes into subservience to the goals of material advancement. The process of human alienation is the natural outcome of three-dimensional man losing the perspectives of his two important dimensions. This is like a three-wheeled vehicle which had lost all but one wheel, and to stay in balance in this condition with its ever-increasing burden

[50]P.D. Ouspensky, *op. cit.*, pp. 105-36.

it must accelerate on the same path or else disintegrate. This indeed is the predicament of human society. Under the best conditions modern societies committed to consumerism are highly vulnerable. Vulnerability flows from the impermanence of knowledge and instruments which accelerate human society towards its economic goals. It also flows from the high speed at which you cannot afford to have accidents. But above all it is the price which many have to pay to keep the few in a state of affluence.

Every major technological innovation, be it a nuclear power plant, a supersonic jet or a communication network or control of the human organism, must be balanced by a high level of human and social responsibility to contain the processes of reversal. When a techno-economic system is controlled by a few and has to be protected from the many, it has a limited survival value. When such processes break through the barriers of social organisation to attain antisocial objectives, they, along with all the other elements which constitute this process, become counterproductive. Such counterproductivity manifests itself in many different ways, including inflation, unemployment and mass poverty. Paradoxically, the corrective decisions are outside the power of those who have to pay the greatest price and rest with those who have most to lose if they take the right decision.

In this realisation the individual awareness of monasteries is losing its meaning and purpose. Awareness has to be socialised and must come to those who are the target of the consumerist machine. Controlled gluttons must be aware of the bottomless pit through which human and physical resources find their way into the junkyards of eternity. Proliferating literature on the grandiose techniques to bring about societal change in the external world, while depriving man of his sensitivities and awareness and leaving the inner core untouched, is at best an exercise in futility.

Only through consciousness from within will the world be able to cast aside the superficialities and the burdens of a one-dimensional culture. Fear, insecurity and impermanence are the hallmarks of a sensate culture and are hurdles to realising that "being within being" which lightens our path to all corrective effort and provides the inspiration for creativity. But this is moving into the ivory towers of monasticism, where in the confines of the outer space, beyond the reaches of human problems and sufferings, the divinity of science sends its benedictions to the victims of consumerist passion, to the beneficiaries of the armament programme, for the satisfaction of the intellectual curiosity of their fraternity.

"Forgetfulness of Being"

This duality between consciousness in the higher reaches of science and the instruments of knowledge as transferred to the processes of unidimensional development ultimately leading to the total "forgetfulness of being" causes the human crisis. Fragmentation of knowledge, and the continuous extension of each fragment on a narrower and narrower spectrum, has contributed significantly to making the technological society. But as probing the atomic and subatomic world proceeds further the limitations of classical ideas are becoming increasingly obvious. This calls for a radical revision of many of our basic concepts.

> Eastern mysticism provides a consistent and beautiful philosophical framework which can accommodate our most advanced theories of the physical world. . .Western thoughts of the dualism between mind and matter, between body and soul. . .This separation of mind from the body and then given the futile task of controlling it is causing an apparent conflict between the conscious will and the involuntary instincts. This inner fragmentation has projected itself in an entire spectrum of human thought, life and activity, leading ultimately to the series of social, ecological and cultural crisis.[51]

In Eastern thought all things and events the senses perceive are interrelated and connected and represent different manifestations of the same ultimate reality. A desire to identify oneself with this ultimate reality is the cornerstone of Indian and Eastern thought.

But as the sensate culture makes inroads into the sanctuaries of the Eastern psyche, a strange duality comes into being, seeking not integration but excellence on two self-neutralising desires and activities. This is yearning for the fruits of integration and fragmentation at the same time. The physical man desires material rewards and the spiritual man his Nirvana.

The evolutionary processes must either follow the path of the

[51] Fritjof Capra, *op cit.*, pp. 12, 21, 23.

integrated man, attaining within himself and his environment a synthesis of all the dimensions, or society must integrate within itself the various dimensional disorientations and imbalances to contain the unidimensional march towards total disintegration.

Indian society has over the millennia attained this objective by containing the processes of fragmentation through individual discipline and the societal arrangement. The individual's continued search for the ultimate reality, either through perfection of his work or direct psychic experience or through a process of correcting planal disorientation with outside assistance, helped to achieve some understanding through control of the various dimensions. Superimposed on this was the social organisation which integrated the various activities and dimensions to keep society in a state of dynamic or static balance.

The objectives and attainments of the technological society were furthered and accelerated through a deliberate process of first bypassing and then eliminating the balancing factors of the second and the third dimension so that the non-material elements do not become a drag on man's one-dimensional material objectives. The results are there for all to see. In the midst of an ever-accelerating speed all talk of new international economic order or new world order models is only a last-ditch effort to rearrange the one-dimensional, unidirectional world of economic man from falling apart.

And nothing seems to work because of this duality between the inner and the outer reality, between the physical sciences and the higher consciousness, between professions and actions. The thoughts and actions of today carry in them the seeds of tomorrow. That is why Gandhian thought stressed the need for becoming a living model of the era we wished to create. It is time we cast aside our illusions that it is not the direction that needs change but the speed of change that needs acceleration. Clearing up environmental pollution alone will not do, the sickness is of the consciousness.

> ...the basic difference between Eastern and Western dialectical handling of the problem is that the West seeks the solution within the framework of abstract thought and the East beyond it, for the simple reason that the West regards the pairs of opposites as ontological and the East does not.[52]

[52] Amoury de Reincourt, *The Eye of Shiva*, London, Souvenir Press, 1980, p. 135.

In essence the difference between Eastern and Western culture springs from the continuous advance of spiritual Eastern aims against the material aims of the West. While the East searched for the shortest route to higher consciousness Western thought was preoccupied with ideas of evolution. And this search led to the advance of astronomical philosophy, the physical sciences on the one hand and the biological sciences on the other, and thus laid the foundations of the modern conception of evolution—orderly and progressive development governed by certain exact but unknown laws.

The dualism in Western thought, that is the separation of material man from the reservoir of higher consciousness, led to the uncontrolled acceleration of the continuously fragmenting unidirectional search for the ultimate. This search through human intervention on the evolutionary path has strayed from its cosmic origin, and in this process not only has the future of humankind been jeopardised but the synergetic fountainhead which provided the vision, inspiration or instinct for change is being lost except to project inexorably on the same unidimensional, unidirectional path of material advancement.

Into Blind Alleys

Our inability to relate the frontiers of the new knowledge to our cosmic origin is leading us into blind alleys. This is further emphasised by the counterproductivity of many techno-economic phenomena and the outright reversal of the multipliers in many technologies. So the human search for the ultimate on one of the fragmented, unidimensional pathways in the multi-dimensional infinite universe has lost its moorings. The future is neither leading us towards the utopia of Buckminster Fuller's More with Less nor towards Teilhard de Chardin's "ultimate self-subsistence pole of consciousness" but into a new kind of ecologically polluted wilderness where even the dreams of the future are lost. "When your children cease to dream dreams and lose their vision of the future, your nation will perish...For the first time in history Western civilisation suffers from an absence of positive and generally accepted images of the future."[53]

[53]Robert T. Francoeur, *Images of the Future—Twenty-first Century and Beyond* (ed.) Robert Bundy, New York, Buffalo, Prometheus Books.

Less than a century ago Nietzsche predicted in his preface to *The Will to Power* the advent of nihilism, with modern science as its most important symbol, thus:

> For some time now our whole European culture has been moving as towards a catastrophe with a tortured tension that is growing from decade to decade, restlessly, violently, headlong, like a river that wants to reach the end, that no longer reflects, that is afraid to reflect.[54]

While another savant, Sri Aurobindo, visualised the vulnerability of the new techniques of material advancement when he conjectured that "Europe prides herself on her practical and scientific organisation and efficiency. I am waiting till her organisation is perfect, then a child shall destroy her."[55]

Through the ages, through various mechanisms, including religion, the human urge was to get into right relationship with the sacred world as the source of cosmic order and therefore as the key to the perpetuation of life as expressed in the return of the sun, the seasons and so on. Creation was a cyclic and recurring event. It had to be re-enacted ritually at each moment of crisis if the world was not to slip back from order into chaos. In this cyclic process "when God was mentioned, fertility was always implied."[56]

This also implies that

> celebrations and rituals are not merely symbolic performances but are actual parts of all the cosmic events that are being celebrated. Thus does man act out his preordained part in cosmic life, emphasising the necessary coordination between himself and the play of natural forces.[57]

In this cosmic dance, in this manifestation of primal rhythmic energy of infinite power, humankind with all its energy, resources

---

[54] Friedrich Nietzsche, *The Will to Power* (ed.), Walter Kaufmann, New York, Random House, 1967, p. 3.
[55] Sri Aurobindo, *Thought and Aphorisms*.
[56] John Irwin, *The Stupa*, a series of lectures in New Delhi, December 1978.
[57] Amoury de Reincourt, *op. cit.*, pp. 48-49.

and wisdom is an infinitesimal speck. But when we in our arrogance begin a process of intervention in these forces, and that also not as seeker after knowledge, understanding and truth but as manipulator and exploiter for individual profit or even for common good, it does not require great genius to predict the consequences of such action. We have already lived through many of these consequences and many more of grave proportions in their different manifestations are aggregating in all parts of this world, breaking loose wherever we cross the threshold of the cosmic reason.

The population explosion, the crisis of environment, the massive aggregations of heat and the changing climatic balance, the energy crisis, human degradation through external influences of power, the techno-socio-economic crisis are manifestations of the same delinquence in our relations with the cosmic order. An affirmation of nothingness of the forces under human control in the vast expanse of the universe, this is the point from which we have to plan our retreat to sanity, involving action on an entire spectrum of human activity.

Respecting the Cosmic Order

Interference with cosmic order in all its manifestations must cease. The first step is that no aspect of this order should be exploited for group or individual profit. It should be approached in a spirit of reverence rather than conquest—to search, to seek but not to exploit. Nature is placing its own hurdles, taking revenge, wherever we interfere with its balance to achieve short-term material objectives. We are only skirting the fringes in the understanding of the great universe, and the next step in our understanding cannot be reached within a dualist conceptual framework, that is within the present idiom of Western science.

Among the great devaluations of our times that of organised religion is perhaps the most significant. This has largely been brought about by the massive institutionalisation of religion and the failure of these institutions to enable "the meek to inherit the earth." There are a few instances where religious institutions played a role as initiators of change, but that effort was largely to subvert change and strengthen the forces of status quo. The inference is obvious.

Can the Teilhardian concept of progressive unification of mankind and movement towards the convergent structure of evolution as it seeks out its cosmic centre be sustained in an environment of manipulation of cosmic laws on a unidirectional path to the detriment of the larger human interest?

Can we aspire for such a state

> In the midst of a war of arms, a war of commerce, a war of ideas and cultures, a war of collective personalities, each seeking to possess the world or at least to dominate it . . . where every method is justified which leads to success, and even peace is a covert state of war.
>
> . . . And all life not capable of this culture and efficiency must be eliminated.[58]

Advanced technology is highly vulnerable, and unless such processes operate within a harmonious and just environment and with common consent they could be used against the interests of the community at large and would require to be protected against nuclear terrorism by fascist regimes. George Orwell visualised in *Nineteen Hundred and Eighty-Four*[59] the prospects of nuclear terror and the emergence of fascist regimes to protect society against such eventualities.

What will be the implications of compulsive intensification of high-energy, high-technology productive processes in the face of the growing unemployment and resources crises in the affluent countries? What will be the cosequences when similar processes of consumerism are launched to include over 2 billion people in the developing societies demanding the right to work within the accepted value systems propagated world-wide by the affluent societies and the elites of these countries? Can runaway consumerism be contained through the existing politico-socio-economic framework?

Can the roots of insecurity arising out of the techno-economic processes and the consequent social breakdown be contained by the massive proliferation and sophistication of offensive and defensive weapons? Would it be possible to maintain wide techno-economic disparities and at the same time assure the free flow of

---

[58]Sri Aurobindo, *The Human Cycle*, Pondicherry, Sri Aurobindo Ashram, 1971, p. 43.

[59]George Orwell, *Nineteen Hundred and Eighty-Four*, New York, Harcourt Brace and Company, 1949.

energy and resources through oceans of poverty to a few islands of affluence with nuclear missiles?

Many techno-economic phenomena are reaching points of counter-productivity, and many others are reaching stages of outright technological reversal. In other words, the socio-economic costs of technologies to the community at large have overtaken the multiplier effects of new technologies. Most paths are leading into blind alleys and those which appear possible may at best be profitable for an individual, an organisation or a country but disastrous for a community as a whole or for humankind.

Have we reached a point of no return in our commitments to this course? This is the human dilemma in the closing decades of the second millennium.

PART TWO

2. Crafts to Consumerism

CRAFTS

The basic feature of human-oriented production is creativity. In creating articles of utility craftsmen do not merely exhibit the level of their competence in handling tools and materials. They express the intensity of their emotions, a dedication to form, colour and other aesthetic parameters, and the level of commitment to their environment. With increasing intervention by the machine

> The industrial object tends to disappear as a form to become indistinguishable from its function. It is diametrically opposite the work of art (in which the meaning is to be useless but beautiful). Crafts work is a mediation between these two poles.[1]

The culture of the crafts has therefore a much deeper significance for the human psyche and its integration with the environment. "Handicraft itself was the mediating factor between pure art and pure technique, between things of meaning that had no other use and things of use that had no other meaning."[2]

The driving force in the process of creative productivity was not the generation of surplus value. That came with the intervention of the machine which not only bypassed creativity and freedom and provided speed, uniformity and precision, but above all changed the social organisation to make it an appendage of the larger techno-economic structure.

When some segments of a techno-economic organisation generates rapid surpluses other parts of the structure cannot remain viable in techno-economic terms. It has to become a part of the overall

---

[1] Octavio Paz, *Use and Contemplation—In Praise of Hands*, New York, Graphic Society, 1974, p. 21.

[2] Lewis Mumford, *Art and Technics*, New York, Columbia University Press, 1960, p. 30.

system where "instead of lengthening the life of the product and lowering the cost to the user they raise the cost to the user by shortening the life of the product and causing him to be conscious of more stylistic tricks that are without any human significance or value."[3]

Resistance to this trend cannot be sustained. "The more the worker expends himself in work the more powerful becomes the world of objects which he creates in face of himself, the poorer he become in his inner life, and the less he belongs to himself."[4]

INTERMEDIATE TECHNOLOGY

Intermediate technology belongs to a kind of culture which lies between an era of creative productivity and the growth addiction of our times. Some may regard it as a retreat from the compulsively innovative autonomous technologies, while others may see in it a progression from the culture of the crafts to initiate the so-called modernisation processes in communities which cannot cope with the imperatives of the post-industrial societies with their creative tools. And between these two opposite poles, between two mutually neutralising cultural extremes, stands intermediate technology.

Some of the rich see in this vague intermediate point the road to sanity. The poor glimpse a new hope for the future. Both are unable to arrive at this point because of their inability to create the kind of environment in which intermediate technologies can take root and thus make a perceptible difference in the lifestyles or the cultural patterns of the affluent and the needy.

But there are many islands within the different socio-economic systems where either because of human perseverance or natural protective processes technologies belonging to neither culture have survived for periods of time despite hostile environments. These are exceptions rather than the rule.

On the one hand, many high-energy, high-technology productive processes are becoming socially and economically counterproductive, thus resulting in increased unemployment and diminishing returns. On the other, millions of unemployed in the developing

---

[3]*Ibid.*, p. 80.
[4]B. Bottomore (tr. and ed.), *Karl Marx, Economic and Philosophical Manuscripts—Early Writings*, New York, McGraw Hill, 1964, p. 22.

societies are barred from productive work because in the midst of the emerging consumerist passions and the rapid surplus-generating systems of production the tools of crafts and intermediate technologies and losing their survival value and, even worse, their social acceptability. In the process, inbuilt compulsively innovative techniques are proliferating to serve the interests of the major beneficiary, the dominant class within the politico-socio-economic system, whether in developed or developing societies.

Whether the culture of intermediate technology can hold its own in such an environment is a fundamental question. The only reason for hope that one can perceive is the growing resources and energy costs and counterproductivity of a broadening spectrum of technological processes, both in social and economic terms.

Countries which can resist compulsive temporary surplus-oriented innovations may one day find that their greater strength lies in what they have held on to rather than what they have allowed themselves to be swept away with. Success does not always lie in rushing in to act, and it is often more profitable not to act when the time is not opportune.

> Once we have achieved the right form for a type object, it should keep that form for the next generation or for the next thousand years. Indeed, we should be ready to accept further variations only when some radical advance in scientific knowledge or some radical change in the condition of life has come about, changes that have nothing to do with the self-indulgent caprices of men or pressures of the market.[5]

Continuous innovation of new technologies to protect, preserve and advance the surpluses generated in exchange value or market value productive processes is making an entire generation of people in the affluent societies redundant and/or unemployed. In the developing societies, even with the relatively limited introduction of imported high-energy, high-technology convertors, the productive processes have passed into the hands of an elite whose interests lie in further extending and accelerating the very same processes. Generation of large surpluses and their distribution among relatively few beneficiaries in the system has only helped limit employ-

[5]Lewis Mumford, *op. cit.*, p. 83.

ment opportunities to a small fraction of people who can operate the system.

Hundreds of crafts and techniques which can no longer be protected in the market economies are rapidly moving into the archives of museums. They belonged to a system of production which was closely intertwined with the life of the community, where techniques were transferred from father to son, from master craftsman to apprentices, where there was no distinction between aesthetics and the materialist.

This entire social system is now in total disarray. It is breaking into fragments to fall in line with specialisation in productive techniques, with no alternative tools and techniques provided to the homeless, directionless victims of these processes, the only survivors of a dying culture.

Because of the overwhelming odds, what is happening almost effortlessly between high technologies and craft techniques in a developing socio-economic system is being achieved through a relentless process in the international exchange-value economic system. Caught between the triple straitjackets of foreign exchange, armaments and resources, technological innovations are aimlessly and compulsively extended to protect national states from themselves, their imaginary friends and enemies, both within and without.

But many of these technological processes are becoming counter-productive in socio-economic as well as political and technological terms, and in this perhaps lies our hope. Self-containment of aimless proliferation of techniques can serve the purpose of directing attention to the debris of ecological destruction, waste, alienation, aimless acceleration, disintegration and unemployment which the adventurism of the last three decades has left behind.

To the developing societies it may well provide a breathing spell from their concern with international illusions of progress to their own national realities.

Postwar affluence, built around high technologies, limitless consumerism and exchange surpluses, also created pressures for the wider distribution of these surpluses, larger acquisition and use of energy and other resources, and wider dispersal of markets and trade. In this process, the entire international system is being transformed into one or other stages, of consumerism and high-waste economies. As a consequence of this there are countless casualties, the most important being the right to employment and security and the technological stability of the productive process.

Technological anarchy has contributed greatly to the massive migration of talent from the developed to the highly developed, the less developed to the developed, and from the poor to the rich countries. With some counter-flow the alienated are in search of integration, a British scientist and Indian doctor in the United States, a Turkish taxi driver in Germany and an Indian manager, plumber, carpenter or cook in the Middle East, a "guest worker" from the South to the North.

Behind all this to-and-fro movement are the values attached to the different technological levels and the question of supply and demand in different environments. These processes are as much a part of the world system as the compulsions to innovate breeder and fusion reactors to meet energy shortages or to send man to the moon to keep space scientists employed, or to keep on training doctors, engineers or technicians at a high cost in India and then put them in a brain drain pipeline rather than providing opportunities to use them for the uplift of hundreds of millions of the poor. Containment of this indiscriminate proliferation of technologies is therefore just as important as orderliness in the brain drain processes in the international market places and the rural urban exchange.

Affluent economies have also come to mean high-cost economies, and as these economies move towards counter productive technologies their competitive position, except perhaps in the wasteful areas of defence and space, become highly vulnerable to the productive processes in relatively low-cost economies. The emergence of Japan, Korea, Hong Kong, Taiwan, Singapore, and more recently India and China, as competitive factors in many high-technology and medium-technology consumer products is a case in point.

So the affluent economies have few options. They cannot sustain their high-production, high-cost, energy-intensive and resource-intensive system in isolation. They cannot allow the system to be overwhelmed by low-cost economies, by resource limitation, by unemployment and social unrest. They cannot afford to slow down their one-wheeled, single-track, high-speed system for fear of collapse. Thus, every escape route leads to the proliferation or armaments and war hysteria.

The developing countries, partially in self-preservation but largely to emulate those considered more successful, are also committed to a capital-intensive, resource-intensive and energy-intensive and employment-restrictive system of development which, while intensifying the unemployment problem (capital/output ratio has been rising), is in many ways benefiting them in international competition because of the relatively low cost of their products. As such, they are posing a challenge to the productive apparatus in the affluent countries. This challenge comes from:

> —The growing vulnerability of the markets of high-cost economies because of the relatively low cost and acceptable quality of a wide variety of consumer and industrial goods now emerging out of developing societies.
>
> —The needs of developing countries for energy and other resources in their developmental processes. The rising world-wide scarcity of materials and the escalation of their prices, and the acquisition of resources which now lie fairly substantially within the poorer parts of the world are becoming a major factor in world politics.
>
> —Some developing countries such as India are rapidly building up a large reserve of trained technical manpower to meet their own needs. Some of these countries are also making an important contribution to meeting the trained manpower needs of other countries.

It is therefore obvious that technological innovation and its integration with the productive processes is not just a factor in isolation, or a neutral process, but is part of the politico-socio-economic system within a state and in the larger international system. Each level of technology needs its own milieu, its own system of organisation to take roots.

As personalised craft techniques were replaced by the factory system of production the social organisation of society and its politico-economic institutions also underwent radical changes, though often delayed. When mechanical looms made thousands of weavers jobless, society had to react to bring about change. The modern techniques of mechanisation, rationalisation and automation are making an entire generation of people jobless. How will the system cope with such problems? Can intermediate technology representing another moment in culture take root in such an environment?

Gandhian Approach

The Gandhian approach to development was that nobody should create a surplus over his daily needs, and that this would assure enough food and other basic needs and leisure for all. Gandhi expected all productive effort to be a labour of love for the common good in which there would be neither rich nor poor. This is totally contrary to growth in market or exchange economies of increasingly high technologies and large surpluses. It is presumed that intermediate technology is to extend beyond the culture of crafts so as to accelerate and extend the technological processes to some intermediate point to reduce the drudgery of work and create surpluses and thus enlarge the area of welfare through enhanced consumption of a relatively large variety of goods. Can we then draw a line beyond which surpluses cannot be created? Hence when we accept a graduated increase in surpluses and growth rate the Gandhian system of economics becomes unsustainable.

What happens is that as intermediate technologies, starting with a lower level of surplus generation, accelerate this rate, higher and higher accumulations are ploughed back into the system to increase continuously the capital intensity of the productive processes. So, theoretically, the intermediate technologies of today will one day become the high technologies of tomorrow, low capital intensity will similarly become high, low surpluses will become large accumulations and present-day India will become tomorrow's United States.

If these assumptions are correct, intermediate technology is only a stop-gap arrangement to enable those who cannot cope with the present level of capital intensity to pick another optimum point which they can relatively afford better till they can catch up with the capital input/output ratio of the developed societies.

But how will this be achieved without restricting the freedom of choice of work or productive effort, or level of technologies, the surpluses they will generate, the salaries and wages they will command. Even in developing countries such as India the introduction of high-technology machines in a few key industries or in small sectors or some major industries create wage differentials, giving the appearance that we are living in two different societies.

The havoc this creates with crafts, the cultural disorientation it brings about, and the feeling of helplessness, disillusionment and dissatisfaction it generates in relation to the tools in use sets the crafts and intermediate technologies apart from the environment of consumerism and mark them out to be eliminated through a process of attrition.

Thus whatever be the politico-socio-economic orientation, we cannot strengthen the symbols of consumerism and at the same time yearn for a culture of crafts. We cannot allow productive processes to ride the tiger of continuing obsolescence and indiscriminate wage differentials, and at the same time avoid compulsive pressures towards the capital intensity of the productive processes.

We cannot seek international export markets to assure the viability of our economic system without at the same time being pushed towards seeking parity, if not a higher level of excellence, in our own technological development. This is not only true in the world community between groups of communities but also within national states.

What is in question is not the desirability of introducing intermediate technology, but its capacity for survival. We are all climbing towards an illusion on technological steps, and we either tumble all the way down to a culture of crafts and in this process break our necks or perhaps shatter our illusions regarding the ultimate price of a technological society. But we cannot stand in the middle and hold on to our hopes of an intermediate point between somewhere and nowhere. We cannot create islands of rationality in the midst of a technological wilderness. We cannot attain stability of productive processes with wandering technologies.

The economic foundations of intermediate technology were shattered with the destruction of craft culture long before intermediate technologies came into being, and this havoc has now reached out to the lowliest of hamlets in the remotest parts of this minuscule globe of ours. The only hope for intermediate technology now rests not on economic foundations but on human foundations, of protecting what is left of man. It lies in a new human orientation of the technological processes.

We must slowly alter our symbols and values so that technology does not merely represent an outside stimulant, propelling humans on to accelerate every process to exploit every resource, but projects itself onto the centre of the stage, not to manipulate the physical and the human environment but to synthesise within its own essence of man into a new amalgam of human knowledge—humanology.

Techno-economic factors alone will be irrelevant in bringing about such a basic transformation, centres of human awareness must also be reached to break away from the hypnotic effects of consumerist modes of life. It is not possible to get back to an earlier social organisation. The technologies we innovate should not only be appropriate to our needs but also to the times and the social order we wish to attain and stabilise.

High-energy technology converters are the outcome of a continuing process of centralisation, aggregation and concentration. This process must decelerate, the old linkages must be broken and new ones established so that the higher levels of technologies, instead of destroying everything, could be integrated into an economically viable combination of various levels of technologies reacting favourably on each other within self-contained rural republics, or nuclear communities in the urban areas.

One of the characteristics of such communities would be their decentralisation with regard to the satisfaction of as many of their minimum basic needs as possible in the immediate environment.

Elimination of economic incentives or big wage differentials in favour of high technology operators in such a decentralised system would serve the dual purpose of a freer choice of work and the initiation of processes of creative innovation. It would help contain the compulsive, often forced, trend towards multiplying the desire and apparatus for unbridled consumerism.

It would help develop an economically viable synthesis of an entire range of technologies within a self-contained system. A wide diversity of techniques from crafts to many levels of intermediate and super-high technologies will further the processes of production, innovation, creativity and self-expression, not out of economic compulsion but human choice. In larger human terms this could set in motion processes for a four-dimensional development.

A wide variety of the energy and resource needs of such communities could be met through solar and bioenergy, agriculture and livestock development programmes and recycling of waste. And all this could contribute to the emergence of a new social order where citizens could live in harmony operating different technological levels of innovative and productive apparatus or seek satisfaction in creating beauty and utility through their crafts. Intermediate technology or humanology has a very vital role to play in providing the linkages for such a transformation.

COUNTERPRODUCTIVITY

To a society in the throes of consumerism nothing seems to make sense except to cope with its compulsions to assure continuity and further the desire to extend its consumerist frontiers. And in this process all the instruments of knowledge and resources are pressed into service. The logic of deteriorating environment, dwindling resources, disorientation of the human psyche are of no concern except as problems to be overcome with still higher doses of human and other inputs. Only the objective and the framework are sacred while all else is dispensable in this process.

It is an irony that the preemption of the resources of other vulnerable systems freely form a part of the calculations to assure the safety of societies which stand committed to patterns of high consumption development and a rigid system for the organisation of production and distribution. In achieving these not only have many commitments reached points of no return but even the techniques have reached a point of alarmingly high stress.

Techno-economic imperatives apart, all other aspects are getting devalued to the point that these are being made subservient to the primary concern—the viability of the economic system and its continuity on the path of growth. And this is not only the concern of the principal beneficiaries of such development but also its willing and unwilling victims.

The Strategy

During the last many decades, numerous factors have contributed to the growth and stability of the productive processes. Among these are:

An undisturbed unidimensional growth of the techno-economic system, regulated through the safety valves of recession, depression, overemployment and under-employment.

Aggregation of profits through acceptance of smaller returns on larger turnover and markets.

Controlled and uncontrolled obsolescence of consumer products, capital goods, techniques and human inputs.

Enlargement of non-utility production such as defence and space equipment, armaments race between client countries and inciting and directing controlled wars.

Creation of monopolies, price control, inflated international price variations and differentials to balance losses in one market with larger profits in other through multinational operations.

Balancing losses in one product against profits in others through multiproduct diversification and multicompany conglomeration. Price manipulation of raw material and finished products to the advantage of manufacturing societies.

Political control of backward, resources-rich societies through military dictatorships and willing or complacent elites.

Technological innovations to replace old products with new.

Manipulation through psychological techniques, new desires, social compulsions, novel hardships, pleasure-potent addictions and systematic arousal of the worst consumerist passions.

Curtailment of working hours in socially useful productive units, extension of the socially less useful service sectors, massive enlargement of social welfare schemes and unemployment benefits.

Finally, economic and financial manipulation of the economies and of interest rates through intervention by international institutions.

These and many other strategies have evolved during recent decades to keep the politico-socio-economic systems on an even keel and protect them from threats within and without, real or imaginary. These strategies are also meant to sustain the moral of those who operate the system and to affirm that there were always technological and other solutions round the corner to maintain its viability and expansion.

Indeed, it is increasingly admitted that many economic processes are approaching points of diminishing returns. But it is argued that this does not constitute a real long-term threat to the stability of the system, and that there will always be an economic upturn. All such maladies are considered the outcome of economic failures rather than unproductive policies, technological slowdown rather than ill-considered use of new technologies, jealousy of others rather than our own greed, concessions to man rather than subservience to machines, aggression by others rather than manipulation and deceit by ourselves.

But what is the reality? Many of these maladies spring from the equation of all human rights as political rights by some and economic rights by others. The outer limits of our political rights is now narrowing to the selection of highly promoted politicians as our leaders. Freedom of choice between highly promoted articles of consumption is now regarded as economic independences. As this human evasion and self-deception continues many political-social-techno-economic institutions and processes are becoming counter-productive.

This phenomenon manifests itself in many ways. While the economic factors may appear to be relatively more readily measurable and the technological terms more easily discernible, their impact on human affairs is largely latent and invisible. It is difficult to pinpoint this or to relate its origin and source to the end-product.

The Unpredictable Element

There are many variables which determine the course of economic activity. Price and availability of raw materials, the salary and wage structure, dimensions of the market, linkages and relationships with other sectors of the economy, mechanism of the input-output relationships, and depth of promotional activities.

Any one of these factors can swing the pendulum between increasing and diminishing returns. These are largely short-term or temporary phenomena, normally subject to financial and other manipulations such as control of demand and supply and the price mechanism.

But within a social system the most unpredictable consequences are those of technological change which introduce the processes of expansion, obsolescence and replacement at the same time. They affect an entire range of parameters such as markets and the work force. Each new technology affects one or all the parameters. It brings about drastic changes in the employment market and causes qualitative changes in manufacturing techniques. And some of these are all-engulfing and irreversible changes.

In the process of economic survival technological frontiers are often extended to a point where the sole contributory factor is that of a competitive advantage through saving manpower costs without any other significant advantage to the overall economic system. At this point the processes of diminishing returns reach their outer limit and react no more to manipulation and become irreversible.

Any further projection of the economy results only in counter-productivity in socio-economic terms. The political and gross social cost to the community may far outweigh marginal advantages in sustaining the socio-economic system through the triple straitjacket of resource limitation, foreign exchange needs and defence expenditure.

In some instances where the economy finds itself at the first stage of diminishing returns we may be simultaneously reaching out for chronic unemployment. This is indeed the red signal of social counterproductivity, which in turn pushes the system to an acute state of political instability, racial tension, brain drain and often assumes various other manifestations outside the framework of the consumer-oriented planning mechanism.

When the processes of counterproductivity make their appearance in a sector of society, they start affecting the entire range of input-output relations, the apportionment of societal surpluses, increasing costs and diminishing benefits for the same level of investment. One of the most visible symptoms of approaching counterproductivity is growing immunity to all known remedies to contain inflationary and deflationary pressures and unemployment. Every remedy becomes contraindicated for the disease it is expected to cure.

Behind all these processes are changing technologies, innovated to serve the imperatives of a one-dimensional techno-economic system. This system is ever hungry for increased competitive advantages resulting from cost reduction and manpower saving through a higher dose of automation. Its vital role is to improve product acceptance and thus serve the larger purpose of protecting, preserving and advancing consumerism. Every new effort is to assure the continued growth and stability of the system.

But all the elements through which this objective is expected to be achieved ultimately become a threat to the system itself. When the techno-economic processes cannot provide the desired escape routes the other available routes only tend to lead to blind alleys. Thus begins a continuous process of greater and still greater effort with an ever-diminishing response, larger and larger investment with an employment squeeze. Increased efforts are made to produce in saturated markets under environmental constraints and spiralling costs.

Productivity Lag

Productivity changes in recent years have been attributed to a variety of reasons including changes in work ethics and workers' mobility towards service industries. But most researchers attribute the extent of change due to these factors to less than one-tenth of 1 percent.

The growth in output per man hour has fallen off between 3 percent in the 1960s to only half that much in recent years. Yet much of the American industry is capital intensive. In such industries labour productivity may be a minor issue. More important is the productivity of plant and equipment, energy efficiency and the field for materials. The broader measure of output per unit of input is called total factor productivity. Harvard economist Dali Jorgenson and Frank Gallop of the University of Wisconsin have used sophisticated analytical techniques to produce some total factor productivity data. The annual averages express a general downturn after 1966 which worsened after 1973. Adverse trend has further accelerated after 1973.[6]

An average downturn of over 40 percent in productivity increases when estimated industrywise may reflect a massive downturn in some industries with gains in others largely due to automation that is at the cost of employment.

Two major contributors to the downward trend have been construction and extraction industries while electronic industry continues to show an upward trend at a very high cost. The manufacture of silicon chips production line which cost US $2 million in 1972 now costs US $100 million.[7]

Whether it is printing and publishing, paper making or petroleum refining or aircraft production or food industries billions of dollars are being spent on automation and computerisation and in meeting environmental regulation. All these add to the cost of production, the social cost of unemployment and making the techno-economic

---

[6]Edward Meadows, "A Close Look at Productivity Lag," *Fortune*, 4 December 1978.

[7]"Science and Technology Review," *The Economist*, 20 January 1979.

system more and more rigid and increasingly less amenable to manipulation and control. Market saturation also limits innovative possibilities.

Marginal technological changes may improve the competitive position of one industrial unit or another, but in the ultimate analysis they do not add to the well-being of an overall techno-economic system. The US Department of Labour places the US at the bottom of productivity increases in the industrial countries.

The same story is repeated on a broad spectrum of technological change, starting with revolutionary changes through innovations to increasing investment and diminishing returns to a stage of counter-productivity, and from there on to total reversal. "Due to inadequate assessment and consideration of social consequences of rapid technological change, and in haste to milch technology to immediate economic advantage environment is being turned into a physical and social tinder."[8]

And society is being converted into an ecologically polluted, spiritually disabling synthetic mirage.

The acceleration of every technological process disturbs some political, economic or social balance. Through the processes of technological reversal, the socio-economic and ecological cost of many technologies are becoming greater than the economic multipliers achieved through the use of such technologies.

Economic indicators as symbols of excellence are being rapidly exploded, and the reverberation of such processes of reversal are felt on a very broad spectrum of human affairs. Inability to see the totality of effect of techniques is the primary reason for the blind reach towards the counterproductivity of technical processes. According to Ellul all these techniques form a whole, each part supporting and reinforcing the other.[9]

The phenomenon of counterproductivity also speeds in the same manner. It is an illusion to believe that we can take the positive and discard the negative aspects of technological change. Each new machine "disturbs" the equilibrium of production, and then there is need to create many more machines[10] to restore this balance.

[8] Alvin Toffler, *Future Shock*, New York, Random House, 1970, Bantam Books, 1971, p. 429.
[9] Jacques Ellul, *Technological Society*, New York, Alfred A. Knopf, 1965, p. 194.
[10] *Ibid.*, p. 194.

Little by little the whole edifice is constructed. The technical movement is strong enough to break down all barriers to progress and thus further accelerate the processes of counterproductivity.

In free market economies an overpromotion of consumer goods, to retain or expand the share of the market, overautomation to secure a competitive price advantage may be an excellent policy at the micro level, but is counterproductive at the macro level. It usually ends up in greater dissatisfaction among the deprived and anger among those who are rendered surplus to the techno-economic system.

The Prime Mover

Unless counterproductivity intercepts the process or alters the course of development all developing societies will be one. There will be no difference between India, Chile and Greenland. Technique is the prime mover of the rest.

Only ceaseless technical progress on a broad spectrum can compensate for the causes of depression which become manifest in mature economies. The other possibility would be the horizontal proliferation of productive processes in interlinked developing societies lost on the path of consumerism. This may help to contain the counterproductive processes for brief periods, but in the long term it would further accelerate the processes of resources depletion and unemployment and otherwise become socially counterproductive.

It may be argued that theoretically all systems are subject to inherent or intrinsic or natural (or physical) constraints or limits, and within these limitation all processes of counterproductivity may be considered temporary or impermanent and can be corrected. To these processes would belong limits such as the speed of light, absolute zero temperature and absolute vacuum. Ratio of output to input, measure of efficiency or probability are also inherently limited to unity or 100 percent. Then there are ecological or environmental limits as well as those to the human metabolism.

There are many other limits such as the efficiency of harvesting crops and conversion of energy. There are also time-dependent constraints, and it is generally presumed that by their removal many prerequisites for the success of advanced technological systems can be met. But the cost of development is an increasing function of the degree of departure from the existing technology, and this in turn may be circumscribed by the economy constraints of the market-place.

Many technologies which contributed massive economic multipliers only a few decades ago are in the course of time becoming increasingly counterproductive. The technological processes are totally divorced from the disturbances that their introduction can generate in the political-socio-economic and ecological systems. So a variable in an area of technology may display wide fluctuation at a micro level while the macro systems are likely to change relatively smoothly and continuously, and without violent fluctuations. The stability of a macro system (variables) is partly the result of the operation of the law of large numbers. Further, the macro variable is likely to deviate relatively less from its main or centroid than any components. As an example, fluctuations in gross national product (GNP) will be much smaller than the mean fluctuation in individual income.

In recent decades, particularly from the 1960s, there has been an aggregation of various negative factors in different systems. These sub-macro system changes have remained largely invisible because of the over-all impact of rapid technological changes, economic growth and the expansion of welfare. These also remained invisible because of the apparent predominance of positive elements such as increases in GNP, growth in employment, world trade, international adjustments, economic equalisation, factors between affluent countries such as USA, EEC and Japan on the one hand and USSR and the East European countries on the other, and also relatively easy transfer of resources and technologies to the developing world.

But simultaneously with the positive factors negative factors were also in operation. Their overall impact on the world systems was however relatively small and the cumulative effect of many sub-macro systems became increasingly obvious in the early 1970s.

To this category belonged rising wages and accelerated technological change, largely directed towards labour-saving devices in increasingly competitive markets and cosmetic changes in production to gain competitive advantage. Another dominant factor in this period was the aggregating commitment to the production of offensive and defensive weaponry and war effort. All these factors lead up to growing constraints on employment and inflationary pressures through the diversion of massive resources to nonproductive and wasteful expenditure.

Overcommitment to research development and production of armaments diverted too large a percentage of resources to areas which placed technological constraints on large sectors of the consumer goods apparatus, thus limiting the expansion of the system to maintain a healthy growth in employment.

> When technical stagnation occurs, it would result in the regression of the economy and deep crisis. Only ceaseless technical progress can compensate for the causes of depression.[11]

It also became socially counterproductive in letting loose a revolt of the youth against what was considered an unnecessary and wasteful tragedy. Defoliation of large areas of Vietnam highlighted the destruction and criminal neglect of environment in the social system. It accelerated the wasteful use of many vital raw materials and energy, forced the flow of resources to super-high, employment-limiting, capital-intensive technologies against employment generating technologies.

The froth of these decades of neglect surfaced in the Vietnam War not just in the United States but in the entire world system. The counterproductivity of many processes became obvious. Beyond a point tools become destructive and institutions counterproductive.

Grand Finale

This counterproductivity throttled the flow of resources commensurate with the needs of the developing societies, and widened the technological gap between desirable and available technologies. Similarly, sophisticated elites beholden to international trends in the midst of diametrically opposite socio-economic needs, appeared in the developing societies, thus starting a counterflow of aid in the form of brain drain from the developing to the developed countries, counterproductivite for both.

The grand finale of all this has been the aggregation of ecological hazards, inflation, unemployment, resources crisis, massive commitments to unproductive armaments and waste, social unrest, alienation. Any solution to these problems further aggravates the others, or is contraindicated in their solution. Steps to contain

[11] *Ibid.*, p. 151.

inflation cut across employment-generating programmes. Inflation brings down the value of currencies, further aggravates negative trade balances and disturbs international trade.

Armament reduction programmes increase unemployment, disturb trade balances, reduce GNP, upset sensitive balances of power and endanger trade routes for raw materials and energy. Free trade flows between the developed and the developing countries endanger high-cost industries in the affluent countries and low-technology, low-production industries in the developing countries, thus restricting the further expansion or productive apparatus in the midst of an explosive unemployment situation. And yet the elites in the developing societies continue to share the fantasy that the growth of the rich to hyperabundance will help their cause.

> Recent trends where the leaderships of the developing societies on one side are endeavouring to maintain technical progress, and are on the other pushing for decentralisation, will find the exercise self-negating, and counterproductive in more ways than one.[12]

The most effective high-technology socio-economic systems are rapidly moving towards extreme centralisation. The liberal democratic front, which is another name for decentralised influencing of political choices, no longer affects the hard core of the centralised socio-techno-economic systems which operates its own code of conduct, steel frame and linkages. Choice of parties or personalities has only a marginal influence on the working of the basic structure of management and efficiency. Whenever and wherever it intervenes it constitutes a threat to the system.

Recent trends have constrained its abilities to circumvent the steel frame of high technology linkages within the system and have established the retreat of the effective liberal frame. Countries like Japan, Germany and USSR have evolved their own protective mechanism to curb intervention by the political process, while USA and France are still struggling between the imperatives of a technological society and the need for reversing the highly promoted emotional commitment to the liberal frame. There is hardly any hope for the liberal frame to prevail in the ultimate analysis. "Today

[12]*Ibid.*, p. 194

the question is not of liberty but how to keep the illusion of liberty."[13]

Britain carries a much greater burden of commitment to the processes of dissent. As such, her problems arise from inability to firm up viable (sustainable) technological processes in the larger Western techno-economic system. Repeated intervention by her political processes in the techno-economic structure of society, and recurring compulsions to compromise the techno-economic system to secure political equilibrium, has led to a strange dichotomy in the system. Britain desires to be in Europe, but it cannot cope with its techno-economic realities. She wishes to have a liberal frame, but cannot reconcile it with her African policies and investments. Her Commonwealth configuration is strained by her immigration policies and conflict of interests within the larger Western community. Her path to prosperity is barred by liberalism, her pursuit of liberalism and a place in the sun are eclipsed by Black Africa. Every road to the future is leading to blind alleys.

Politics of Populism

The developing countries have their own cross to carry. Between the need for rapid growth and modernisation on one side and the politics of populism and promises on the other, neither are the requirements of high technology development met nor is there democratic decentralisation to accelerate rural and regional development. All this is leading to the rapid aggregation of socio-economic problems, to which both political and technical processes are contributing.

The introduction of various levels of technologies into the techno-economic system has created a new power elite which is endeavouring to consolidate its gains through political processes, while extreme forms of populist politics are exacerbating the very tendencies which negate the techno-economic organisation of a welfare state. The situation in countries like India, of continental proportions and with regional, religious, caste and developmental differences, has become far more complex.

While the desirability of rapid techno-economic organisation is widely understood the organisational framework, the sense of responsibility and many essential prerequisites for such a develop-

[13]*Ibid.*, p. 194.

ment are entirely absent from the planning frame. Also absent are the techniques and the will to organise compulsive and cooperative endeavours without which no meaningful development can take place. Whether it is Mao's cultural revolution or a total revolution, these have failed to firm up to the demands of a technological milieu.

Big-power ideological rivalries have not helped. In the midst of entirely different conditions, another moment in time and culture and a different psychological frame, the protective umbrella of big-power trade, techniques and armament is offered and willingly accepted by the elites of developing societies. An environment of consumerism is being promoted in situations where even basic needs have not been satisfied. Instead of contributing to the processes of rational organisation of productivity within resource limitation the elites are busy sowing the seeds of confrontation.

Many processes are thus becoming counterproductive long before arriving at the point of full realisation of the available potential. Much time is spent in "maintaining a facade of public and private morality—preoccupied most of all with the voter—to justify itself at every stage"[14]

Overcentralisation of the power structure creates its own problems. When the processes of centralisation are stretched beyond the point of relevance to organise and operate a high technology system it becomes counterproductive. This is brought about by the brittleness of the system.

In the Second World War the German war machine was overcentralised after initial successes. Even small reverses started running through the entire system, magnifying its disabilities, causing demoralisation of the total system, creating panic among its operators, enlarging the areas of vulnerability, shadowing the credibility of the powers and hastening the disintegration process.

Responsible democracies can on the other hand operate in a system of checks and balances, on a meaningful synthesis of rights, responsibilities and duties. The technological imperative can be satisfied through strong subsystems like space agencies, nuclear commissions and industrial organisations operating within the larger or total system. A subsystem can quite often operate at a much higher level of excellence than the total system. Through

[14] *Ibid.*, p. 228.

large monetary incentives, sophisticated management of high-calibre personnel and efficient management of man and machine relations, such systems can operate as independent constituents.

The people in command may shift from one subsystem to another, but they are only shifting within the same steel frame with an identical language and rules of the game, and only to maximise the effectiveness of the particular subsystem in relation to other subsystems. But as the subsystems reach a high level of efficiency and develop linkages with other subsystems, their influence on the overall system continues to aggregate till it becomes dominant.

When the system becomes rigid the processes of diminishing returns commence, leading to counterproductivity and then reversal. The system then needs new politico-socio-techno-economic arrangements to continue on its path of expansion and growth. It also needs new techniques to anticipate human reaction.

> To make supportable what was not previously so and not in modifying anything in man's environment but by taking action on man himself.[15]

This is usually the ultimate stage of a totally centralised, completely integrated new kind of authoritarian human system.

Human intelligence cannot resist propaganda and manipulation of its consciousness. A series of protective reflexes organised by techniques immediately intervene. They create a certain predisposition among the masses and act upon human consciousness, leaving man with the illusion of complete freedom.

All these techniques are today serving the larger purpose of sustaining the third stage of consumerism, and also increasing acceptance and containing revolt against ideas on which the fundamentals of consumerism rest. The weapons are largely the same whether this is to be achieved through the defence of democracy or dictatorship. The end-results achieved are also the same. The human effects of techniques are independent of the ideological end to which they are applied and achieved through a process of involuntary psychological collectivisation—a way of life.

[15] *Ibid.*, p. 321.

Gross National Product

One of the greatest socio-techno-economic distortions of our times has been brought about by the misuse of the term gross national product. The ultimate consequence of this is that the economies of greatest waste become by a strange coincidence and misrepresentation the economies with the highest GNP. If we were to reduce this to the benefit accruing to individuals and communities in a rising GNP, we may have another story to tell.

Let us start with food. If we take 3000 calories as the minimum a human adult should consume as food in certain proportions of proteins, carbohydrates and fats, and if this food were to be consumed in the form of vegetable proteins, animal and vegetable, oils and carbohydrates, the GNP of a community would be a factor, say X. If similar caloric needs are met by animal proteins, polyunsaturated fats and factory-processed carbohydrates, the GNP of the same community would improve by a factor of say 5X.

Further, the energy cost to the community to achieve perhaps a lower level of nutrition and physical well-being will increase by a factor of 5-10 depending upon the communities under comparison. Apart from all the other negative factors, the work is transferred from the home to the factory, and thus all the effort which goes unreflected in the GNP of a developing community becomes an important contributory factor to the GNP of affluent societies.

Similarly, if a family were to have vegetable proteins, fats and cereals and transform these at home, or to have a steak dinner even at a medium-priced restaurant, the difference in the GNP increase may be of the order of as much as 1:10.

Another wasteful cost which contributes extensively to GNP is distribution. A relatively middle class farmer in India goes round his field and digs up a few vegetables, withdraws rice or wheat and refined butter from his store, takes wood or cowdung from his backyard, buys salt and spices from the village grocer and contributes almost nothing to GNP as against his counterpart in USA who drives into a neighbourhood store and buys processed foods of a wide variety. The processing, handling, transport and distribution costs of his purchases may have increased GNP twenty-fold while the commensurate welfare and quality of life in real terms may not even be twice as much.

This is not just a matter of excluding the contribution of the household sector to GNP. It is the inclusion of a great deal of waste, inefficiency and duplication of effort which becomes a part of GNP in most affluent countries. What came into being as a process of natural division of human economic activities has become a psychopathic symbol of superiority and success.

So the processes of large-scale mechanisation, automation, increased investment costs, material and labour costs, continue. If finally the illusionary cost of the end product drops a few percent, that becomes the justification for more rapid movement on the same path, often leading to overproduction and rapid increases in servicing and marketing, particularly advertising costs. And these costs often more than neutralise the benefits from excessive mechanisation and automation. The processes of counterproductivity have by now set in and GNP rises are largely an index of growing inflation, static or diminishing employment and mounting costs.

What is true of food is equally valid in other areas such as transport. GNP rises in direct proportion to waste in the transport of people and goods, at least this has been the experience of the last few decades, long before the sudden rise in energy costs distorted the picture totally out of recognition. The energy investment, resources and ecological costs of creating and maintaining an infrastructure for two-car or three-car families, as against the public transport system and its contribution to GNP, does not need repetition.

Another important factor bloating GNP is the rising cost of medicare. When a doctor nets an income of $ 100,000 a year, when a hospital bed costs $ 100-200 per day, when the cost of medicines includes research and promotional costs to serve the needs of a small fraction of the population, GNP rises much faster than when "barefoot doctors" bring medicare to the sick and the aged. When aged citizens are transferred to old people's homes, GNP rises much faster than when they are cared for by their families. With the division of the human body into spearate systems like cardio-vascular or circulatory, nervous or digestive, each handled by a specialist, GNP rises much faster than when the patients are attended to by a family doctor.

New Limits to the Quality of Life

While new diagnostic and curative techniques and equipment have considerably enlarged the capabilities of the medical profession to alleviate human suffering, they have taken medicine farther and farther away from those who need it most. New drugs have helped eliminate mass killing epidemics and diseases, and this has added considerably to the population. Starting from a low base of average human longevity, largely through the containment of infant mortality, the ceiling reached and the extension of the average human life span has almost halted in the case of affluent nations.

The approaching biological limits of the life span, the backlash of wonder drugs, emergence of new strains of viruses and bacteria immune to known remedies, the environmental tensions, ecological disturbances and the pollution of air, water and food, all contribute to the limitations on the quality of life and the consequent containment of longevity and the increasing hazards to human life. The new designs are new only in terms of novelty and not improved quality of life.

So the counterproductivity of these processes is manifesting itself on a very broad spectrum of everyday human existence. The massive increases in population and demand on limited resources in land, minerals, water, energy, metals and construction materials present an inscrutable dilemma for the Third World countries.

In recent years, the bulk of research and development effort and allocation of resources has been devoted to extending the frontiers of knowledge to conquer diseases like cancer, of the cardio-vascular system and other mass killers which are the direct outcome of the physical and social environment in which human beings are required to function. While medical science endeavours to reach out for the frontiers, a large mass of humanity, even in the most affluent country, lives under the constant dread of diseases without remedy. The costs of even elementary cures and remedies are steadily getting beyond their reach.

The mass of humanity saved from infant mortality and mass killing epidemics in the developing countries are languishing in poverty, malnutrition and the agony of curable diseases in unhealthy hygienic conditions with little medical attention. The medical fraternity of these countries congregates to man hospitals in urban centres or in the affluent world. This significant trend of aid in reverse is a clear symbol of the phenomenon of counterproductivity of higher medical education in developing societies. For the individual it is a passport for upward mobility, for the community of deprivation and neglect.

Medicare available in most developing countries is restricted to the urban elites.

The health budgets of poor countries are heavily weighted toward modern hospitals that cater to the urban elite...less than 20 percent is spent on preventive medicine accessible to the rural and urban poor. According to a World Bank estimate, some 800 million people have no access to even minimal health care.[16]

The system of advanced medicine is making it impossible to maintain a human being's physical welfare through a single intermediary and doctors now fear to prescribe medicines because of the consequences of their action on human organs outside their line of specialisation and control. A substantial proportion of the income of the medical fraternity in the United States is going towards their protection in the form of insurance from the consequences of decisions taken in performing their professional duties. What could be more symbolic or representative of the growing counterproductivity of our techniques of medicare? If the frills are discarded, there is no correlation between sky-rocketing costs and what we get in return.

The entire human system has begun to operate towards the manufacture of problems and a search for their solution. In few other areas of human endeavour is this more prominent than in health care and medicine. Diminishing returns are reaching out towards counterproductivity through mercury detergent and DDT pollution, through food additives, smog and antibiotics. Newer technologies at higher and higher costs are becoming progressively less effective in containing these hazards and reducing them from the fruits of technologies now in use. The use of psychedelic drugs is going beyond human physical welfare into a new kind of intervention in the human psyche, an attempted conditioning of a person's future relations with his environment.

New genetics is racing towards evolving a new body of knowledge to give greater control over human life, disease, longevity, appearance, activity and behaviour, and all these are having a profound effect on medicine. Complete genetic mapping is on the horizon. The real problems of poverty, suffering and disease have been left way behind while we struggle with problems and issues beyond our comprehension and farther beyond our control.

[16]Colin Norman, *Soft Technologies, Hard Technologies*, Washington DC, World Watch Paper 23, 1978, p. 19.

When means have outgrown ends there is no knowing where the processes of counterproductivity will find their destination and what will be the consequences of this uncontrolled drift to the future of humankind. One of the unalterable facts of human existence is death and the span of human life. So it is with cultures, which have their own life span. If we alter this life by acceleration or living it up the processes of reversal and destruction also arrive with speed. And this speed is determined by the outgrowing means or the thoughtless acceleration of technological processes.

As technological advances continued to push back the point of counterproductivity not only was an illusion of progress sustained but in fact further fostered the belief that such progress would have no outer limits. But now the processes of counterproductivity are manifesting themselves in a broad spectrum of human activity and in the satisfaction of a variety of human needs.

Diminishing Returns in Agriculture

Food production is being accelerated through the simultaneous use of less land and diminishing manpower but with increasing use of energy, fertiilsers and pesticides. In a period that the population of USA grew 34 percent, agricultural production increased 45 percent and the use of energy by the use of nitrogenous fertiliser increased 65 percent, the harvested area declined 15 percent and yield per acre 77 percent. Peasant tradition resisted innovation and the old agricultural system preserved its stability. Once technical innovations make their entry into agriculture the ultimate end is setting in motion many counterproductive processes. The immediate impact has already been mapped out:

—The adjoining areas get water pollution.
—Increasing erosion of the soil because of deep ploughing and excessive use of nitrogenous and other fertilisers as well as deforestation.
—The kilo-calories of energy of fossil fuels actually used works out at many times more than the energy in the form of food obtained for human consumption.
—Drastic reduction in employment in agriculture, with particularly disastrous consequences in the developing countries, without alternative sources of employment.

—Large migration of population to urban areas leading up to an explosive urban problem and the aggregating charge on financial, energy and other resources, concentration of trained manpower in urban centres and large-scale deterioration of the rural communities.

So the processes of counterproductivity have far-reaching influence beyond agriculture production itself. They reach far into the socio-techno-economic mechanisms of society, its trading relations with the rest of the world and its pattern of brain drain.

Just as the extension of agricultures to new lands runs up against diminishing returns, so do the development of water resources and increasing use of fertilisers.

Crop yield increase predictably with each increment of chemical fertiliser—rapidly at first, than more slowly until they eventually level off. At 40 kilograms per hectare of fertiliser each kilogram yields 27 kilograms of corn. With the second 40 kilograms of fertiliser each kilogram yields 14 extra kilograms of corn. For the third and fourth 40 kilogram increment the additional yield of corn is nine kilograms and four kilograms respectively. The fifth addition of 40 kilograms yields one kilogram of corn. As one kilogram of fertiliser if far more expensive than a kilogram of corn the processes of counterproductivity take over long before these levels are reached.

Similar characteristics of counterproductivity apply to many other crops like wheat, rice and potatoes. There may be minor variations in the response of different crops, but there is no basic change in this pattern.

For instance, world food production increased 130 million tons in the 1950s and fertiliser production 13 million tons, in other words each additional ton of fertiliser increased food production 10 million tons. This ratio changed to eight in the late 1960s, seven in the late 1970s and to less than six in 1975.

While the worldwide average ratio was approaching points of counterproductivity it had already reached this position for many in some countries, particularly Western Europe, USA and Japan. The growth of the fertiliser industry is already on the decline. Natural limitation on water and sunlight ultimately place a ceiling on its use.

Considerable attention was directed after the Second World War to increasing the world supply of marine proteins.

> Between 1950-1970, the catch increased by an average of 5 percent yearly, far outstripping population growth and sharply boosting per capita supplies of marine proteins. But in 1970, the trend was abruptly and unexpectedly interrupted. Since then, the catch has fluctuated between 65-70 million tons.[17]

As catch exceeds regenerative capacity the productivity of scores of ocean fisheries is falling. While investment in fishing has continued to rise there has been no perceptible increase in catch. "Since 1968 there has been a substantial decline of 40 percent for herring and 90 percent for halibut."[18]
Ocean fishing has reduced the catch below the maximum sustainable yield in 27 of the Atlantic region's 30 fisheries.

> Since the 1972-73 debacle, when the catch dropped to a few million tons, the Peruvian Government has controlled fishing vigorously in an effort to restore fishery productivity. As of 1977, these efforts have met little success.[19]

> The OECD in its review of fisheries in 1975 reports that the total gross tonnage of the world's fishing vessels over 100 gross registered tons (GRT) has grown more than 50 percent in the six years to mid 1975. During the same period the catch did not increase at all, which means that the catch per dollar invested fell precipitously.[20]

Fishing is a classic example of the phenomenon of counterproductivity in an ever-widening spectrum of techno-economic activity. We therefore need to take into account not only diminishing returns in economics but also negative returns for overexploiting nature.
Similar trends have become discernible in the search for new oil sources and in mining because of the continuously diminishing quality of the available resources and inaccessible ore deposits.

[17]Lester R. Brown, *The Twenty Ninth Day*, New York, W. Norton and Company, 1978, p. 18.
[18]*Ibid.*, p. 20.
[19]*Ibid.*, pp. 20-22.
[20]*Ibid.*, p. 166.

The phenomenon of counterproductivity is also accelerated by double-digit inflation in most economies. This, coupled with economic stagnation and increasing unemployment, is rapidly closing many of the options for social rearrangement we anxiously seek.

The cost of oil and other sources of energy and wage increases are pushing beyond productivity gains and market expansion. The broadbased phenomenon of counterproductivity, embracing many aspects of human activity from food production to mining, energy prospecting and scientific and industrial research are not reacting to the known fiscal and economic remedies and are unable to undercut the prevalent and rising cost structures in most economies.

As such, the economies of yesterday are dying and the economies of tomorrow will be able to borrow neither the system nor energy and resources of today's world to make a new beginning. With the erosion of the technological multipliers in the pace-setting economies the new remedies out of the present malaise may lie in entirely new designs for living.

Soap has been replaced by detergents, requiring three times as much energy for its production. In addition, mercury is required to produce chlorine for detergents, and this element is released into the environment as a pollutant.

Soap has no pollution record while detergents have a bad environmental record. When pressure built up in the mid 1960s biodegradable detergents were introduced, but these were found to be even more dangerous and killed fish in the waterways. Phosphates added to combat hard water further worsened the problem of environment.

Similarly, it is not the increase in the number of cars which is the cause of our environmental and energy problem. While petroleum consumption in certain countries increased 60 percent lead entering the atmosphere in the same period increased 400 percent.

To make motor cars run faster their compression ratio changed from 5:9 in 1946 to 9:5 in 1968. Low-powered and low-compression engines were displaced although high-compression engines are less efficient at low speeds, and this is precisely the condition which they perform in traffic jams. So pollution increases with the increased number of cars, with miles travelled, with high compression and low engine performance because of the addition of tetraethyl lead to prevent knocking, particularly at low speed. Over

50,000 tons of toxic lead went into the air in 1946, and the quantity increased to 280,000 tons by 1970.

Nuclear Promise Unfulfilled

In the aftermath of the Hiroshima nuclear blast few other technologies showed greater promise as viable sources of energy for the future as nuclear energy. In course of time the acquisition of nuclear reactors for power generation and research became a status symbol and a qualification for acquiring membership of the exclusive nuclear club. But in an environment of cold war the genes which at birth produced nuclear weapons became more predominant, and the temptation to use this technology for offensive weapons was far more overwhelming than the development of its peaceful uses and containment of its hazards.

We are thus confronted with a situation where the causes of concern because of accumulating radioactive waste, rising scale of balance of terror and widening dimensions of proliferation far outweigh the promise of fulfilling humankind's future energy needs. Plagued by the spectre of shortage of nuclear fuels and the unending search for fuel-saving breeder reactors and also fusion power have made yesterday's promise of nuclear power a very expensive problem for tomorrow. On top of all this, the dangers of uncontrolled proliferation and nuclear terror have made atomic development the most counterproductive of technologies of the late 20th century.

After decades of neglect in search of the nuclear illusion attention is once again focussing on the comfortable reserves of old King Coal. The occupational hazards of coalmining have become an important social cost, which continues to rise even with greatly improved techniques of mine safety.

> Black lung disease alone costs the US exchequer over $1 billion a year. Coal's most obnoxious drawback has been its smoke. Electrostatic precipitators remove more than 90 percent of the soot and fly ash from coal boilers. While as a result of this large particles declined remarkably, the tiny particles that escaped are the greatest hazard and can be carried down into the lungs.[21]

[21] Tom Alexander, "New Fears Surround the Shift to Coal," *Fortune*, 20 November 1978, pp. 58-60.

One of the major environmental hazards from the use of coal is the increasing quantities of carbon dioxide released into the atmosphere. Carbon dioxide in the atmosphere acts as a oneway filter for energy from the sun to create a greenhouse effect. Since this gas is practically opaque to infrared the sun's heat gets trapped. All fossil fuels—coal, oil and natural gas—produce carbon dioxide when burnt, and for a given amount of heat coal produces about 24 percent more carbon dioxide than oil and 76 percent more than natural gas.

It is estimated that the atmospheric load of carbon dioxide could double in the next 60 to 75 years, and the end result of this could be an average world temperature increase of two to seven degrees Fahrenheit. This rise would not be uniform and the polar region might experience increases of as much as $12°F$, while temperatures might not alter perceptibly along the equator. This could bring about serious changes in wind-flow pattern, rain and agricultural productivity.

Unidimensional Education

All processes of preparing human beings to serve the objectives of a high-production and high-consumption technological society are not educational. They are the product or a part of a machine which can perform as efficiently as a gear or a motor or a computer programme. As the capabilities of these machines are enhanced so must the capabilities of their human operators be modified and upgraded.

As machines become obsolete so must their linking human capabilities become obsolete and be discarded. This process cannot be termed education. It is the continuing unidimensional perfection of the human part of the machine. If this part does not fit into the machine and does not work, a new one must be found.

This process is as intricate as the machine itself and is as specialised, but has a short life. In most affluent societies it is subjecting increasingly large sections of the less endowed or less privileged population to perpetual backwardness, and the more fortunate part to a psychological vacuum which only machines can fill.

The real purpose of education is to develop human faculties to innovate on an entire spectrum of human existence, their immediate environment as well as in the larger human frame. For such education to be equitable the entire human race without exception must be reached. Education in a technological consumer society follows trends in obsolescence and counterproductivity similar to those of the techno-economic process it serves.

That is why according to Margaret Mead "it must respond not to the present but to the future needs of societies, it is necessary to forecast constantly and as far as possible in advance the evolution of the vocational structure." And this process continuously pushes the educational structure towards redundance and counterproductivity.

While the processes of counterproductivity are overtaking the entire spectrum of human affairs its impact on education will be reflected in the long-term human future. Unless this transformation, the foundation of all other changes, takes place well ahead of other changes, humans cannot even dream of a possibly more desirable future.

If total human being H at a certain level of evolution could be represented by an integration or a sum total of the various attributes, that is physical (Ph), mental (M), aesthetic (E), psychic (Ps),

$$H = Ph \times M \times E \times Ps$$

the proportion of different elements or attributes may vary in different societes, individuals, moments in culture or time or stages of evolution, but within human limitations the factor H may be assumed to be constant.

> Time as you measure it may be different from my time, mass as you measure it may be different from my mass; speed and momentum and energy may be all different; it is only the relations between them that remain the same for us both.[22]

And broadly speaking these variations in different attributes constitute the cultural differences between social organisations. It is not a question of the superiority of one or other cultures. It is a historic process of evolution in which one or the other aspects get overemphasised because of lack of balancing factors in the social organisation. But none of the aspects can be pushed beyond the balancing factors of human limitations which mercifully bring into play counterproductivity in human terms.

[22] Jacob Bronowski, *Twentieth Century Images of Man*, New Delhi, USIS, pp. 6-7.

The Deeper the Illusion the Graver the Counterproductivity

The illusion of superiority many societies or subsystems within a society carry are only a reflection of the vulnerability or approaching counterproductivity of the elements around which such illusions are created. An economic recession is an economic phenomenon, but insecurity is a human phenomenon. While the importance of human phenomena is realised and attempts are made to regulate them through the media and several other human techniques, the depth of phenomena which aggravate these into depressions is less appreciated.

These are proofs, if any were needed, of the failure of the social organisation to assess the points of approaching counterproductivity of the human phenomenon. Any one of the human limitations can trigger the breakdown of the human system, the techno-economic phenomena being only the outer manifestation of a much more serious malaise. The computer programmers keep examining the veracity of their programmes on the human future and then wonder at the lack of response of the human mechanism to their studies.

It is being repeatedly established that only an insignificant proportion of human mental capabilities are put to use, but many persons in the course of human history have attained psychic and spiritual levels outside the comprehension of most in this age of affluence. We have bartered away the factors E, Ps to achieve physical and mental development, i.e. Ph and M.

The contribution of these elements is limited to the extent that they can be made subservient to the larger accepted societal purpose of the unlimited enhancement of the factor Ph. But Ph and M, like mass in Einstein's theory of relativity ($E=Mc^2$) are the most limited elements in the human situation H. In the total E the square of the speed of light C^2, like Ps, makes an infinitely larger contribution.

The endeavour to convert the limited, i.e. Ph and M, into unlimited elements and the unlimited elements in the processes of human evolution, i.e. E and Ps, to the limited has been the greatest disservice to humankind. Societies with the greatest such imbalance, irrespective of the outer manifestations of affluence and well-being, are in reality in the greatest crisis. To project every point of retreat to the points of counterproductivity is an invitation to disaster. Their manifestation may vary from one society to another or one politico-economic group to another and their intensity may vary from tolerable to unbearable.

But the emergence of the phenomenon of counterproductivity can no longer be denied in any social organisation or system. Counterproductivity is in terms of economic theory in vogue. "No economic theory is eternally valid. Every period demands its own. The problem has a solution in a certain arrangement."[23] But there are societies which have committed themselves to a social organisation in which no new arrangements are considered possible.

These societies have reached a stage of techno-economic commitment where no reversal appears possible without bringing the entire system crashing down. In such societies Ph and M are reaching their outer limits and the elements E, Ps are no longer free from subservience to Ph so as to be able to seek liberation from their malaise.

These are societies that may reach points of irreversibility in social action. They are not just a threat to themselves but in the process of nurturing their illusions and in search of their own salvation can become a threat to all humanity.

There are in absolute terms no uncommitted societies. Each society has a level of commitment. So long as human processes reach a point of reversal and when such points relate only to a relatively small segment of society, there is still hope of a peaceful rearrangement. So long as the element Ph alone reaches its outer limits and when the elements M,E, Ps are relatively free to seek new solutions societal transformation to achieve new points of equilibrium may be considered possible. Such transformation is only possible in uncommitted societies because counterpoductivity is only in terms of the rigid ideological frame, and new societies have the option to create a new framework for action.

TECHNOLOGICAL REVERSAL

When the effects of technological multipliers in economic processes are neutralised by the socio-ecological costs of technologies the process of technological reversal commences. This process usually makes its appearance at micro levels where the effects of one technology after another are neutralised by newer technologies

---

[23]Jacques Ellul, *op. cit.*, p. 239.

with lower and lower multiplier effects till it reaches the point of total neutralisation and reversal.

When this effect spreads to a broad spectrum of the economy its impact is felt in the entire system. Unless the technological multiplier effects continuously overtake the reversal factors in key areas of the techno-economic system the system loses its resilience and is unable to stem the tide of aggregating reversal, thus leading to total stagnation with regard to key parameters of growth such as employment and social welfare. And this usually results in the regression of the economy and deep crisis.

The total technological inversions at the micro-level weighted for impact in major areas of development, determine the technological state of society. A system may be very highly developed yet be in a very poor technological state, not in absolute terms but in terms of its ability to provide multipliers in the techno-economic system.

On the other hand, a developing society with a very low capital of technologies may have many options and a wide potential to accelerate the developmental processes through the introduction of new technologies, even technologies which have reached points of reversal in another environment.

Factors which contribute most to accelerating the techno-economic processes are often also responsible for the phenomenon of technological reversal. Introduction of chemical fertilisers contributed to rapid growth of food production, but further use of them contributed to increased salinity and erosion of the soil.

Pesticides caused danger to human and animal life. The development of plastics, while improving performance of many areas of productivity and utility, simultaneously increased the quantum of non-biodegradable pollution. Continuous innovation created new goods and services while resulting rapid and continuing obsolescence have spawned a waste land of goods, mothballed airplanes, ships and military hardware, nuclear waste, automobiles, throw-away plastic materials and thousands of others, consumables and intermediates.

As socio-psychological processes are stepped up to promote and meet the challenges of a high-consumer society, obsolescence and discardability record a growth rate no less than that of the production of goods.

The loss of materials and labour the community sustains in

discarded goods is assuming colossal proportions. Quite often the GNP of a nation and the total capital of goods discarded increase at an equal rate. In other words, a sizable proportion of the labour and material employed in production processes goes towards aggregating waste rather than contributing to human welfare.

Starting with the early 1950s, electric power doubled every ten years in most industrialised countries. Production of goods, solid wastes and pollutants also doubled in the same period. An attempt has been made to assess the implications of such development in the next few decades, and at exponential rates of growth these problems are likely to assume staggering dimensions.

Every single technological process casts its own shadow of certain natural technological consequences. In generating electricity massive quantities of heat are released into the environment.

Similarly, for every 100 units of heat removed by an airconditioning unit over 125 units of heat are dissipated into the environment. The cumulative effect of such large quantities of heat may go beyond the capacity of the natural processes to neutralise, with consequent ecological disturbances.

> Civilisations commonly die from the excessive development of certain characteristics which had at first contributed to their success. Our form of industrial civilisation suffers from having allowed experts to make growth and efficiency, rather than the quality of life, the main criterion of success.[24]

Cyclic wastes are human, plant, animal and other wastes that return or cycle back to the system. These normally biodegradable wastes are usually neutralised by natural processes. But often because of rapid and concentrated generation, as in large urban centres, they accumulate beyond the point of normal dissipation and may require chemical or mechanical handling.

These can be cycled back to the system. Metal scrap can be reclaimed back to basic metals for use again, while gas, petroleum, chemical or some other offensive wastes could be neutralised mechanically or chemically at a cost.

There are many wastes which cannot be cycled back into the

---

[24]Rene Dubos, *A God Within*, New York, Charles Scribner and Sons, 1972, p. 233.

system by natural processes or at a reasonable cost. The half-life of many of these wastes often runs into hundreds of years, and the aggregation of such materials in the environment are a hazard to animal and plant life. This category of wastes, including heat from power plants and industrial wastes such as mercury from chemical and fertiliser production, plastics, pesticides such as DDT, waste from nuclear plants. Most of these wastes are a major health hazard and at the same time an irreplaceable accompaniment of advanced stages of industrialisation.

Mathematically, the following equation would represent the total addition of various types of wastes in an ecological system:

$X = (A-a) + (B-b) + C$, where

X = the cumulative addition to the system of pollutants beyond the capacity of natural and adopted processes to neutralise.

A = the total or waste pollutants of the cyclic biodegradable type generated in the system.

a = the extent to which the waste pollutants of the cyclic type can be neutralised by the natural processes in a given environment.

B = Wastes of the semicyclic type which can be recycled into the environment or into the production cycle at a cost, like reconversion into metals of scrap waste and purification of certain effluents.

b = the waste materials actually cycled back or reclaimed in a non-polluting or reusable form.

C = wastes which cannot be recycled into the system at a reasonable cost or where infiltration into the system can be ecologically serious. These are plastics wastes, DDT and other pesticides, nuclear wastes such as unprocessed fuels, strontium 90, industrial and chemical wastes, mercury and gas released into the atmosphere, lead tetraethyl and many others. The value X is subject to further change because of two factors:

1. Neutralisation of pollutant wastes, internally due to the time factor, usually negligible because of the long half-life of such material.
2. The overall cumulative ecological effect of technological and economic growth.

Hence the equation:

$$Z = Pe + (X-x) \times N$$

Z — represents the total cumulative pollution of the environment, taking both the base and the incremental factors into account.
Pe — threshold or base pollutants in the environment at the time of assessment.
$(X-x) \times N$ — is, the incremental factors due to economic and technological growth.
x — neutralisation due to time factor assumed negligible.
N — is the multiplier due to economic and technological growth, and its value could be assessed as follows:

$$N = (1+GR)^{n-1}$$

GR — annual growth rate in percent
n — number of years
with x 1 as negligible, the equation can be expressed as follows:
$$Z = Pe + NX$$

In a totally backward or primitive, largely rural agricultural society most pollutants cycle back into the system and 'a' is always larger than 'A'. Hence no ecological disturbances or deterioration take place.

In a developing society in the process of industrialisation or large-scale agriculture development

A = pa, where
(p) is the pollutant factor and can be anything from 1−1.2. Corrective processes can contain this level of ecological impurity.

When (p) factor varies between 1.2−1.5 the natural recycling processes would need 10-20 years to correct the excessive generation of pollutants. A (p) factor of above 1.5 would be a matter of immediate concern.

B — is directly related to the level of industrial development in a society and can be correlated with either per capita income or GNP or the ratio between industrial and agriculture production, or with other measures such as the use of steel and other metals. For instance 0.5−0.6 metric tons per capita of steel is brought into use in USA every year, and of this about 0.2 tons turn up as plant scrap and 0.4 tons enter the inventory in use yearly.

The estimated inventory of total steel in use per capita is 15 tons, which after providing for scrap corrosion and other factors is likely to be of the order of 9.4 tons per capita.

Similarly, energy equal to 14 tons of coal equivalent is introduced into the system every year.

C—is generally linked with advanced stages of industrial development. It is therefore zero for a backward society.

For developing societies which have launched on high technology development the factor will vary to the extent of the ratio of high technology development to total development and would include:

Nuclear fuel processing and storage.
Thermal dissipation in nuclear and thermal plants. Ecological effects of hydroelectric development such as soil erosion.
Generation of nonbiodegradable wastes such as plastic and nuclear wastes, mercury chemicals and fertilisers, oil, pesticides, noise (aviation and machinery).

TABLE I

Assessment of Value of X^*

	Factors of pollution assuming minimum percentage for backward and maximum, 100% for post industrial societies	Assumed neutralisation capability of natural or adopted processes
Cyclic Type	$A=0-1$	$a=0-1$......
Semic-Cyclic Type	$B=0-1$	$b=0-0.5$ (assuming
Non-biodegradable	$C=0-1$	$c=0$ economic neutralisation of up to 50% of waste)
Cyclic	Semi-Cyclic	Non-Biodegradable
I. Backward Societies		
$A=0.3$	$B=0$	$C=0$
$a=0.3$	$b=0$	
$A-a=0$	$B-b=0$	

*i.e. cumulative addition to the system of pollutans beyond the capacity of natural and adopted processes to neutralise in societies at various stages of development.

II. Developing Societies
 A=0.6   B=0.1   C=0.2
 a=0.6   b=0.09
 A−a=0   B−b=0.01   C=0.2
 X=(0+0.01+0.2)=0.21

III. Industrial Societies
 A=0.7   B=0.7   C=0.6
 a−a=0   B−b=0.4
 X=(0+0.4+0.6)=1.0

IV. Post Industrial Societies
 A=1   B=1   C=0.8
 a=0.6   b=0.2
 A−a=0.4   B−b=0.8
 X=0.4+0.8+0.8=2

TABLE II
Assessment of Value N

$$N=(1+Gr)^{n-1} \quad \ldots 3$$

A Value of factor N for growth rate of 5% and 10% for various time Scales—Equation (3)

	Number of Years			
	5	10	15	20
Growth Rate 10% (1+0.1)	1.464	2.35	3.79	6.11
Growth Rate 5% (1+0.05)	1.21	1.55	1.98	2.52

$$Z = Pe + NX \quad (4) \quad \ldots 4$$

TABLE III
Factor of Incremental Pollution in Societies at Various Stages of Development with Growth rates of 5 or 10%, i.e. Volue of NX

	Number of Years			
	5	10	15	20
I. Backward Societies				
10% Growth	0.000	0.000	0.000	0.000
5% Growth	0.000	0.000	0.000	0.000
II. Developing Societies				
10% Growth	0.3014	0.4935	0.796	1.283
5% Growth	0.2541	0.3255	0.4158	0.529
III. Industrial Societies				
10% Growth	1.464	2.35	3.79	0.611
5% Growth	1.21	1.55	1.98	2.520
IV. Post Industrial Societies				
10% Growth	2.93	4.7	7.6	12.22
5% Growth	2.42	3.1	4.0	5.04

Table III shows that there is no pollution of any consequence which natural processes cannot contain in backward societies. In post-industrial societies, on the basis of the same assumptions, pollution can increase over 1200 percent at 10 percent growth rate and 500 percent at 5 percent growth rate over 20 years.

This shows the order of magnitude of the ecological problem in rapid developmental processes.

Reversing Factors

With rising environmental pollution and its health hazards increasingly large sums of money will have to be diverted to control it. This will particularly hit countries with much greater reliance on new technologies rather than those developing countries with other parameters of economic growth such as captive raw materials or markets. Japan and the United States will be particularly vulnerable in such a situation. Pollution control investment will be particularly heavy in nuclear and thermal power generation, paper, chemicals, petroleum and such other industries.

Pollution control expenditure on the US paper industry grew from about $90 million in the late 1960s to over $650 million in the mid 1970s—a sevenfold increase.[25] This accounted for nearly one-third of capital investment in pulp, paper and paperboard industries around 1975. In Japan such claims are diverting capital from further industrial expansion and considerably reducing Japan's economic growth. Merely satisfying the conditions laid down by the environmental agency would cost an additional $2 billion.

To reduce noise pollution to a more tolerable level will require airlines to invest $ 5 billion to $ 8 billion over the next five years. This would amount to more than $30 dollars per head of US population or more than the cost per capita of India's sixth five year plan. The need for such investment will grow to 500 percent of investment at present at an annual growth rate of 5 percent and to 1200 percent at a growth rate of 10 percent by the year 2000. The implications are obvious.

The multiplier effects of technologies was a major factor in the acceleration of developmental processes. The greater the incentives the faster the speed of technological change. After going through a period of intense activity and massive contribution to the processes

[25]Cester Brown, *op. cit.*, p. 180.

of economic growth technological processes reach a kind of plateau where fundamental technological changes in specific areas are no longer possible. Technological multipliers become inoperative and overadvertising and "hidden persuaders" take over to assure the continuity of economic processes. These operate over a period of time in advancing the interest of one competitor against others or the preference of one product over another. But in the overall balance the net gains to the system and society are at best marginal.

By this time the technological multipliers start approaching zero, and the cost to the community in wasted materials and effort and in sustaining and promoting the viability of the system would have increased manifold. To this must be added the ecological, unemployment and other social costs. At this point the contribution to GNP is illusory. Technologies are confined to their deathly decline as the processes of technological reversal have gone beyond repair.

From the beginning of the 1960s there has been nothing new of any significance in the automobile industry except cosmetics and novelties. All we have seen and experienced is the acceleration of speed at the cost of additional lead tetraethyl in the engine and the increasing use of high-energy intensity materials such as aluminium, chromium and plastics and increased quantities of nonbiodegradable waste. Fossil fuels have been increasingly used and the processes of waste accelerated.

Many processes of technological reversal are obvious, many others not so obvious, but the options to alter this situation through new technologies and new concepts are becoming increasingly limited. Replacement of large automobiles with a small electrically operated model may generate multiplier effects in the storage battery and some other industries. But engine building, metal and associated energy and other industries would face a major dislocation, and these effects could be equally disastrous with the development of a public transport system.

Replacement of the railroad industry by road and air transport brought about profound changes in the input-output models in the economy of the United States. But the air transport industry is now reaching a point where it can add to the speed of travel of a few but cause the discomfort of a sonic boom to many.

The energy cost per man-mile is also increasing geometrically with speed, and so old technologies run to their death. New ones cannot take birth because of the forced sterilisation of the innovative processes. This could also mean that while multiplier effects would be operating in some economies or parts of some reversal effects will operate in others.

Escape Routes

Today hundreds of technologies and the economic processes that they stimulated, sustained and multiplied are reaching various stages of reversal; from incipient to advanced, i.e. from zero multiplier to total reversal. There is no end in sight for these processes and hope for the birth of innovations is also receding because the massive economic commitment to existing technologies does not leave much room for manoeuvre. Indeed, the socio-economic costs of their replacement would be many times more serious than continuation on the same path.

As more and more productive processes based on these technologies run into blind alleys or downward slides advanced societies resort to a variety of human techniques to assure the viability of the system, or take the escape route of promoting massive defence expenditure on marginal technologies considered politically acceptable or desirable.

Perfection of the instruments of destruction are now reaching ridiculously comic proportions. The ability to destroy millions with finesse is regarded as the hallmark of civilised societies. If the past is any guide the ultimate in the process of reversal and nature's justice would be that every weapon will ultimately be used against the innovating country. Escape routes for economies under siege, as for armies in war, often lead to disastrous consequences. Economic, social, ecological and resources costs of following these escape routes are assuming monumental proportions. They are leading one society after another towards unpredictable consequences of the steps they are taking to stem the rising tide of technological reversal.

Is the phenomenon of technological reversal the natural projection and consequence of technological innovation? Or is the rapid movement towards reversal the outcome of our failure to assure adequate renewal of socio-economic institutions so as to contain the milching of technologies to their demise? Some of these issues may have already gone beyond the point of relevance for affluent nations but are still highly significant for developing societies. In most such societies technological inputs have had very little to do with productive processes.

Whenever such inputs have taken place their effect has largely been superficial or unidimensional. For example, the introduction of fertilisers and pesticides helped agricultural production to increase, but the effects of such increases on the larger socio-economic system have been marginal. They may have helped to increase the prosperity and welfare of certain segments and some pockets in a country, but their impact on the larger economic scene has been largely insignificant.

Introduction of high technology in certain basic industries may increase production, enhance capabilities, change attitudes, reduce imports, raise GNP, but the overall benefits touch only a small section of the population. There can be no better proof of the role of socio-economic organisation on containment of technological multipliers in the economic system than the start of the processes of counterproductivity and reversal at the very beginning of the developmental processes, when not even the basic needs of a small fraction of the population have been satisfied. Many productive processes have reached overproduction in the midst of shortages and inflation in the midst of glut.

No Options for the Committed

There is an important distinction between the exhaustion of the multiplier effects of technologies in a highly saturated situation, leading up to rapid reversal, and a comparable situation in respect of a small segment of the system in a developing society. In the first situation there are hardly any options; in the second the options are wide open. Exercise of the limited option in the first might mean a major dislocation of the system, while in the second dislocation will be restricted to those sectors which benefit from such development.

The story of development in the last three centuries is woven round a continuing series of innovations. There has been a high tide from full control of productive tools in the age of crafts to a helpless subservience to tools in consumerist development to a rapid aggregation of fortunes, from an aggravation of poverty and want, from the elimination of disease to accumulation of pollution.

Behind every process of the multiplication of wants and their satisfaction, of the acceleration of technological processes and their reversal, of the buildup of arsenals of highly destructive weapons and manoeuvres for human rights, there has been somebody's gain, somebody's power, somebody's need for energy and resources. Every process of socio-economic transformation thus gets sidetracked and continuation on the high road to reversal appears far less serious to the decision-makers than disturbing the continuity of the high-speed processes. Hence no corrective action is taken or appears possible. And all that beneficiaries and the state need is justification.

In reality the brutal reversal we are witnessing at present is essentially a return to long tradition. Power is power, but it cannot be exercised without at least the appearance of justice. Doctrine is charged, therefore with the task of furnishing power with the semblance of justice. We repeat it has not always been so. But since at present power is technique, these intellectual constructs no longer have any usefulness beyond supplying justification.[26]

Elites in developing societies are hypnotised by the consumerist syndrome. They are more concerned with acquiring the highest available technologies than with the processes of reversal, more with goods than with their ecological backlash, more with accepted norms of modernity than with the compulsive needs of their own societies. In the result we see acceleration and reversal at the same time, high-speed machines and aggregating unemployment, superhigh technologies bulldozing the culture of the crafts.

Every time the need for employment loses out, every time man falls by the wayside, the machine marches on. As Nietzsche said, "A matter that becomes clear ceases to concern us." Only in the early 1970s did the inadequacies of affluent high-technology societies to meet the new challenges begin to dawn.

The growing crisis of resources, unemployment, inflation, adverse trade balances, the armaments race have placed the affluent societies in a tightening straitjacket from which there appears to be no escape. The abilities of many socio-techno-economic institutions to meet the problems which face developing societies are being equally called into question. Also questioned is the ability of the so-

---

[26]Jacques Ellul, *op. cit.*, p. 284.

called advanced societies to set the pattern for development for others when their own system is unable to cope with problems arising out of their own strategies.

When so many aspects of a system run into a crisis is it worth following such a system? The big-power confrontation almost everywhere, the armament race, the treatment of minorities in the affluent countries, the open support for military dictatorships, one debacle after another in controlled wars and the ruthless cornering of world-wide resources have undermined both the physical and moral authority of affluent societies to set the pattern for the future of their own countries and in developing societies.

Unemployment

Perhaps in no other area of social concern has the phenomenon of technological reversal made a greater impact than in unemployment. The rapid increases in productivity in the US, Western Europe and Japan and other countries after the Second World War was brought about by the rapid growth and modernisation of their economies with massive technology, capital and organisational inputs. These were easily absorbed by the world economic system.

But the continued indiscriminate acceleration of high-energy, high-technology productive processes, coupled with inbuilt inflationary trends, high capital intensity of equipment and consequently major wage differentials within and between societies has placed most advanced societies in an unemployment straitjacket. This social cost is nothing but a consequence of the phenomenon of technological reversal.

The energy costs, resource limitation, wage structure, inflation market saturation, research and development costs, protective trade barriers against dumping, ecological limitations, adverse trade balances are blind alleys leading up to a stone wall against which political and economic leaders stand and make heroic pronouncements for a new economic order while tens of millions around the world are entering job markets to exercise their right to work within the prevalent value system, a system of production and consumption ceaselessly promoted through the international communication networks.

What happened in factories in the 1950s and 1960s is now being reproduced in the area of white-collar jobs by cybernetics, copying machines, pocket calculators and other innovations. The entry of large numbers of women into the job market has introduced another destabilising element in techno-economic systems. Inability to match the skills of large segments of the youthful population to new job requirements is adding to the social costs of both developing and developed societies. About 20 million jobless workers in the highly industrialised countries of the Western world are today reversing the processes of affluence in socio-economic terms.

India's labour force increased by over 60 million in the 1970s. Rapid industrialisation with high-energy, high-technology tools has further aggravated the problem of urban exodus, brain drain, big wage differentials and social unrest.

Over 15 percent of the labour force is unemployed in Pakistan, Sri Lanka, Malaysia and the Philippines, over one-third in Bangladesh, and one-fourth in Indonesia.

The International Labour Organisation has projected that about 30 percent of the labour force will be partially or wholly unemployed in 1980. Up to the year 2000 about 30 million new jobs would have to be created every year.

While Western Europe mitigated the hardships of reversal processes by sending back "guest workers", these workers have now become a major social problem in their home countries.

This crisis of unemployment has not caught us unawares. It was inherent in the techno-economic policies and strategies of the post-war period and rooted in the limitation of the world's resources and environment and, above all, human greed. The future we thoughtlessly projected is now reversing on us. "Maturity consists in the discovery that there comes a time where everything is reversed, after which the point becomes to understand more and more that there is something which cannot be understood."

Technologies to exploit natural resources such as coal, oil and gas took more than half a century to backfire or reach the point of reversal, while nuclear energy with more intense intervention in the natural processes has backfired in less than a decade. Much greater care is therefore required to plan the use of new sources of energy such as solar energy or bioenergy by avoiding overconcentration and developing new use patterns rather than pipe the new sources into the time-worn, wasteful pattern.

As if by a continuous and inexorable process, increasingly large sections of the techno-economic system are reaching a technological dead end. The polestar of the technological societies is hidden behind dark clouds, and as more and more old and new technologies approach the reversal point both developed and developing societies are bewildered about their future course of action. Only the developing societies have some options open. And this is saying a great deal in the concluding two decades of the 20th Century.

3. Energy

INSTRUMENT OF POWER

In the last two decades energy has become the single most important instrument for the exercise of political and economic power. The protection, exploitation and trade in energy has led to the emergence of many regional and international power centres and spheres of influence in one form or other. Energy lobbies play a crucial role in determining foreign and trade policies, and they are always in a state of flux and changing the course of superpower relations.

The discovery of energy resources within hitherto relatively unimportant states in politico-economic terms has given such states a new status in the eyes of their neighbours and often exposes them to the hegemonic designs of the superpowers. Whenever such a discovery takes place in a developing society, as is more often the case, it turns out to be its misfortune. Such countries and their resources then appear in the calculations of major users to be protected and preserved as an integral part of their own economic systems.

Thus West Asia was integrated into the Western economic system to ensure an uninterrupted supply of energy to the market economies and their client countries. Later, integration with the economic system alone was not considered secure. So the entire region had to be developed into a defence system, which in turn made it the target of those against whom this system was directed. The recent happenings in Iran are simply the story of oil energy. An unfortunate owner of oil resources has collapsed there under the weight of his own oil and the armaments required to protect it from the designs of client and neighbouring countries. Wherever the commitment to oil in the energy use pattern of a country enlarges its internal and external security becomes highly vulnerable to outside factors.

The techno-economic systems which emerged from the industrial revolution were based on coal, the energy resource of Britain. Most innovations, whether in transport—*i.e.* steamship or steam locomotives—or in productive processes through steam engine-based machines, were linked with mining, transport or utilisation of coal. These processes were further extended to the continent of Europe. The far-flung colonial empires, with imperial power centres in Europe, were controlled and manipulated through coal-based energy converters and products and power derived from them.

Emergence of the internal combustion engine in the latter half of the 19th Century (1875-1880) and its predominance over the steam engine as motive power by the first three decades of the 20th Century shifted the techno-economic balance of power from Britain towards the United States.

Since the United States relied largely on its own oil resources she had a definite edge over the imperial European powers, which largely depended on oil energy from their colonies. The collapse of the colonial powers after the Second World War and the emergence of the United States as a superpower owes a great deal to the new oil and energy technologies.

The power and prosperity of post-war Europe and its automobility was based on imported energy, largely through the control of West Asian resources. The exponential growth and the continuous reduction in doubling time for the use of oil energy has made the European countries increasingly dependent on West Asian oil. Similarly, a steadily rising proportion of the oil energy needs of the United States are met through imports of oil.

Exponential growth in the use of energy, change in the energy use pattern towards oil, fresh emphasis on research in and development of technologies based on liquid and gaseous fuels and, lastly, current shortages and rising prices have added to the distortions and uncertainties of the world-wide energy picture. In this process local or regional availability of fuels has been ignored and everybody, including the developing countries, is becoming committed to this irrationality of pushing the use of liquid and gaseous fuels.

Even under threat of shortages and the long-term uncertainty of supplies, massive pipelines and tankers are crisscrossing the globe and carrying this coal equivalent to Newcastle. With every price increase, every throttling of supplies, shipping and hundreds of other industries are thrown into disarray, threatening in turn the stability of the entire world-wide techno-economic system.

This confusion is worse confounded as nuclear and oil interests and lobbies distort the ecological image of coal. While the environmentalist lobby is giving a hard time to nuclear development powerful interests are busy staking their options on every conceivable source of energy, old or new, and influencing governmental energy strategies towards serving their own profitability rather than the long-term national interests of their own and their client countries.

Similar distortions and contradictions are being introduced into the energy use pattern and policies of developing countries. Instead of tapping their own locally or regionally available resources and developing technologies to optimise their use, these countries are indulging in unfavourable world-wide commerce in oil and nuclear processing plants.

Through a process of natural justice, affluent societies, generally the greatest beneficiaries of such policies, are becoming their worst victims. Having first latched themselves, then Europe and Japan, and now many countries of Latin America, on to an energy use pattern of high waste, high risk and high conversion, the United States now finds itself in an energy straitjacket. The only escape from it will lead to massive trade deficits, the diminishing value of the dollar, unemployment and threats of deep economic depression and international confrontation. And all this without any long-term solution in sight.

Between overpromotion of energy technologies relating to fusion and nuclear power and new sources of energy—such as solar energy on one side and its denigration by special interests on the other—there is utter confusion concerning the available future options. The role that a particular source of energy is expected to play in future is first blown out of proportions and then shot down for its inadequacy to fulfil that role.

It is often proposed that any future source of energy should fit into the role that is at present served by the existing sources of energy. Nuclear energy is thus expected to propel automobiles and aircraft and solar energy is expected to replace oil, gas and coal in electrical grids. In other words, the evolutionary processes through which technologies and equipment emerged around a given source of energy are now expected to be yoked to an altogether different source of energy, with different characteristics and economic parameters.

On an overall basis, the greatest contribution of liquid fuels to human social organisation has been mobility. The greatest contribution of nuclear energy in view of the ecological and economic parameters can only be centralisation, that of solar wind and biomass energy decentralisation, and that of geothermal and wave energy regionalisation. It is only through an adequate assessment of the basic characteristics of an energy source that its economic, social and ecological parameters can be optimised.

The need for selective centralisation and massive decentralisation to achieve desirable socio-economic objectives in developing societies and the inability of any one of the sources of energy to fulfil all human needs would require a much deeper understanding and assessment of roles of both old and new sources of energy. Centralised energy sources and decentralised societies will be a contradiction in terms. When the very lifeblood of an economic system in a decentralised organisation is subject to control from a distant source decentralised structures become unsustainable.

Sociologists like W. Fred Cottrell see "energy as the organising principle around which social scale institutions and values are crippled and destroyed."[1] Hence, whenever there is a transition from one source of energy to another, or a dominant source of energy recedes, the entire socio-economic system becomes unstable.

A new techno-economic infrastructure needs to be evolved to satisfy the characteristics of the new dominant energy source and the requirements of the new energy use pattern. "The changeover necessitated the radical uprooting of an entire way of life. The way people made a living, the way people got around, the way people dressed, the way people behaved, the way governments governed—all of this was turned inside out then upside down."[2] The world system has gone through many such transitions in the 17th, 18th and 19th Centuries, but none of these equals in scope, dimension or speed the one we are going through today as a result of the shakeup of the techno-economic infrastructures committed to oil. The attempted hasty changeover to nuclear power seems to

---

[1] W. Fred Cottrell, *Energy and Society*, New York, McGraw Hill Book Company Inc., 1955.
[2] Jermy Rifkin, *Entropy*, New York, Viking Press, p. 22.

have aborted.

The bulk of the present world-wide oil energy infrastructure is devoted to the consumerist mode of development wherein the system not only operates towards increasing consumerability and accelerating production processes but also intensifies trends towards high-energy converters, thus continuously lowering the efficiency of the entire energy system through conversion, transmission and distribution, as also the acceleration of speed, narrowing down diversities of energy use and various other factors.

In this process many techno-economic systems are compulsively committed to a particular energy source, build expensive and vast infrastructures, and are thus left with limited manoeuvrability in effecting orderly transition from existing to new sources of energy. Such systems are and will remain in a continuous state of ever-growing crisis.

Energy Policy and Management in Agriculture

There can be no energy policy relating only to a sector of the economy. Energy used in agriculture cannot be treated separately from that used in other sectors. Often a sizable proportion of this energy, such as for the manufacture of fertilisers, machinery, pesticides, transport, is used at points far away from the scene of agricultural production and under a different set of priorities. Energy policy must incorporate the entire techno-economic system, which in turn must be related to or be the outcome of the total developmental strategies and the overall nature of the problem.

The parameters of the demographic and unemployment realities of a society, the outer limits of its energy and other resources, and the ecological limitations must be accurately defined. For instance in the case of India, the fact that her population will most probably reach levels of over 1000 million by the year 2000, with over 60 percent still living in communities of fewer than 1000 persons, must be faced. India will have to provide an additional 150 million jobs in the prevalent value system.

As high-energy societies reach out towards points of technological reversal on a broad spectrum of techno-economic effort and to points of no return in their energy use pattern, it is time that developing societies should take stock of their options in formulating sustainable energy policies.

An infrastructure for energy in the rural sector, as commonly understood, means linking villages with an electrical transmission system. All plans for extension or enlargement of this infrastructure are related to setting up hydro, nuclear or thermal power stations. But in reality the infrastructure for energy means much more. It is far more complex and involves many special considerations. Basically, the extent and type of energy introduced into a rural system determines the type of development which takes place. For instance, if electrical energy is introduced into the entire system, it would become highly capital-intensive and inefficient at the point of use. And to a great extent this energy would depend on fossil fuels and nonrenewable energy sources.

A commitment to the use of these resources at the very commencement of rural developmental processes would mean the extension of high-energy, high-technology, high-cost urban development processes to the rural areas. Over the coming decades these countries will find themselves committed to a type of techno-economic infrastructure which even the more affluent nations find difficult to sustain or reverse.

Therefore, firstly, developing societies must take a look at the total rural energy system of which agricultural needs are a part. Long-term stability of any socio-economic system will depend on its ability to stabilise its growth objectives at levels that energy consumed can be continuously renewed or replaced. And this can only be achieved if the energy downgraded or rejected in one part of the system can be used in another.

Secondly, such societies have to establish the optimum level and types of energy inputs into the agricultural rural system and the consequences of departure from these optimum levels in terms of production, employment and other social costs, considering the long-term objectives and short-term compulsions.

Annexure A indicates the energy needs of a typical rural community of 1000 persons in India. Energy use generally falls under the following categories:

Domestic needs such as cooking, water supply, hot water for bathing, washing, lighting.
Social services—road lighting, schools, transport, hospital or dispensaries and other public institutions.

Sustaining and increasing agriculture production. Generation of employment—processing of agricultural produce, workshops, house construction and materials, general industrial and production activity, transportation of goods (inwards and outwards).

Thus, it is obvious that the infrastructure for energy for such a community would have to be so designed as to supply needs very economically and not just electricity for lighting, kerosene for cooking, diesel for tractors and power pumps. Cooking can be done most efficiently with methane gas or wood, both renewable energy sources. Lighting can be provided with electricity or methane gas. Irrigation from wells will be undertaken with the help of electricity or methane and crop drying with solar energy, a renewable source. In agricultural production alone the extent and type of energy used depends largely on the nature of agriculture and the strategy for production.

Annexure B indicates food energy yield versus mechanical energy for various inputs into agriculture. In subsistence agriculture in most parts of India, the bulk of the energy used is consumed by human beings in the form of food or, in the case of draught animals, as cattle feed. The average energy output/input ratios in such a situation are quite high, often 15:1, while in the case of high-energy intensity agriculture the ratio comes down to 1.5:1.

Annexure C gives comparative output/input ratios for different energy intensities in agricultural production. Some important conclusions that may be drawn from this assessment are:

(a) To meet India's projected food needs of 250 million tons in the year 2000 the natural systems, left to themselves without any energy subsidy form outside, would require about 1000 million acres (400 million hectares) of land against the 350 million acres (140 million hectares) now under cultivation and about 100 million acres (40 million hectares) which can be brought under cultivation by the turn of the century.

It is just not possible to achieve adequate food production targets and thus support India's population through subsistence agriculture alone. A more intensive use of land and for meeting seasonal labour shortages would call for energy inputs beyond what man and animal can provide. With a large land area and its low occupation the gross energy needs for a high-calorie, high-protein diet are relatively low. But with a very large population, low availability of land and high unemployment as in India energy-intensive agriculture is not economically viable.

(b) The extension of medium-energy intensity agriculture can help to realise production objectives without enlarging the area of unemployment beyond manageable limits, and no more than 70 million acres of additional land would be required to be brought under cultivation by the year 2000.

(c) About 60 percent of the energy in medium-intensity agriculture would be contributed by human labour and draught animals. This is towards supporting employment, reducing hard physical labour and furthering the objectives of a livestock-energy economy.

None of the three alternatives in *Annexure C* can therefore be exclusively applied to solve the wide complexity of India's food, energy and employment problems. Up to AD 2000 there will have to be an integration of all three possibilities, that is marginal use of high energy intensity agriculture should be made to urgently fill the gaps in food availability.

Subsistence agriculture would have to be practised to keep farm labour employed till alternative opportunities for work are created. But the maximum effort will have to be directed towards medium-energy intensity agriculture, and also towards optimising employment and production per unit of energy consumed. Or in other words, the widespread use of high-energy converters to save man-hours of work would have to be restricted.

Medium energy intensive agriculture with an output/input ratio of over five appears the only logical policy for agriculture in the Indian context. On an India-wide basis, with an estimated rural population of 615×10^6 in AD 2000, this works out at:

Energy for agriculture (medium energy intensity agriculture)	$= 16.0 \times 10^6$ tons of oil equivalent
Energy for domestic and other purposes	$= 66.5 \times 10^6$ " " "
Total	$= 82.5 \times 10^6$ " " "

Livestock Energy Economy

It would appear that by recycling agriculture and animal waste and using the full potential of our livestock-energy-economy all the needs of medium-energy intensity agriculture and over one-fourth of the need for all the other domestic energy requirements of rural communities can be met through local effort. By transferring some needs such as energy for biogas plants, domestic water supply and drying crops to solar energy the use of traditional energy sources can be further reduced.

To achieve this objective at the highest degree of efficiency and minimum cost the operations of biogas plants would need to be optimised. Among some causes of the erratic behaviour of biogas plants are variations of temperature. Solar heating of the biomass through simple technologies can make an important contribution in this regard.

The aggregated energy inputs to agriculture have risen manifold over the decades, but food production has not increased in the same proportion. Energy studies have revealed some very important facts. These are:

—Output/input ratios plunge drastically with high-energy agriculture. In some countries more than five units of energy are consumed to make available one unit of energy in the form of actual food consumption.
—In subsistence rice production in India the energy output/input ratio is approximately 15 against high-energy agriculture in the United States of about 1.3, that is, for equivalent production, USA uses about 12 times as much energy.
—With relatively higher energy inputs in rice production in the Philippines, the output/input ratio is about 5.5.

The form in which food energy is ultimately consumed is also significant. For instance, in some countries the output/input ratio for wheat is 3.3 at the farm gate, but by the time the wheat is handled, processed and distributed and reaches the point of consumption, the ratio goes down to 0.525. The ratio for potatoes is 1.57, 0.734 for a kilogram of milk, 0.14 poultry and 0.05 for high-energy fishing with trawlers. The energy output/input ratio in the case of dairying varies between 0.3 and 0.5, and that of meat cattle 0.6.

We may therefore conclude that the massive use of high energy converters in agriculture and the extensive use of animal proteins in affluent countries with very low output/input ratio are increasing the energy cost of feeding the growing population manifold.

AGRICULTURE/RURAL-BASED ENERGY SYSTEMS

Forest Resources

Among some important energy options available to India and many other countries are preservation and expansion of forest wealth. There are many factors to support such a contention. Climate, the high incidence of solar energy and many varieties of fast-growing trees make many developing countries ideally suited for exercising such an option.

But at the rate at which this wealth is being destroyed India is expected to be left with hardly any forest resources by the end of the century. According to some estimates, around 200 million tons of timber is cut and used as firewood every year.

This figure may reach 400-500 million tons by the year 2000. Not even a fraction of this is replenished through reafforestation programmes. In Madhya Pradesh alone less than 1.5 percent of the value of the firewood removed is spent on reafforestation. The national average of reafforestation against deforestation is estimated to be 15-16 percent.

Trees provide cooking fuels, building materials and many other commercial products. In addition they perform important ecological functions in cycling water, oxygen, carbon and nitrogen and stabilising the hydrological system, reducing the severity of floods preventing soil erosion and helping hold the topsoil in farm fields. Trees are an efficient method of collecting and storing solar energy in three dimensions.

Among many varieties of fast-growing trees (five to seven years) casuarina, ku-babul and eucalyptus are some that are better known. Some of these trees can provide up to 50 or 60 tons of wood fuel per hectare per year. In other words, phased planting of such trees in the vicinity of villages or on both sides of the highways can have a major impact in meeting perhaps the most important energy needs of rural India, accounting for about half the total energy consumed in the form of firewood.

Assuming an average per capita requirement of 0.4 tons, a village with a thousand people will need 400 tons of firewood, and about eight to ten hectares of land from the village common will suffice to meet this requirement. The other ecological advantages of preventing soil erosion and desert extension apart, this will provide employment for about 1500 mandays a year.

A nation-wide programme of reafforestation would involve a five-pronged attack covering energy, unemployment, soil erosion, pollution and flood control. In 20-25 years about 60-75 million hectares of largely unproductive land would have to be reafforested, which would require 900 million-1000 million mandays of work. This would be the cheapest and most effective method of collecting and storing the energy of the sun.

In recent years, a number of interesting proposals for converting wood from these energy plantations into metallurgical charcoal or liquid fuels such as methanol and/or ammonia through pyrolisis have been made, and some of them have considerable merit. But first things first. Let us first assure ourselves that we fulfil the task of creating the raw material base, or else we may end up in further accelerating the processes of deforestation and consumerist modes of production.

Agriculture-based Liquid Fuels

A new energy system being processed and promoted converts foodgrains and other food crops such as sugarcane into ethanol for nonfood purposes to keep automobiles on the road. The potential for this is so great that the world's entire food production cannot fulfil the requirements of the present number of automobiles. The implications of this are obvious: agricultural production will move from the mouths of the hungry to the automobiles of the affluent who will be able to pay a much higher price for this basic resource, already in critically short supply. Massive intermediate investment apart, with rising oil prices the choice of converting grain to liquid fuel will become increasingly more attractive.

But the energy cost for both agriculture and processing for the manufacture of one litre of ethanol fuel is around 6000 kilocalories (KCals) for sugarcane and over 4500 KCals for tapioca. After taking credit of energy from agriculture waste such as bagasse, a net energy input of about 3000 KCals will be required to produce a litre of ethanol, while the calorific value of ethanol is around 5260 KCal, giving an output/input ratio of 1.75/1.

For maize as a source material for ethanol the energy gain is only marginal. These energy balances could be improved through the use of solar energy. Sugarcane provides the highest alcohol yield per hectare of 3600 litres. Cassava/tapioca can yield over 2000 litres per hectare. The capital cost for each gallon of ethanol produced from sugarcane is higher than that of grain crops.

But cassava/tapioca rapidly exhausts the soil and yields can only be maintained by outside fertilisation, in other words by further reducing the energy output/input ratio. All this leads to devising a new food system to rotate crops between food and energy, with all the inherent risks of further reducing plant varieties and thus accelerating the trend towards monocultural impoverishment and vulnerability of the economic system.

India uses about 2 million kilolitres of petrol for cars and commercial vehicles at present, and this is likely to increase to about 10 million by the year 2000, that is one-third of the present level in Japan. This would require 150 million tons of sugarcane—against present production of 170 million tons—or 60 million tons of tapioca/cassava against present production of around 6 million tons. An additional 2-4 million hectares of land would have to be brought under cultivation of these crops. In short, it would require about ten to twelve times as much crop land to keep a small to medium automobile on the road as to keep one person alive on a slightly higher than subsistence diet.

Ethanol has the ecological advantage of being a clean fuel and acts as an octane booster. In some very special cases it acts as an adequate replacement fuel. But in the present context, with increasing population, malnutrition and rising food prices, it would be a dangerous diversion of resources of capital, energy and agriculture to bail out a techno-economic-energy system that is becoming rapidly obsolete.

Livestock and Waste Energy Economy

Among the known alternatives the only biomass conversion system that can provide a steady supply of clean fuel for rural household and agricultural needs is anerobic fermentation of animal plant and human waste. Biogas (methane) is an excellent fuel for cooking, lighting and operating machinery, generating electricity and operating absorption refrigeration system.

To assure the maximum use of animal, plant and human wastes and economies of scale in a decentralised rural system village-scale plants with capacities from 50-150m³ upwards offer a better approach to the problem. This is particularly so where village priorities call for water pumping and other mechanical functions against gas for cooking purposes alone. Many parameters such as temperature, alkalinity (PH), sludge liquidity, scum buildup and carbon-nitrogen ratio require to be controlled within optimum limits to assure efficient performance. Such optimisation would be easier to achieve in community-sized as against family-sized plants.

By dropping human waste directly into digesters and mechanical handling of animal waste the cleanliness and sanitary conditions of a community would improve considerably. Then of course there is an additional bonus of nitrogen-rich slurry with a nitrogen content of 1.5-3.0 percent.

India has over 175 million cattle—generating about 770 million metric tons of dung every year. If this is processed in community biogas plants along with other livestock and plant waste it can generate about 30-40 billion cubic metres (900-1500 billion cubic feet) of gas yearly. The heat value of this gas will exceed that of 15-20 million tons of oil equivalent. The nitrogen content of the dried sludge will be over 2 million tons, with an energy-saving potential of 2-4 million tons of oil equivalent.

Similarly, if the agricultural waste of some principal crops such as wheat and rice were to be taken into account it adds up to more than 100 million tons of oil equivalent. Similar value for sugarcane waste such as bagases and leaves are over 25 million tons of oil equivalent. All these and other wastes provide a wide range of opportunities such as anerobic fermentation to generate methane gas, conversion into ethanol by fermentation; gasification by pyrolysis or direct use as fuel.

Over half a million acres of land in India are covered by water hyacinth and other water weeds, and over 40 percent of this area is in Bihar alone. This easily digestible raw material can be fed into the digester either by itself or in combination with cowdung. It has a high gas yield and rapid fermentation possibilities at relatively low temperatures. Its calorific value is higher because of the larger proportion of combustible gases. A ton of water hyacinth has on an average 10 percent yield of compost. A ton of its compost contains 20.5 kilograms of nitrogen equivalent, 105 of ammonium sulphate, 11 of P_2O_5, 69 of superphosphate, 25 of K_2O equivalent and 50 of muriate of potash.

According to some studies in the major cereal-growing areas in the northern states, agriculture accounts for only 14 percent of the total commercial and noncommercial fuels, diesel for irrigation, trucks, pumps and tractors accounting for 4.3 percent, while energy for nitrogen comes to about 10 percent. Biomass fermentation in digesters can contribute significantly in meeting the fertiliser and energy needs of agriculture (1.8 tons of oil equivalent is required for every ton of nitrogen).

Direct Uses of Solar Energy

Most of the R & D effort in new sources of energy is directed towards satisfying the existing energy use pattern, that is to provide large concentrations of energy to assure the maximum use of the existing techno-economic infrastructure. And in many instances it does not fit into the characteristics of the available new sources of energy, particularly solar energy.

The principal characteristics of solar energy are abundance, diffusion and intermittance. While abundance generates hope in the ability of solar energy to meet a sizable proportion of energy needs attempts to overcome its basic characteristics—its diffused nature and intermittant availability—through high concentration and storage is expensive, with costs often increasing geometrically with the extent to departure from the available intensity and insolation and periods of storage.

We must thus incur high infrastructural costs to link solar energy to an existing techno-economic structure. As in the past, future structures of this type would have to be tailored to an energy source and not an energy source to an existing structure if it is to be economical. For instance, we could not connect a coal-based steam engine system with oil or gas and keep it efficient. An internal combustion engine had to be innovated.

Similarly, in the case of solar energy, new concepts and technologies will have to be innovated. Quite often, with a change of energy source complete retooling of the technological structure of a society becomes necessary, in other words a social revolution of wide dimensions. Lack of understanding of this revolution and the manner in which it would affect new societies could lead the innovative efforts of hundreds of solar scientists into a blind alley. It is in this framework that the role of solar energy for rural and agricultural development strategies has to be examined.

Firstly, there is no existing technological structure in the rural areas of developing societies worth the name, which means that they still have some techno-economic options.

Secondly, an entirely new energy use pattern can be innovated to limit undue transformations of energy, which at the requisite temperature levels and in most energy-efficient forms can be provided to attain the lowest capital intensity per unit of energy. While fulfilling these prerequisites a sizable proportion of the energy needs of the rural communities can be satisfied. In this process a basic characteristic of solar energy, its diffused nature, could be overcome.

Thirdly, the intermittence of solar energy is no major handicap in a rural context.

The entire rhythm of rural life for centuries has centred on the cycle of the seasons, and the needs for energy are quite often greatest in periods of optimum availability of solar energy. Pumping water, refrigeration, drying crops and desalinating water are some examples of needs matching availability. Even if this were not so no great harm would be done if the rhythm of life followed the patterns of seasonal availability rather than the rigid patterns of the accelerated pace of consumerism.

Solar energy by its diffused nature therefore fits in with our need to decentralise the socio-techno-economic system, in other words to satisfy the energy needs of the more than 500,000 far-flung rural communities. But along with new energy systems we must innovate new designs of living. Merely hooking up an energy system with strong characteristics for decentralisation with a highly centralised energy-intensive social system will not do. We cannot retain the contours of a socio-techno-economic system based on fossil fuels with solar energy.

The world is not running short of energy. It is running short of oil. With our commitments to the oil infrastructure relatively small, we still have many of our energy options open to enable us to integrate our techno-economic system with a broad spectrum of new energy sources. We are also in a position to effect the thermodynamic matching of our needs with the most appropriate energy source so that expensive, high-quality energy like nuclear or thermal power, oil or other fossil fuels are not wasted on tasks which could more efficiently be performed by the renewable energy source of the sun in all its manifestations, including biomass.

An integrated energy system developed around solar energy, recycling waste, biomass agroforestry could while satisfying a broad range of compatible agricultural and rural energy needs, make an important contribution to improving the quality of soil, preventing soil erosion, bettering sanitary conditions, health and employment prospects.

Over a period of time these processes can be further extended to convert many agricultural surpluses and wastes into ethanol, or wood through pyrolysis into methanol and ammonia. Most highly developed countries with an irreversible commitment to an infrastructure based on liquid fuels and a techno-economic system based on high-energy, high-technology agriculture are in no position to alter their course rapidly. But most of the pathways to the future are still open to us.

Energy Perspectives for Urban Future

A basic feature of all urbanisation is the process of concentration. This process engulfs an entire spectrum of urban life, such as concentration of population in limited areas, concentration of power structures, transport and communication systems, of manufacturing and commercial activities and employment, education, training and medical facilities. Behind all these activities is the concentration and aggregation of energy, concentration not just in the sense of high-energy, high-technology converters in transport or manufacturing but also in terms of wasted energy aggregated, degraded as goods and in junkyards.

A variety of materials are used in constructing buildings. Apart from the energy used in construction, each kilogram of material such as cement, steel, aluminium, plastic, glass, bricks consume large quantities of energy in the production process. Annexure D shows the quantity of energy required to produce some important raw materials.

If the total energy used in creating and maintaining an urban socio-techno-economic infrastructure were to be estimated it would amount to astronomical figures of consumption and waste. The energy cost of sustaining an integrated rural community in a relative state of welfare is less than one-fifth of an urban-based system. Rapid urbanisation, leading up to a megalopolis stretching hundreds of miles is therefore often based on the premise that our resources are unlimited and that technology will find newer and better answers to the ever-growing energy and resource problems.

As the urban areas get larger and more widespread, the supply of energy in various forms and for a multiplicity of uses has to be brought in ever-increasing quantities from distant places, often from distant countries. This further increases the cost of bringing energy to points of use and can become quite critical, often leading to the breakdown of advanced energy systems in periods of emergency. So energy concentrations in an urban community are determined by many factors such as concentration of people, of movement of people, communication systems and services of inward and outward goods traffic, of food supplies (another form of energy), of work-places, entertainment, dispersal of biodegradable and nonbiodegradable waste.

To top it all, there is concentration of wealth and resources as a magnet for further concentration and aggregation of the very same processes. The energy needs of metropolitan areas and urban communities are not therefore just measured in terms of satisfying day-to-day energy needs but in terms of the entire process of energy cost, investment and aggregation.

These processes of energy aggregation do not operate in a vacuum but in a highly volatile energy system. The control of such a system is an intricate process and can often become critical to the extent of endangering the politico-socio-economic system.

Urban Problem

The twin sisters energy and technology are the most important instruments for accelerating and aggregating all processes within a politico-socio-economic system, not just transport or machines, and play the same role between the urban and rural areas in a country as they play between affluent and developing countries in the larger world context. The implications are serious enough internationally because they lead to international instability, exploitation in the use of resources, political domination and neocolonialism, but with the urban exodus become explosive within a country. It would accordingly be fair to say that the use of high energy and high technology in the processes of consumerist production, and thus energy aggregation, is perhaps one major factor in creating what is termed the urban problem.

This problem does not begin in a city. Its roots lie in the rural areas, and often big urban plans and planners are its cause. This problem starts when population pressures on the rural areas increase and a drive begins to increase production in the shortest possible time.

This can only be achieved through the use of high-energy converters which start a trend in rural areas of using the highest available technologies, including mechanisation, to improve land yields. This results in increased food production, but with a simultaneous reduction in the number of the employed. And as this process accelerates and as food production increases, strangely the ability of rural areas to employ more people shrinks at the same time.

Simultaneously, this process launches countries on the first stage of consumerism under pressure of meeting the basic minimum needs of the community, and emphasis in manufacturing techniques shifts from production by the people to production for the people. This process remains within manageable limits in the first few decades of development, but when the second stage of consumerism begins planned obsolescence, energy and technological intensity of the production processes, the cost per workplace, all force the trend towards reducing employment.

So the kind of problems posed in urban development processes are how to stop the flow of people to urban areas, how to provide employment for those who are there, and how to do it within our resources. The tragedy of the situation is that having gone thus far it is not possible to provide jobs in terms of the old value system. Jobs have to be created in terms of our value system today, and this is far beyond our reach. Factors which encourage a massive rural-urban shift include:

A system of education that promotes a value system which cannot be satisfied in rural areas. People are not equipped to perform functions called for in a rural environment and fit them only for certain types of jobs in urban communities.

Introduction of high-technology, high-energy converters in agricultural production and increase in population are forcing people into urban areas in search of employment.

Wage differentials and other incentives increase beyond a certain point pressure towards a shift from rural communities to higher-wage urban centres.

Rural communities lose the economic base to support schools, doctors and the social services.

These and many other factors have been responsible for population growth in metropolitan and urban areas. But behind this all, in one form or other, are misapplied energy and technology policies framed with the sole objective of achieving rapid increases in production without any consideration for long-term politico-socio-economic consequences.

Distribution of energy for productive processes in many ways determines distribution of welfare. The differentials in energy concentration and use between urban and rural areas tend to bring about similar differentials in distributing welfare between communities.

Energy Policy Planning

Optimisation with regard to use pattern involves policy decisions on sources of energy, which in terms of economic parameters is considered the most energy-efficient and cost effective. Locally available energy sources may appear to be less cost-effective in relation to another source to be transported from a distance, but may in actual fact be more efficient in economic and energy terms when transport and other costs and subsidies are aggregated.

Increasing energy concentrations beyond the point of need, or temperatures higher than those actually required, tend to make the energy system inefficient, less cost-effective and more capital-intensive. The use of electrical energy in applications where energy is required in thermal forms is perhaps the most energy-wasteful process. Apart from the capital costs of conversion and reconversion, efficiency drops at every step. And all steps reduce thermodynamic availability at the points of use often by as much as 80 percent.

An important consequence of high-energy concentrations is that energy always has to be brought from outside sources. Problems of transport, storage and distribution of energy often shift the trend towards the use of energy in relatively more desirable and manipulative forms. In other words, the choice shifts from oil, coal, wood and such other energy sources to electricity. This must either be generated from imported oil or coal, which increases handling costs, or hydroelectric power, which in turn means large transmission and distribution networks, reduction in efficiency and high capital costs. The other possibility is to set up nuclear power stations, which are more costly. Then there are the ecological hazards resulting in growing compulsions for shifting away from larger population concentrations.

While the highest temperatures and energy concentrations should be supplied through nuclear energy the other sources will fall at various points in the spectrum to be tapped to match the needs and availability of the process. The general trend has been the proliferation of innovation around oil and gas. Internal combustion engines, turbines, hydroelectric power and other types of high-energy converters have been growing in number, size, speed and efficiency of conversion to electricity.

Today, as the importance of the internal combustion engine recedes with the reduction of oil supplies, considerable effort is being directed towards retaining the energy use pattern and the technology structure with the help of methanol, ethanol, requiring outside energy subsidies, nuclear energy or new sources of energy such as solar, wind or geothermal. But new sources can fill the role of the old fossil fuels at a very heavy cost since their equipment, basis of design and energy use pattern are fundamentally different.

Thus over the years an entirely new technological structure will have to be innovated and raised around new sources of energy to meet the emerging socio-economic needs of developing societies and the socio-techno-economic and ecological compulsions of affluent nations. Indeed, increasing concentration and transformations are not the right answer to the satisfaction of future energy needs. The solution lies in apportioning the optimised role of every available energy source within an efficient pattern of energy use. The new developing nations, with a relatively lower level of commitment to the technologies of existing resources, have therefore a much better chance of rearranging their energy use pattern than the highly committed affluent nations.

Sacrifice of ecology and efficiency to speed and then its attempted reversal has been a highly wasteful process. Social and not commercial compulsions must necessarily dictate the energy strategies of the future. High-priced labour, cheap energy and automation, trend setters of economic growth, are leading to a rapid depletion of resources, pollution, unemployment and crime.

In planning the energy economies of the future, the energy costs of defensive and offensive weapons cannot be ignored. This would be like letting an elephant go by and holding on to its tail.

Wherever the energy source has changed, this has been accompanied by changes in value system and social structure. Overwhelming concern with status quoism in social institutions usually distorts the use pattern of new sources of energy. Decentralisation of use will be the cornerstone of new sources such as solar energy.

National socio-techno-economic behaviour must correspond with that required ideally to exploit the new energy sources. Each value system calls for varying types and quantums of energy. Unless human society can replace energy used up in the living process it cannot survive ultimately. An unbridged and permanent deficit would make life impossible. In energy planning for urban areas, places of work will have to be brought near population concentrations, thus assuring minimum use of transport and nonrenewable sources of energy.

There should be a shift towards the planned organisation of productive units in smaller communities. And as far as possible products of daily use should be produced within or close to these communities. There may be many areas in which such arrangements may not be possible, but there must be some logic in the situation.

Energy Subsidy

In this context availability of energy resources in nature does not always mean that it is only a matter of time when these can be extracted and used. The cost of outside energy subsidy to extract and use one unit of energy is steadily rising, and it must be derived from the increasingly scarce reserves of other kinds of energy, and this carries with it steadily increasing energy costs. For example, to get 1000 KCals of energy through coal gasification we require a primary resource of 2050 KCals and an external energy subsidy of about 138 KCal. Similar figures for high-grade oil shale are 1238 and 483 KCals.

Against this, Middle East oil requires only 40 KCals for extraction and 40 KCals for shipment, say to Europe. Similarly, North Sea oil would require about 100 KCals for extraction, and electricity generation is at best 36 percent efficient. In nuclear fission, these figures are about 7500 KCal and 450 KCals respectively.

Every commitment to the existing fossil fuels or overreliance on technological breakthroughs in using new sources of energy without taking into account ecological hazards, technology failures or the ever-increasing energy subsidy can therefore lead to unsustainable energy decisions or wide dislocation of productive effort. In the ultimate analysis, energy requirements for extracting and using fuels should be a major factor in any energy policy decision.

New Energy Use Patterns

Energy planning is not an isolated exercise. It is woven into the fabric of a socio-techno-economic system. The tools and technologies of a society are determined by its energy source. Changes either in the type of use pattern of energy has far-reaching implications for the entire socio-economic system and its relationship with the world trade and defence system. To talk of new sources of energy, or energy conservation exercises or restraints in energy use, there should therefore be first discipline within the economic system. More than energy policies, the techno-economic system such policies support need examination.

Each source of energy can, in terms of its characteristics play an important role within a given energy use pattern. Optimisation of the pattern in the framework of new developmental strategies in uncommitted societies can help to achieve multipronged objectives such as increasing energy efficiencies, reducing energy transformations and energy costs, diversifying energy resource use and enlarging long-term energy perspectives, containing ecological hazards and, above all, directing a larger and larger proportion of energy needs to new and renewable source of energy.

All this would not be possible in societies where the fundamental compulsions are towards continuity of the existing energy use pattern within the straitjacket of ever-accelerating consumerist developmental processes. Technological solutions and commercial opportunities in extending our energy or ecological frontiers "are as myopic and dangerous as social science, which assumes that there is no limit to man's aspirations. And yet the overwhelming majority placed emphasis on discovering technical solutions rather than limiting production and consumption."[3]

Each energy source, old or new, has its own role to play in the future. An ideal situation would be to enlarge the role of the new and renewable source of energy and limit that of fossil fuels and nuclear energy within a desirable and efficient framework, and design a sustainable energy use pattern ideally suited to the basic characteristics of different sources of energy.

The available sources of energy will determine lifestyle in the coming decades. It will not be possible to order the source of energy to match lifestyle. Similarly, technologies for energy use will have to be innovated around available sources. These sources cannot be tailored to fit an established energy use pattern.

Many of the cost, efficiency and ecological limitations of an energy source could be contained by optimising its use in terms of its characteristics and then evolving a synthesis of such "use-optimised sources" to innovate new lifestyles of the future. And ultimately it would be an ideal mix of the available resources in a given environment. It would relatively be much easier for uncommitted societies to achieve this objective.

An understanding of the role of different energy sources in terms of their characteristics and limitations could contribute vastly towards rational use of the emerging and existing resources and the design of new lifestyles, tools and technologies.

Nuclear Energy

After the euphoria of the 1950s and 1960s nuclear fission became a subject of considerable circumspection in the 1970s. Doubts about the continued projection of nuclear power into the future arose from many factors:

—Diminishing resources of nuclear fuels, particularly uranium, in terms of the projected requirement.
—Ecological hazards of operating nuclear power stations and handling highly radioactive wastes as a byproduct of such power generation. (A typical 1000-megawatt reactor produces yearly 30 tons of fuel rod assemblies that are highly radioactive.)
—Plutonium 239, the isotope used for bombs, and also produced

---

[3]William R. Burch Jr., *Daydream and Nightmares*, New York, Harper and Row, 1971, p 110.

in breeder reactors, is widely thought to be the deadliest element in reactor wastes and has a half-life of over 24,000 years.

—Fear of nuclear proliferation to the extent of accumulating bomb-grade residues in many hands, thus first laying the foundations of nuclear terror and then the emergence of dictatorial regimes to contain such terror.

Very little attention is paid to the possibility of reducing the proportion of plutonium in processed enriched uranium so as to limit its effectiveness as an adjunct for nuclear armament. Similarly, processing steps could be altered to prevent the complete separation of plutonium from uranium, thus resulting in diluting the plutonium content of nuclear fuels.

While there may be technological possibilities to contain the proliferation hazards of nuclear power the success of such endeavours rests largely with the major nuclear powers, who will have to sell their credibility along with technological solutions to contain proliferation.

Ecological factors have been blown out of proportion by environmentalist groups, and armament factors by those who have acquired such weapons. In this process the positive aspects of nuclear energy as a possible contributor to the energy pattern of the future are being cast aside.

Nuclear energy, in terms of its characteristics, has an important role to play in meeting the concentrated needs for both thermal and electrical power, in providing the energy base for large power-consuming industries such as aluminium, for operating thermal energy-based heating and cooling plants for large concentrations of people, for generating hydrogen as a power source, and a large number of similar applications.

This would help in achieving economies of scale in basic sectors of the economy, and also in containing ecological and security hazards to a few selected centres rather than cancerous growth throughout the techno-economic system. Socially, because of residing in isolated high radiation-risk colonies, attractive incentives regarding working conditions and incomes are justified for operators. The entire development of nuclear energy could thus be built around its main characteristics of high risk, high-concentration economies of scale, and very high temperatures.

Irrespective of success in containing, or perhaps at best partially neutralising, the radiation risk, the future of such an important power source must remain in doubt till the problem of waste disposal is resolved at socially acceptable levels.

This lack of confidence in our ability to handle this problem competently was compounded by the mishandling of the first light-water fuel reprocessing at West Valley, New York, where 600,000 gallons of liquid radioactive waste was accumulated and stored temporarily in carbon steel tanks.

America's second commercial reprocessing project was also unsuccessful. The General Electric facility built at Morris, Illinois, with a special feature for recovering weapon-grade plutonium also had to be abandoned.

The French Government plant at La Hague, at the tip of the Cotentin Peninsula, is the only commercial reprocessing plant operating in the West and has a capacity to reprocess 2400 tons of nuclear waste.[4] The plant has had a number of accidents. (The British reprocessing plant at Windscale was closed in 1973.) In April 1979 France formally opened a billion-dollar, gas-diffusion, uranium-enrichment facility at Tricastin, southern France. This plant was built in partnership with Spain, Italy and Belgium. But the accident at the Three Mile Island nuclear power plant in USA has once again brought the fundamental question of nuclear safety to the forefront.

Nuclear reprocessing halted in the United States in 1977 and discharged fuel has been accumulating since. Although demonstrated technology for disposing of high-level nuclear waste is claimed to exist, nobody has yet taken the basic decision to use it for fear that radioactive material would eventually enter the ecosystem.

Uranium Resources

Real rich reserves of uranium are probably limited to 3 million tons. Present estimates put annual world uranium demand, excluding that of the centrally planned economies, at:

1985	65,000 tons
1990	100,000 tons
2000	180,000 tons.

[4]Edward Goldsmith and Nicholas Hildya, La Hague, "Chaos Reigns Supreme," *The New Ecologist*, 1978, No.6, pp. 205-7.

If used in reactors of the present type these reserves would provide a fuel value of less than the known oil reserves. But if the same reserves were to be used in breeder reactors the fuel value of the available reserve would improve by a factor of over 200. This could improve further with reduction in refining costs.

The available uranium reserves are less than 1 percent of the fuel value of the available coal reserves, but if used in breeder reactors they would be 2.5 times the actual coal reserves. The reserves would improve further because of our ability to use the high extraction cost reserves which could provide us with a fuel value equal to 2 million gigatons of coal. Similarly, the fairly extensive thorium reserves could also be brought into use through breeder reactors.

If one ton of natural uranium is required per installed Mwe as the initial charge and the refuelling requires 0.3 ton per year by installed Mwe, most of the rich reserves would be exhausted by the year 2000, even with a modest nuclear programme.

For example

if the 250 tons of plutonium likely to be available from the predominantly burner reactor programme by 1985 were used to fuel say 80,000 Mwe of fast breeder capacity, it would be almost doubled by the year 2000. The lead time required, however, means that the fast breeder programme would add little to the overall plutonium inventory by the end of the century.[5]

It is not therefore possible to start a breeder programme at will to preserve the available uranium resources for any length of time, particularly when power needs have doubled in less than 12 years and may do so in shorter periods of time in the future, particularly in the developing societies.

Even under the most favourable conditions the plutonium doubling time to sustain such a breeder programme would be twice as long as the growing needs for power. But if the big-power nuclear weaponry programme were to be discontinued and pluto-

[5] S.E. Hunt, *The Nuclear Power—National and International Considerations*, Journal of the Institute of Nuclear Engineers, March/April 1978.

nium were to be directed towards power generation, there will be a better chance for sustaining such a programme, ecological factors permitting.

No Longer King Coal

Total world production of all types of coal in 1977 was 3400 million metric tons, of which hard coal represented 2500 million tons, or about 70 percent. More than 75 percent of world output is mined by six countries—USA, USSR, China, Poland, Britain and West Germany. India is one of the larger producers of coal among the developing countries. USA mines about half the coal produced in non-communist countries while USSR and China produce about 80 percent as much as USA.

The geographical distribution of coal among the nation states is extremely uneven, and this is even less equitable than oil in respect of the developing countries. The continents of Africa and Latin America have just about 1 percent of the world's coal reserves and most developing countries have hardly any. While Soviet Russia has 63 percent of the world's hard coal and lignite, the United States claims 18 percent, China 11 percent, Europe 6 percent and India just over 1 percent. Use of coal has been falling steadily in all markets. In non-communist countries it declined as a primary energy source from 23 percent to 10 percent in 1960-76.

Coal is largely used to generate electricity, which accounts for more than 75 percent of the coal consumed in USA, 57 percent in Western Europe and 18 percent in Japan.

Because of its bulk and costs involved in transporting it, only 8 percent of the world's hard coal production (190 million tons) moved in international trade, largely as coking coal for the steel industry. Japan was the largest importer of coal for this purpose.

Of all the fossil fuels available for exploitation reserves of coal are by far the largest. The world energy conference survey of energy resources (1976) estimated total resources of all types of coal at 11,500 billion metric tons. Of this only 1300 billion tons qualify as known and measured reserves, and of this 740 billion tons were deemed economically recoverable when these studies were made. Of such reserves, USA has 31 percent, USSR and Eastern Europe 26 percent, Western Europe 17 percent, China 15 percent and Australia 6 percent.

Recoverable tonnage, taking all factors into consideration, comes to about 600 billion tons of hard coal, enough to meet requirements for about 200 years. This is equivalent to the energy content of 3000 billion barrels of oil, which is four to five times the known reserves of oil.

Apart from the unpredictable and uneven distribution pattern of coal reserves this mineral suffers from various other handicaps. "It takes seven to ten years to open a new coalmine, at least a decade to prove a major new mining process commercially, a generation to develop a new way of using coal as a fuel and a generation to replace outdated power plants with the latest available technology."[6]

The high costs and risks of underground mining resulted in a shift towards large-scale strip mining. A mine in Campbell County, Wyoming, produced over 13 million tons of coal in 1977, and another one is planned in West Germany to achieve a production of over 1000 million tons. Massive machines weighing thousands of tons mine and rip daily over 35,000 cubic metres of coal, which is then carried away in 100 ton haulers for processing and shipment through pipelines as slurry or by rail.

These ugly mammoth structures escalate the hazards of coal dust beyond permissive limits. Also, both the economic and energy costs of coal mining are rising, and new capital-intensive mining operations are steadily passing into the hands of powerful, highly diversified oil companies.

The long-wall mining techniques of the last quarter century are reaching the point of counterproductivity. New electronic brains built around micro-processors are used to control operations in underground mines to sense radiation, hear ultra-sounds and microwaves, to avoid wasteful cutting of rocks, to perform chemical analysis and position machines automatically. Integration of all these elements would increase mine safety and increase productive efficiency manifold. But it would also dramatically reduce manpower for the same level of production and increase costs.

From the point of view of highly developed societies reliance on coal will be tampered with rising capital and energy costs of mining, declining employment in the energy industry and the timelag in developing new mines to meet rising requirements and to

[6] *The Economist*, 6 January 1979, p. 59.

replace other fossil fuels, particularly oil.

There are many other technologies of burning coal at various stages of development to replace oil, especially in steam generation in small industrial boilers. One such technology, fluidised bed combustion, could help meet variable demand and effect economies in small-scale power generation.

Technologies for the converting coal into liquid fuels and to bring its use to a level of efficiency high enough to compete with oil cannot be expected to fructify till the end of the century.

Another system of high promise is magnetohydrodynamics, but it will take long to prove its technological and economic viability. It works by preheating compressed air to 2500°F and expanding the resulting hot ionised plasma through a super-conducting magnetic field to generate direct current, which has then to be converted back into alternating current. Both technological hazards and many conversions and reconversions place this technology far into the future.

Costs of converting coal to liquid or gaseous fuels vary between 150 and 300 percent of the price of available products. To date there has been no credible effort to convert coal on a large scale into oil and gas except perhaps as some kind of insurance against unforeseen eventualities. South Africa is constructing with some outside support fairly large facilities to gasify coal with steam and oxygen and converting this gas into various products, including oil.

The greatest hurdle in the way of using coal as a transient fuel from the age of oil to new, renewable sources of energy is its environmental record. There is a growing belief that a heavy commitment to using coal could trigger irreversible changes in world climate and consequently agricultural productivity and our ability to feed the growing world population. All fossil fuels—coal, oil and natural gas—produce carbon dioxide when burnt, but coal produces about 25 percent more than oil, and 75 percent more than natural gas.

As a result of the accelerated burning of fossil fuels, the CO_2 in the atmosphere could double over the next 70 years. This could cause a 2-7 degrees F rise in the atmospheric temperature, which in the polar regions could increase by as much as 12 degrees F with little change on the equator. The pole to equator temperature differences determine the path of the winds and as a consequence thereof the extent of rainfall. A variety of other feedback mechanisms could amplify the greenhouse effect with many unpredictable consequences.[7]

Reversion to a coal-based economy is plagued by just about as many uncertainties as nuclear energy, economically, technologically and ecologically. In spite of these reservations, coal, because of the extent of its economically recoverable reserves, is possibly the only fossil fuel with the potential to tide us over the period of the decline of other fuels of the same type, particularly oil. This would be even more so if fear of the ecological hazard, technological inadequacies, economic viability and terrifying potential of nuclear energy continue to aggregate. But this would undoubtedly require a massive infrastructure to open up new mines within the economic environmental and safety constraints.

Perspectives for the Future

It is becoming increasingly obvious that the energy challenges of the future cannot be met by nonrenewable fossil fuels in a situation of rapid exponential growth of consumption. On the basis of the present state of technologies and expected developments in the coming decades, the energy picture of the future can be projected as follows:

The next five-ten years (1985-90): Use of oil and gas will be curbed and that of coal extended. Nuclear fission will continue to play a limited role in this period. Technologies for bioconversion and solar energy used for cooking, lighting, heating water, heating and cooling of homes, and some industrial uses will improve considerably. But the overall use pattern will at best remain limited. Costly production of gaseous and liquid fuels from coal, shale and lignite will make limited advances.

The next ten-twenty years (1990-2000): Improvements in fastbreeder reactors will further extend the use of nuclear fission, but in the larger context its use will be limited. Part of the need for liquid fuels will be met through the liquefaction of coal. Use of oil and gas will however peak off. The areas of solar energy use will expand, and bioconversion through biomass and recycling of animal plant and human waste will make rapid strides in India, China and

---

[7]Tom Alexander, "New Fears Surround the Shift to Coal," *Fortune*, 20 November 1978, pp. 50-60.

many other countries, and will thus encourage trends towards the growth of integrated rural communities and possibly provide some respite from the exodus to urban areas.

Technological advances will be effected to bring about high-temperature, high-intensity solar energy development which would open up new areas of solar power, both mechanical and by direct photovoltaic generation through solar cells. Use of hydrogen as fuel will become important. Many offshore islands may have nuclear power plants generating hydrogen and oxygen through electrolysis of water, and hydrogen may make an important contribution as a clean fuel in a broad range of applications.

The next 20-40 years (2000-2020): It would appear that in this period clean fusion power may become a reality. An era of large earth and space stations generating solar energy to meet the needs for concentrated energy and extensive use of hydrogen, ethanol and methanol will become an important factor in the world energy picture. Hundreds of thousands of self-contained, integrated rural communities satisfying their own food and energy needs with renewable energy sources are expected to come into being, thus relieving to a considerable extent the pressure on the centralised energy system.

Annexure—A*

ESTIMATED ENERGY NEEDS OF A RURAL COMMUNITY

Population—1000
Area under cultivation—400 hectares (1000 acres)

Application for which energy required	Preferred source of energy—in order of preference	Basis of estimation	Annual energy requirements million cu. ft. of gas	Estimated electrical energy
Phase I:				
1. Cooking	Gas, solar, wood, coal, kerosene, electricity	7.5 cu. ft. per person/day	2.75	
2. Lighting				
(a) Residential	Electricity—gas	3 mantles of 2.5 cu. ft. per hr. for 2 hrs.	1.09 ⎫	25w/person (25 kw) 36000 kw. hr.
(b) Street, public areas	Electricity—gas	100 mantles for 3 hrs. of 2.5 cu. ft.	0.27$_5$ ⎭	
3. Domestic water supply	Electricity—gas	7.5 gallon/person/day	0.135	(4 kw) connected 6000 kw. hr.
4. Maintenance of optimum temp. in bio gas digester	Solar—gas	20% of gas produced mostly from solar energy, 5% from gas	0.165	gas
			4.415	
5. Irrigation from wells	Animal, electricity, gas—solar	Grain yield of 5 tons a hectare or total of 2000 tons	5.00	(0.45 × 10^6 BHP hr. at 25% efficiency)
6. Other direct energy inputs	Gas, oil—electricity	Grain yield of 5 tons a hectare or total of 2000 tons	1.54	(0.14 × 10^6 BHP hr. at 25% eff.)

*J.C. Kapur, *India 2000* A.D., p. 44.

Analysis

Domestic load	4.250	mil. cu. ft. of methane gas
Irrigation load (if through wells)	5.00	mil. cu. ft. of methane gas
Other direct energy inputs such as supplementary fertiliser, fuel, for machinery, tools, transportation and processing	0.45	mil. cu. ft. of methane gas.
	9.70	mil. cu. ft. of methane gas

Annexure—B*

FOOD ENERGY YIELD vs. MECHANICAL ENERGY USED**
EQUIVALENT TONS OF COAL PER TON OF FOOD GRAIN

	Equivalent tons of coal per ton of food grain	Ratio of mech. energy used to food energy produced
Irrigation from wells	0.195	0.167
Chemical fertiliser	0.156	0.134
Fuel for machinery	0.104	0.089
Farm tools and machines	0.055	0.047
High yield seeds	0.008	0.002
Plant protection	0.003	0.001
Crop drying	0.016	0.013
Transport	0.009	0.008
Storage and marketing	0.003	0.002
Food processing	0.065	0.056
	0.614	0.519

*J.C. Kapur, *India 2000 A.D.*, p. 42.
**Computed from Gerald Leach Roger Revelle Studies.

Annexure—C

OUTPUT/INPUT ENERGY RELATIONSHIPS FOR HIGH ENERGY INTENSITY MEDIUM ENERGY INTENSITY AND SUBSISTENCE AGRICULTURE

Nature of energy input input/acre	Output of rice per acre	Output/ input ratio	Area of land under cultivation 1975	(i) Area, (ii) man years and (iii) energy requirements for producing 250 M.T. of food grains (estimated population 850 M)*	Breakdown of energy inputs	Remarks limiting factors in achieving desired levels of food production through available energy alternatives
1	2	3	4	5	6	7
High Energy Intensity Agriculture. With labour inputs of less than 12 hours and all energy inputs of 0.6 tons of oil equivalent	2.3 tons of rice (0.78 tons of oil equivalent)	1.3	350 m. acres (140 m. hectares)	(i) Area of land $250/2.3 \times 10^6$ $= 109 \times 10^6$ m. acres $= 44 \times 10^6$ m. hectares (ii) Hrs. of work $109 \times 10^6 \times 12$ $= 1308 \times 10^6$ man hrs. assuming 1800 hrs. of work/yr. $= 0.73 \times 10^6$ man years (iii) Total energy required $= 109 \times 10^6 \times 0.6 = 66$ million tons of oil equivalent	(a) Labour $\quad$ 0.024×10^6 (b) Machinery $\quad$ 4.360×10^6 (c) Fuel $\quad$ 11.120×10^6 (d) Irrigation $\quad$ 29.650×10^6 (e) Fertilisers $\quad$ 10.750×10^6 (N 137 kg P 67 kg)	(a) Massive unemployment (b) Unattainable and expensive energy inputs (c) Overcentralisation of agriculture

*See *India 2000 A.D.* (p. 40, Annexure I) by J.C. Kapur.

1	2	3	4	5	6	7
Medium energy intensity: With labour of about 230 hrs., draught animals 110 hrs. and all energy inputs of 0.0385 tons of oil equivalent	0.60 tons of rice (0.21 tons of oil equivalent)	5.5	350 m. acres (140 m. hectares)	(i) Area of land = $250 \times 10^6/0.6$ = 417×10^6 acres = 167×10^6 hectares (ii) No. of man hrs. = $230 \times 417 \times 10^6$ = 95910×10^6 man hrs. = 53×10^6 man yrs. assuming 1800 hrs of work/yr. (iii) Total energy required = $417 \times 10^6 \times 0.0385$ = 16×10^6 tons of oil equivalent	(a) Labour (d) Draught animals (c) Machinery (d) Fertiliser (N $\times$ 5.6 kg) (e) Pesticides and herbicides (f) Pesticides and herbicides (g) Electricity (h) Drying	1.77×10^6 8.35×10^6 3.90×10^6 1.76×10^6 0.22×10^6 1.096×10^6 3.200×10^6 4.800×10^6 65.000×10^6 tons of oil equivalent 16.00×10^6 tons of oil equivalent	(a) Only marginal additions to land under cultivation (b) Attainable increases in energy inputs (c) Unemployment within relatively manageble limit

1	2	3	4	5	6	7
Subsistence Agriculture: (India) Labour 335 hrs. Draught animals 170 hrs. (fed on agriculture waste) and all energy inputs of 0.0065 tons of oil equivalent	0.25 tons of rice	14.75	350 m. acres (140 m. hectares)	(i) Area of land = $250 \times 10^6 / 0.25$ = 1000×10^6 acres = 400×10^6 hectares (ii) Man hrs. = $335 \times 1000 \times 10^6$ = $335000 \times 10^6 = 186 \times 10^6$ man yrs. at 1800 hrs. per year (iii) Total energy = 1000×10^6 = 6.5×10^6 equivalent tons of oil	(a) Labour 6.5×10^6 tons of oil equivalent	Not enough land to attain food production targets through subsistence agriculture

Annexure—D

QUANTITY OF ENERGY REQUIRED TO PRODUCE SOME IMPORTANT RAW MATERIALS

Material	Unit	Energy in BTU/unit
Concrete block $20 \times 20 \times 40$ cm.	Each	30,000
Ready mix concrete	Cu. metre	275,000
Mineral wool insulation	Ton	12 million
Iron & steel		
Pig iron	Ton	1.6×10^6
Galvanised Steel Sheets	Ton	55×10^6
Steel Pipes	Ton	50×10^6
Stainless steel sheets cold rolled	Ton	250×10^6
Alminium plate	Ton	230×10^6
Nuts, bolts, screw	Pound	22,000
Glass plate	Sq. foot	12,000
Wood board	Board foot	5,000
Paint	Gallon	420,000
Cement	Ton	8×10^6
Polyethylene	Pound	63,000
Bricks	Unit	13,000

4. Power Centres

Power is exercised within a socio-economic system through control, manipulation or neutralisation of the instruments of power centres. Although power is exercised for a wide variety of purposes basic motivations swing between the ideals of world peace, national pride and growth on one side and economic gains and, quite often, the naked preemption of political and economic power and self-defence on the other.

Power is centred in decentralised rural communities in developing societies like India in small groups of rich landlords, moneylenders, high-caste sectional leaders and local administrators. Power is often preempted through control of the techno-economic infrastructure or inputs, which strengthens the economic and political hold on the community, and is then related to the district, state or national political processes. Consequently, patronage is received and distributed within the rural system in return for promises to deliver votes in elections.

In the Indian context there is a multiplicity of power centres representing a wide variety of interests: North and South groups, with subdivisions; Right and Left groups with subdivisions; public and private sectors; employers against labour; landlords, farmers and tenants; religious groups—Hindus, Muslims, Sikhs, Christians with subgroups; caste groups with subdivisions, majority community against minority communities; subdivisions in the middle of the road; political groups; rural against urban: pro-West against pro-East; centralisation against decentralisation; rich against poor; state against federal; and district against state.

Before independence Gandhi appealed to the stavistic idealism of the people within the framework of India's social organisation and was able to neutralise many of these micro-power centres representing conflicting interests. In this process he forged the strange conglomeration of the Congress Party into an effective power centre to weaken the hold of the colonial power. The harassed colonial power on its side encouraged the emergence of new centrifugal power centres representing religious and sectional interests such as the Muslim League and the Chamber of Princes, and this ultimately led to partitioning of the country.

India is a conglomeration of all these and many other power centres which in their totality provide direction for the exercise of power on the subcontinent. As many of these centres are mutually neutralising while others are mutually supporting, the ultimate weight and direction of the resultant factor of all the vectors represents the power centre that is India. And in such national systems if the vectors are adequately integrated, the available power of the centre usually remains constant.

Under strong Maoist leadership a multitude of micro-power centres were forged in China into a few sub-micro-power centres such as the Communist Party, the government and the defence establishment. Exercise of power was relatively less complex than in India, and the party leadership exercised power ruthlessly to achieve social and international objectives.

But in less than a decade many centres, such as pro-Soviet against anti-Soviet and supporters of the cultural revolution against its opponents emerged within the system. These have multiplied manifold since the death of Chairman Mao, and variety and complexity have been proliferating since the late 1970s. China's power structure and policies will therefore remain uncertain in the 1980s.

The manoeuvrability of the political system in a democratic society to effect change is directly related to the integration of forces emerging from many micro or sub-macro vectors of forces within the system. For instance, the ability of the political leadership to neutralise micro-level agitation or dissent in the rural or urban systems depends largely on the possibility of its being able to introduce a stronger vector of forces which will not only neutralise the negative elements but provide a positive thrust by integrating other sub-micro power centres in the system.

The synthesis of such forces in a parliamentary democracy is often represented by the numerical strength of members of the national parliament or state legislators representing different interests and views. The manoeuvrability and success of the political process lies in its ability to establish a positive and strong vector of forces in the group exercising power and a similar vector in the opposition to neutralise the undesirable elements in the exercise of such power.

If the political leadership cannot aggregate a positive vector of forces of adequate strength, this means that the micro-power centres in the system, instead of integrating into a meaningful direction, are neutralised to the extent that no positive thrust can be established within the national system.

In a complex system such as India the test of leadership lies in its ability to assess the strength and direction of various micro-power and sub-macro-power centres within the larger political system and through that to:

—forge a positive thrust towards an effective programme for development and growth; and
—relate the national power centre to the world system through a choice of regional or international alignments or neutralisation processes.

Nehru picked up the remnants of the Congress Party after independence as well as its mass base and power centres the organised authority of the government represented. Then by neutralising ideological extremes by promoting nonalignment and a mixed economy he was able successfully to transform a situation of crisis into one of dynamic balance in the country and in its international relations.

Affluent Societies

Power centres in highly developed or affluent countries play quite a different role from those in developing societies. In the process of development many micro-power centres get submerged in the satisfaction of techno-economic imperatives and the protection of interests controlling the means of production in capitalist and socialist states. Powerful industrial, armament and labour lobbies play a far more significant role in the control and exercise of political and economic power than state, regional or racial interests. Emergence of a military industrial complex in the United States or powerful labour unions in Poland are cases in point. Thus the weight of each dominant power centre becomes heavy and direction more precise. In other words the leaderships have to reckon with a few large power centres rather than hundreds of micro-power and sub-macro-power centres. To control the crisis arising from the Great Depression in the 1930s Franklin D. Roosevelt integrated new vectors of forces representing organised labour, the unemployed and intellectuals and forged plans for the New Deal for an effective forward thrust. While the general contours of this power structure remained unchanged for some decades after Roosevelt's death it went through many important transformations, and new power centres have emerged in USA in recent years.

To cope with similar imperatives President Reagan is integrating an altogether new set of power centres representing powerful business, industrial, energy and armament interests without whose support major politico-techno-economic objectives cannot be achieved. The supporters or agents of such interests are often directly, indirectly or surreptitiously represented in major centres of policy formulation in the political system.

Thus the power centre representing the people is transformed to represent interests. But such elites or interests are not necessarily in control; they are only taking advantage of the forces that have their own life span. "And often such interests are supported against the interests of betrayed constituency."[1]

SUCTIONAL—DIFFUSIONAL

When a country can relate its techno-economic or defence system to that of another country or group of countries to its own advantage it exercises suctional influence over these countries. US trade and defence relations with Europe in the Second World War are a classic example of such a role which operated greatly to its advantage in politico-techno-economic terms.

Even its diffusional role of providing Marshall Aid after the war paid big dividends politically and economically by strengthening its allies and effecting their economic unification.

When a major power centre diffuses its economics (technology resources, manpower) and defence (power) and creates a balance between suctional and diffusional elements it reaches a state of power-factor balance. If the diffusional factors, in a socio-economic system are weaker than the suctional factors, the system tends to become an ascending power centre, such as the United States became before World War II and Japan between the 1950s and

[1] Charles Reich, *The Greening of America*, 1970, p. 88.

1970s. If on the other hand the diffusional factors are stronger than the suctional factors it tends to become a descending power centre such as the US in the 1970s.

But when the US accelerated its diffusional role in other states by transferring military hardware, creating military blocs or otherwise through political and economic intervention, the suctional advantages of the 1950s and the 1960s began to be neutralised by the diffusional costs of the 1970s. An overcommitment to a diffusional course, as in Vietnam, became socially counterproductive, reaching a state of outright reversal in terms of many parameters such as in the recent debacle in Iran.

Each power centre has a force of suction and diffusion, often balanced or unbalanced. Some are in balance as Western Europe, others are in diffusional imbalance such as USA. In many instances, such as USSR and USA, diffusional forces predominate while in others such as India, China and Japan suctional forces predominate. An excessive emphasis on one or other of these forces in the major power centres tends to create a state of imbalance in the world system, leading to a world-wide economic, resource or armament crisis.

INTERNATIONAL POWER CENTRES

These power centres use their economic muscle to control agencies for the transmission of information or propaganda. Through intelligence reports, influencing legislators and their world-wide connections they exercise influence far out of proportion to their number and size, and are often in a position to subvert any policy orientation or formulation which threatens to interfere with their interests. Such subversion often reaches far beyond the boundaries of the nation states to which these power centres belong.

The growing crisis of energy, resources and ecology has given further edge to this protective intervention in the affairs of other countries. To assure availability and secure supply lines of energy and resources new power centres have to be created and manipulated in resource-rich countries and along supply routes.

This is often achieved by injecting armaments, manipulating friendly or dislodging unfriendly governments through the organisation of military blocs and groups with common defensive and offensive strategies, and often through engineered wars and revolutions. Other instruments for intervention are trade and aid pacts, supply of armaments and penetration by multinational corporations or state-owned companies and through the dependence of recipient countries on armaments and aid from and trade with the donor countries.

For the developing countries to establish mutually beneficial aid or trade relations with the affluent countries is therefore very complex and hazardous. The overprotective leaders of such countries stand to become targets of interests in the affluent countries or revolutions within their own borders. This often restricts their abilities to seek the most desirable solutions to their problems because the power centres in the system often exercise weight far out of proportion to their real strength or needs as a result of the insidious support they receive from outside the borders of their nation states.

The national leaders have not only to contain, neutralise or strengthen power centres which have their origin within the country but also much larger power centres superimposed from without. So the vector of forces which emerges in the macro systems in developing societies bears no relation to a country's real needs or true power structure.

The leaders of these countries, whether subservient or in revolt against international intervention, spend most of their energy and aid in assuring their own stability and security rather than in accelerating the developmental processes through most desirable and appropriate means. The impact of such strategies on the developed countries themselves is no less serious. In the process of following international policies they often overreach themselves, when the net gain usually turns into a net loss.

Along with expansion of the means of communication and transport the significance of the power centres in the international system has also been growing. Just as penetration by the automobile and raliroads reduced the importance of the local power centres and simultaneously helped strengthen regional and national power centres, steamships increased the significance of a centre operating at the seat of a colonial power for the inhabitants of remote colonies.

The entire colonial structure operated on the principle of neutralising all power centres in the colonies other than those from the mother country. A principle of honour among common interests operated very successfully in consolidating and maintaining distant empires, so much so that even countries like the Netherlands, Belgium, Spain and Portugal could control and maintain large colonial interests through non-intervention and support from larger colonial powers like Britain and France.

This went off very well till other important power centres like Germany, Italy and Japan laid a claim to their share of the pie. In fact, they started the process of massive intervention by breaking the weight and continuity of the suctional and diffusional power centres which operated between the mother country and the colonies. This was brought about by disruption of the means of communication, supplies and trade by attacking, weakening and displaying the vulnerable points of the colonial system.

This process was further aggravated by the emergence of major power centres in the form of mass movements in the colonies which the colonial powers were unable to neutralise and contain. Thus the Second World War accelerated the breakdown of the colonial system. Over the last three decades this process has reached near completion, and the end of the decade of the 1980s might see the burial of colonialism in a form which determined the condition of humankind in the 19th and early 20th Centuries.

But late 20th Century colonialism is assuming new forms and dimensions. Motivations do not however appear to have changed though strategies and techniques are more sophisticated. Many affluent countries have in the tradition and expectations of the colonial era become committed to using humankind's total capital of resources and energy to maintain standards of life which are totally out of tune with the realities of the world in crisis. The real issue concerns the manner in which this world capital will be used to provide the minimum basic needs of the poor half of the world rather than to maintain the affluent nations in the third stage of consumerism and waste.

Present trends are towards seeking the further acceleration of the very same processes, to aim for a still higher level of consumption and thus maintain the validity of the socio-economic systems. But this is not going well because of the counterproductivity and reversal of many processes around which the systems are built.

To assess hundreds of micro-power and sub-macro-power centres within an intricate mosaic such as India and forge these into a meaningful forward thrust is difficult enough, but to relate the overall Indian power centre with a highly intricate world system is literally impossible.

As late as the early part of this century the flow of power, its point of origin as in the recipient country to which it flowed, was well understood. This pattern subsisted for a long time and went through very smooth and well-ordered changes. But this was disrupted after the Second World War, when the balances of power started shifting from one part of the world to another, from one power centre to another, and one set of imperatives to another.

But compulsions of the pre-colonial era were no longer valid and new ones were born. In recent decades both the speed and dimension of change have been so rapid and the movement and strength of the power centres so erratic that it has become impossible to pinpoint the factors which will condition the world of tomorrow.

The deserts of the Middle East, which till a decade ago were just a source of supply for one raw material, have today become the Achilles heel of the world industrial system. Every country is busy aggregating and pooling its resources with other states to assure the continuity of supplies of energy to its own techno-economic system, and to retain the sources of supply and trade routes within their sphere of influence. Energy which fuels the world's industrial and agricultural machines and contributes two of the most vital vectors of power, namely gross national productivity and the defence system, are threatened by curtailment of supplies and skyrocketing costs. The greater the dependence on outside sources of energy the greater the threat to a power centre.

The ascending power centres of yester years, which through their inherent strength and international arrangements had most of the parameters under control, are now obliged to pull in their horns, rearrange international strategies, enhance expenditure on war machines, accelerate innovation of war technologies, redefine their terms of international trade and, above all, forge new alliances more relevant to the present situation than ideological considerations alone. As the supply of resources and energy are threatened, the risks involved in maintaining the centres increase geometrically. Mounting armament costs accelerate this descent.

Emergence of new power centres such as the Organisation of Petroleum Exporting Countries, the nonaligned bloc, the European Economic Community, the Warsaw Pact nations and North-South groups are also bringing about massive neutralisation of the existing power centres.

Accelerating processes of technological reversal and increasing cost of ecological factors in expanding technological frontiers are reducing the value of the power centres in relation to the cost of innovating new technologies. They are also limiting the high-technology markets because of the growing contradictions between decreasing energy resources and increasing capital and energy intensity and the reducing employment potential of new technologies. Growing indiscipline, terrorism and human alienation are destroying the basic pre-requisite in operating high technologies and increasing their vulnerability.

As this is generating centrifugal processes in many social systems, it is encouraging the emergence of interest groups and the further concentration of political and economic power. This monocultural growth of power at a few dominant points in major social systems is reducing safety factors in the power centres. Complex centres usually have a much longer life and ability to survive in fast-changing situations.

While quite often a sizable proportion of resources is directed towards protecting the subversion of systems from without, the greatest enemy, the growing vulnerability and reversal of the system, is within and receives scant attention. Inflation, unemployment, waste, counterproductivity and technological reversal are far more dangerous enemies of the system than guided missiles and nuclear weapons in the arsenals of the opposing power centre.

The support the power centres receive through the economic strength of the system is receding while military hardware is becoming its backbone. This is a trend from which there appears to be no escape, and most major power centres have been caught in the straitjacket of offensive and defensive weapons, while one system after another is being destabilised through social and economic crisis within and intervention from without.

Most countries have not understood the interrelationship of all phenomena. While they can see and congratulate themselves for having engineered the processes of destabilisation in one country or revolt in another or a military coup in a third they do not see the impact or backlash of these actions in the environment where such actions take place, but above all their own countries from where they originate.

The socio-economic price the United States paid for its actions in Vietnam may turn out historically far greater than the suffering Vietnam had to endure in the process. Peace, security and prosperity are the greatest liberalisers of politico-socio-economic institutions while war, tensions and economic disturbances accelerate the processes of centralisation. Therefore, when countries, while professing humanistic or democratic ideals within their own boundaries, encourage military dictatorships abroad, in guiding such dictatorship they encourage similar trends internally.

They ultimately end up with dictatorial centralisation within their own country because you cannot manage international dictatorships in client countries through democratic institutions within your own. Those who are put in charge exercising dictatorial powers see much greater and more rewarding scope for their talents at home.

Diffusional power centres are therefore short-lived in terms of long-term perspectives and wither away rapidly both in social and economic terms as the processes of counterproductivity make their appearance, often leaving the practising countries a shamble. Wars of aggression are an extreme form of diffusional action. Insidious covert operation is another form, though somewhat restricted, almost as surely as war has a highly demoralising effect on the practising country.

The story of the last two decades is one of missed opportunities in development, of irresponsible exercise of diffusional power, breakdown of cherished institutions and emergence in their place of trends pointing towards socio-economic breakdown. For those who chose the path of prosperity also simultaneously chose the path of environmental destruction and waste of limited resources. The only option left is to take the world in their orbit or to explode, and without knowing the consequences they have chosen the first path.

The power centres with the highest survival rating are those where all the factors which condition strength, stability and longevity are adequately apportioned, and their suctional and diffusional characteristics are adequately balanced to create an upward push or ascent. The balancing wheels are energy, raw material resources, manpower, technology, markets. If one or more of these are inadequate the power centre must have the suctional and diffusional strength to fill in the gaps through trade (Japan) or economic or military power (the USA).

A rapidly ascending power centre accelerates consumption of resources, which it draws through suctional and diffusional effort from outside sources in its orbit. It needs a stable social environment to control its upward movement, and it has also to restrict continuously its orbit with acceleration. Broad-based rockets cannot take off, and so a rapidly ascending power centre has to isolate itself from restrictive elements in the social system. A stage is finally reached when the power centre is totally isolated from the social system.

Excessive use of resources, failure to control suctional and diffusional forces, or aimless upward spiral with no provision to decelerate, failure of the social system to support the cost and recoil of the overkill in the system for self-preservation is the cause of the failure of many power centres. The value of a power centre diminishes radically when it starts using machine guns to kill mosquitoes.

When 100-mile-wide countries are bombed with supersonic jets the value of the power centre between the point of kill and overkill is totally redundant. A centre which uses power to the factor of seven to kill where only one is required, or which creates overkill capability many times larger than the real need, therefore has a much lower power of the centre than is generally believed.

Economic Factors

Similarly, on the economic front, when a nation declares a perfectly good automobile or refrigerator or other piece of equipment obsolete and thus endeavours to increase rapidly the value of a power centre in the midst of energy and resources shortages, the true value of its power centre is less by a factor determined by the true life of the equipment in years divided by the years for which it is actually used. Thus GNP is not an adequate index for power centre assessment because for the same contributing element a developing society may get the same power with a much lower GNP as will be obvious from the Table on the opposite page.

Industry	% Contribution to GNP	Life of product years/obsoleted in years	Actual contribution
Automobile	25	12/3 = 4	25/4 = 6.25%
Textile	10	4/2 = 2	10/2 = 5.00%
Electronic	10	10/2 = 5	10/5 = 2.00%
	45		= 13.25%

In a long-term perspective the true contribution to GNP is not 45 but 13.25 percent. Hence in the assessment of the true value of the material elements of a power centre it is not the visual or obvious but the latent, the real, the long-term value that must be considered.

OVERKILL ROAD TO DESCENT

Power does not mean more bombs but how many are required to kill the enemy. According to the accepted value of the power centre, North Vietnam was dead when the United States entered the Indo-China conflict because the measured value of the US power centre is over a hundred times that of North Vietnam. But the integrated value of this power centre is smaller by a factor often because of the visual multiplier of overkill. Technological vulnerability is another element detracting from the power centre. Simultaneous ascent and descent create confusion and disturbances within a power centre, restrict its striking power, make its forward or upward motion aimless.

Diffusional and suctional pressures from other power centres start internal neutralisation of power and weaken the centre. Power centres which are overly reliant on external factors are highly vulnerable in disturbed international situations. Disturbed, erratic, swinging power centres are a constant threat both internally and externally and usually have tangential reactions and are hence very dangerous, often reacting with much greater force than needed.

A stable power centre is much less vulnerable. It would be much more effective with much less power. Neutralising factors are much less predominant. A stable ascending power centre is many times more viable and effective than shooting stars or rockets which burn more power than they generate.

Power Centre Assessment

A power centre can be assessed in terms of its characteristics, state of health or movement with the help of the following tabulation:

1. Category present overall	Superstar	Star	In orbit	Satellite
2. State	Highly stable	Stable	Unstable	Explosive
3. Characteristics	Diffusional	Diff-suct	Suct-diff	Suctional
4. Short-term movement	Ascent	Halting ascent	Halting descent	Descent
5. Long-term movement	Ascent	Halting ascent	Halting descent	Descent
6. Health	Internal power aggregation	Stable retention	Unstable retention	Internal power neutralisation
7. Prediction life in Present form	Very long (20 years)	Long (10 years)		Very short (1-2 years)
8. Projected category in the year 2000	Superstar	Star		Satellite

A power centre is a superstar when it carries in a stable state within itself and/or in its orbit adequate GNP and defence capabilities and resources to back up its own and its allies' interest at a high per capita income level. The only power centres which qualify for this definition are USA and USSR. If reference to a "stable state" were strictly adhered to, even the United States cannot entirely meet the requirement of a superstar. As Japan is highly vulnerable in terms of energy and other resources it could at best qualify as a star. While some countries are struggling for a place in the sun many others are either in the orbit of other major power centres, or can just enjoy the status and the perquisites of a satellite.

As many highly stable or stable power centres are moving into an era of techno-economic uncertainties or a situation of confrontation with other power centres they are effecting big changes in their characteristics, health and viability. The main power centres of the world at present may not necessarily be dominant by the end of the century.

5. Uncommitted Societies: Pace-Setters for Tomorrow

The committed societies have lost their bearings in the blind alleys of consumerist production and are falling apart. In earlier stages of development, the capitalist system, in the process of ushering in the age of consumerism, enlarged the areas of welfare. But in the long run an irreversible commitment to such an ideology determined the social and institutional framework within which techno-economic activities took place. And as these processes accelerated after the Second World War the regulatory mechanisms which determined the outer limits of action, the value system, codes of conduct and psychological supports to assure the validity and the continuity of the system also broke down.

The primary emphasis was on equal opportunity for all, the Protestant ethic of hard work and frugality, and a kind of individualism that knew no frontiers. And so the cult of the robber barons who sprang up after the civil war in USA had to be curbed through social action, the unrestrained growth of wealth in a few hands had to be provided with an orderly frame to lay the foundations of expanding networks of consumer markets.

The class conflict had to be regulated Through process of law in labour relations. The booms and busts in the system had to be contained within recessions and inflation through processes of regulated unemployment, social security and an aggressive promotion of consumerist utopias. The preemption of resources and markets for the benefit of individual nations had to give place to sharing them with likeminded nations. This arose out of frequent confrontation among the capitalist nations to obtain or enhance their share of the spoils.

The first major sequel to the Second World War was to heal the wounds of the defeated nations within the world-wide capitalist system, to bolster up their shattered economies through massive aid and free trade and to induct them as partners and beneficiaries in the world capitalist system. Growing pressures for the liberation of the colonial countries and the rapid neutralisation of the economic advantages and trade preferences of the colonial powers helped remove one of the major irritants in the relations among capitalist countries.

The need for a unified policy towards the emerging nations also contributed towards a commonness of interests and approach. The world capitalist system, with all its contradictions, started working towards a truly ideological orientation. The greatest enemy to the preservation of global capitalist interests was the threat of communism. This threat came from the communist monolith taking shape between Peking and Belgrade.

Aid and alliance directed against the threat from the Soviet Union in one region became, with the Korean War in 1950, a crusade against communism virtually in every corner of the globe. Moreover, largely as a result of the war, the struggle being defined as broadly based anti-communism rather than the original theme of containing perceived Soviet expansion.[1]

The threat also came from the rising expectations in the two-thirds of the poorer parts of the world. The production revolution in Western Europe and Japan, the technological revolution in the United States, the rapid growth of trade among the capitalist countries and the emergence of a powerful common enemy helped forge unified policies both within the capitalist and communist parts of the world.

The world became a vast arena, with two monoliths led by USA and USSR respectively, facing each other. Two major power centres had emerged on the world scene. Alexis de Tocqueville had prophesied the emergence of these two states, the United States and Russia, that had grown in obscurity. "Their starting point is different and their courses are not the same, yet each of them seems marked out by the will of heaven to sway the destinies of half the globe."[2] After putting their own houses in order they were now getting ready for diffusional intervention on the world scene. Their

---

[1] Jane Change, "Is Foreign Policy Consensus Possible," *Foreign Affairs*, Fall 1978, p. 3.

[2] Alexis de Tocqueville, *Democracy in America*, New York, Alfred A. Knopf, 1945, vol. 1, p. 434.

policies were directed towards creating regional power centres of those prepared to be manipulated for considerations of aid and trade. They tried through psychological techniques to cajole and frighten the uncommitted to fall in line so as to protect themselves from subservience to the imperialists or the communists. Western capitalist policies were largely directed at the elites. They presented new visions of human freedom and the wild delights of consumerism. The communist monolith had the general mass of the poorer sections of society as its target. It held out visions of equality, lack of exploitation, economic independence and socialism.

Faced with colossal socio-economic problems, the newly liberated poor and backward societies were learning the facts of life. While the poor dreamt of the end of their suffering the elites in these countries, saw visions of consumerist utopias. In the midst of a world-wide ideological confrontation and compulsions the leaders were hard pressed to choose between the two systems and seek technological and other resources. They clearly saw the nightmares of a new kind of economic servitude and the ultimate subversion of their policies and objectives.

Nehru came out with a new vision of nonalignment with the two major power centres. It was originally intended to be an exercise in political equidistance and friendly relations with both power systems, but ultimately it became a compulsive amalgam of socio-economic and cultural attitudes of a mixture of laissez faire and public sector enterprises, of political democracy and controlled economy, of capitalism and socialism, of the need to meet the basic needs of the many as against the consumerist passions of the few. While India was able to overcome the effects of some of these contradictions, and to an extent had the benefit of both approaches, a Pickwickian situation of falling between two stools arose in the case of many nonaligned societies.

THE AMERICAN WAVE

At the beginning of the 1950s the United States was the most powerful country in the post-war world. The dollar was the most powerful currency, backed by gold and annual trade surpluses of considerable magnitude. It was also the world's storehouse of new technologies. Most of the innovations in science and technology originated in the United States. It had also accumulated a considerable fund of goodwill for its record on human rights and freedom and generosity towards poor nations and the colonial world.

The US policy of democratising Japan and the techno-economic rehabilitation of Western Europe and Japan paid rich dividends in politico-economic terms and led to a further acceleration of techno-economic processes in the US itself.

Its sympathetic approach to the emerging colonial countries as full-fledged sovereign units further reinforced its position as a world leader. The appearance of dazzling consumer products, king-sized automobiles, television sets, modern homes, yachts on world markets, reinforced by US movies, brought about a large-scale cultural penetration of Europe, Japan and many developing countries around the world. The American way of life appeared to become the wave of the future.

The 1960s saw the emergence of Western Europe and Japan. The existence of an infrastructure of basic industries and trained manpower, though considerably depleted and dislocated at the end of the war, was ready to receive massive financial and technology inputs from the United States.

With defence commitments largely taken over by the US and free from any commitment to old technologies and machines which were a shambles after the war, the European and the Japanese techno-economic systems perked up rapidly not only to reconstruct their war-torn economies but caught up in, and in many areas excelled, the armament-committed R & D system of the United States. Through this process these countries, particularly the Federal Republic of Germany and Japan, made massive inroads into US markets for consumer and industrial products. They also staked their claims to the world's raw material and energy resources.

While the US was left with the responsibility for policing the world, of making massive investments in armaments and armament research to retain parity with the communist bloc, providing aid to the developing countries, building up intelligence networks, fighting a war in Vietnam and resisting revolutionary movements in Africa, her allies increased their trade and technology penetrations in her own preserves.

THE NEW NIGHTMARE

The 1970s were even more earth-shaking. The US defeat in Vietnam, the rising cost of arming and policing the world, the Chilean operation, growing inflation and unemployment, racial dissensions, all cost the US heavily in terms of its image as a superpower and the strongest pillar of the Western economic system, and its credibility as a respecter of human rights.

The oil crisis further aggravated these trends. A major producer of oil, the US benefited to some extent and was not jolted as severely as the other countries in the Western economic system, particularly Japan. Indeed, the US oil companies benefited greatly by increasing their revenues manifold with the same supply of oil, and for a time warded off the accelerated decline in the value of the dollar, largely through the export of armament to the oil-exporting countries of the Middle East and the direct transfer of the surpluses of these countries to the US banking system.

But this was at best a temporary respite. With exponential growth in the consumption of oil, with rising deficits in balance of trade because of oil imports and the growing constraints on the export of armaments, the US has lost much of its manoeuvrability in coping with the economic challenges from within and the political challenges from without. Unemployment continues to soar along with inflation: the remedy itself is being transformed into a disease.

The counterproductivity of techno-economic processes on a wide spectrum of human effort, leading to a state of "reversal" in many technologies, is making new investments unprofitable, and in many instances destructive of the environment. Corrective efforts are checkmated by contradictory trends and risks and ultimately by total inaction. It is becoming increasingly uneconomical to maintain industries such as shipbuilding, automobiles, electronic products, textiles and garments. The initiative is steadily passing to other countries such as Japan and developing countries such as India, China, Korea and Taiwan.

The pressures of counterproductive technologies at one end and employment costs and wages at the other are the dilemmas the US faces today. The dilemmas of rising deficits in trade balances, growing resistance to expenditures on armaments in client countries and mounting costs in the US itself, and the inability of the polity and techno-economic system to find viable alternatives without disturbing the Western economic system has attained the proportions of a nightmare for US allies in Europe and elsewhere.

How rapidly can systems move to rearrange their economies in the light of the new compulsions? Will the leaders have the courage and farsightedness, and the vested interests the ability, to see the inevitability and the necessary flexibility to survive such a transformation? Can consumer-oriented societies, after reaching a state of outright waste, revert without techno-economic upheavals to restraint and logic in managing their affairs? This is the biggest question mark before the affluent societies today.

The Communist Monolith

The communist monolith, which shadowed three continents under the arch from Belgrade to Shanghai, developed ideological and personality clashes in the 1950s. The urban-oriented revolutionary leadership of USSR could not see eye to eye with its rural offspring in command of the People's Republic of China. The war-scarred Soviet Union looked at the world from a different perspective from the self-assured revolutionary leadership of China, itching to project its interests and views within the communist bloc. This threatened Soviet hegemony in the councils of international communism.

When the break came in the later part of the 1950s the Chinese leaders engineered a cultural revolution within China to break all bonds with the Soviet Union and avoid ideological infiltration by the Soviets and the Western powers. China succeeded in protecting her ideological virginity from Soviet attacks throughout the life of the protector Mao Zedong. But long before even a single flower blossomed on the grave of the great Mao, post-Mao China fell a victim to the snares of the West. The temptations of a high-technology power system and consumerism were too much for the Maoist chastity belt to contain.

It would appear however that there will be no wedding. But much ideological turpitude and illicit relationships will bloom in the decades before the end of the millennium. China feels assured she can contain and Japanese marital designs and retain her position as the most sought after bride by the economically harassed countries of the capitalist world. Thus she hopes to neutralise any attempts by her powerful and angry Soviet neighbour to bully her into submission.

To the Western world this widening schism between the two major powers in the communist monolith was a welcome respite.

They could now concentrate on USSR and checkmate its moves in the Middle East, Africa and elsewhere. With the growing internal pressures towards consumerism, human rights and liberalisation of polity, Moscow could no longer have all the advantages of a controlled society, just as the Western world could no longer afford the luxury of an unbridled free enterprise system, and multinational penetration and exploitation of unwilling Third World countries.

In this unusual chess game both sides are checkmated. Either they must call off the game and share the rewards or jump at each other's throat. The only option open is to share the rewards as the consequences of confrontation are dangerous beyond belief. In the midst of the temptation of high-technology consumerism every society is losing its ideological purity. The satiated, jaded appetites of the high-consumer societies cannot retreat into the monasteries in search of Nirvana, certainly not after getting the rest of the world launched on this path.

Developing Societies

The post-independence leadership of the Republic of India, headed by Prime Minister Nehru, followed another kind of strategy. Though India declared herself neutral and nonaligned in relation to the major power centres represented by the United States and the rest of the Western world on one side and the communist monolith, including China, led by the Soviet Union on the other, she adopted many politico-techno-economic institutions and practices from both sides. She received aid and technical assistance freely, but steered clear of military assistance (as against purchases) or alignment with either bloc.

A low profile was maintained in all respects except in organising a world-wide movement for political nonalignment. This movement achieved a high level of success in the 1950s, but its success was largely limited to countries like India, while John Foster Dulles insisted that neutralism or "nonalignment was morally untenable in a struggle between the communist and the free world."[3] Thanks to their size, manpower and other resources, such countries endeavoured to develop, and succeeded to an extent in developing, a

---

[3] John Foster Dulles.

techno-economic infrastructure to ensure a modicum of independence.

In the ultimate analysis the weight exercised by a country in the world power game was determined by its level of freedom to make a commitment to the techno-economic imperatives of development. Pragmatic handling of techno-economic processes considerably enlarged the productive base in countries like India. These processes also helped strengthen the hold of the elite on an entire spectrum of development. Largely because of the influence of personalities rather than that of institutions, development in the 1950s and 1960s was marked more by a stop-go approach than by continuity.

Contradictions in techno-economic growth began to surface in an acute form in the 1970s. Increasing unemployment, sharpening economic disparities and massive urbanisation were some immediate consequences of such growth. Inability to reach a national consensus on goals and strategies in the midst of a multiplicity of choices in development considerably slowed the pace of growth.

These choices are now being further narrowed down by energy resources, ecological, human and other factors. It is becoming obvious that the economies of waste in affluent societies cannot continue on their present course, and also that it will no longer be possible to attempt such development in developing societies.

Further, for societies that have already made resource and techno-economic commitments to high-energy, high-technology and capital-intensive techniques of development, a retreat to employment-oriented strategies will not be possible. Brazil is a classic example of a country which has closed most of its options for low-cost, employment-oriented development. Mexico is moving in a similar direction.

Societies which are irrevocably committed to consumerist orientation of their productive processes, and where the compulsions for increasing production get precedence over the urgency for increasing employment, often tend to reach a point of no return with regard to their techno-economic orientation, which can then only be altered through a considerable dislocation of the politico-techno-economic structure.

Urban Elitist Groups

India encouraged the rapid development of state-controlled basic industries, consumer-product manufacturing and matching organisations of scientific, industrial, agricultural and medical research, and education. Paradoxically the benefits of such development remained largely confined to the upper classes and elitist groups. Apart from setting in motion processes of rapid urbanisation it enlarged the area of opportunities within the urban system, thus further accelerating the very same processes of population explosion in the urban sector. The social cost of providing the basic infrastructure and employment opportunity increased manifold. The cost ratios of providing similar opportunities to urban and rural systems reached a factor of over twenty.

These phenomena are, to varying degrees and with some exceptions, true of countries in the three continents of Asia, Africa and Latin America. While indices of welfare such as GNP, education, health, employment, consumption of goods and services, trained manpower, agricultural production and industrialisation have in many instances shown exponential rates of growth over the last three decades, in real terms the benefits have largely been limited to a very small section of society.

These benefits have continued to aggregate in fewer and fewer hands while vast sections have continued to slip into penury and degradation. As in the case of affluent societies which cannot get out of the straitjacket of consumerism and extravagance, the developing countries are unable to contain the rising spiral of elitist development, and are incapacitated to take those decisions which may bring about a reorientation of their societal organisation to meet the needs of the larger sections of the community.

Societies which have encouraged such uneven growth and have developed inbuilt compulsions of unequal distribution need a protective apparatus to contain their disparities. They also need to protect themselves from diffusional intervention by other societies. These factors negate the functioning of democratic institutions, reverse the processes of decentralisation to achieve broad-based (mass-based) development and increase the vulnerability of societies to external politico-techno-economic manipulations.

By the time the elites become aware of the dangers to their polity through such development, it is too late and the vanguard of the so-called democratic processes becomes the willing tool of all kinds of authoritarianism within the systems. And this becomes a simple exercise with the cooperation, connivance or acquiescence of the elites. The choice today is not between authoritarianism and democracy but between two different grades of authoritarianism.

Premature Arrival of Contradictions

A clear solution seems to lie in decentralisation and mass participation, but the compulsions are for centralisation and state control. In the midst of pre-industrial attitudes and infrastructure, where economies demand low-energy, low-technology tools, the pressures are towards high-energy, high-technology tools and resource-intensive and productive processes. Instead of introducing habits of thrift and accumulation of resources and their investment in productive channels, they are wasted in promoting consumerism and fanning consumerist passions by encouraging the habit of spending money before it is earned through consumer credit schemes.

In many developing countries with a high incidence of direct and indirect taxation unaccounted money and cash transactions become a norm for trade. Thus the contradictions which appeared in affluent societies in the advanced stages of techno-economic order in the post-industrial era have surfaced at the very commencement of such processes in developing countries.

"The economy, the polity and the culture," says Daniel Bell,[4] "are ruled by contrary axial principles; for the economy, efficiency, for the polity, equality and for the culture, self-realisation (or self-gratification). The resulting disjunctions have formed the tensions of social conflicts of Western society in the past 150 years." These tensions have already started appearing in the developing societies. But both with regard to commitment to an ideology or otherwise, these have affected only a narrow spectrum of the community or interests and can therefore more easily be neutralised than in the case of committed societies.

Classic Examples

Classic examples of societies which still retain some politico-techno-economic manoeuvrability and consequent options to re-orient

[4]Daniel Bell, *The Cultural Contradictions of Capitalism*, New York, Basic Books Inc., 1976, p. 11.

their systems within a new framework are countries like China, India and Yugoslavia. At the other extreme are societies which have fore-closed all possibilities for independent action by linking their economies with major power centres and opting out for consumerist or centralist techniques of development. They have thus placed themselves in the midstream of political confrontation and economic retrogression.

Israel, South Africa, Chile, Brazil, South Korea and many other developing countries have chosen or have been pushed on to the path of such development, or have otherwise made institutional and resource commitments leaving for themselves little room to move away from their international mentors. This has often subjected these countries to a commitment to solutions totally unrelated to their needs or inherent compulsions, thus contributing to growing instability in many developing societies.

A small nation like Iran committing tens of billions of dollars to the defence of its 34 million people, grovelling at various levels of poverty, was bound to be a nine-day wonder. It acquired neither the ability for self-defence in war nor political and economic stability in peace. It is not strong enough to protect itself in the north, nor is it secure from fear of its potential enemies in the South and West. Its very defence preparedness turned out to be the greatest threat to its polity, the processes of modernisation through centralisation of authority only activating religious, chauvinistic or extremely radical trends.

In the long run, the show of massive high-technology-based physical strength becomes exceedingly vulnerable in the face of poverty, unemployment and free trade. In the late 20th Century people do not commit hara kiri to save royal dynasties or in defence of time-serving allies, or distant benefactors through shady armament deals. When benefits accrue to the people, only then do they fight to keep the supply lines serving their interests open.

It would appear that in the short term the authoritarian regimes of the Left have displayed a relatively greater survival value than dictatorships of the rightist variety. Most proletarian dictatorships, whether in Eastern Europe, Southeast Asia or Cuba, with a much larger base of popular support and participation, with greater ideological purity and sustained by relatively better defined socio-economic objectives, have stayed in power much longer.

The pyramids of power in propped-up military and other dictatorships have their apexes controlled from distant power centres and have very little contact with the power base in their own countries. Such dictatorships can be toppled at will by the controlling power centres. They are always vulnerable to pressures from within and without, and more often than not remain in a state of suspended animation throughout their existence.

Many South American, African and Southeast Asian dictatorships of the recent past and present represent this type of uncertain state. This situation is further aggravated by the acceleration of consumerist-oriented developmental processes where the elites are the major beneficiaries, and the power structure in the social system and the distant controlling power centres act in unison to perpetuate such a situation. That is why most communist societies avoid a consumerist orientation in the first stages of the developmental process. The distinction between free and controlled societies gets blurred in the second and the third stages of development.

On the political level there is a need for mass participation in the decision-making processes. Emerging economic institutions must represent, satisfy and promote the needs of a broad spectrum of the people. At the same time the polity should have the authority and power to bring about social changes to curb the undue pre-emption of benefits of development by the privileged sections of society. Societies should be able to look beyond development to the larger issues of human alienation, ecological protection, preservation of resources and, above all, the long-term human future. The post-war euphoria for new human institutions turned into a mirage because everybody wanted to plant the hybridised seeds of yesterday's world to reap the harvest of tomorrow. They are instead reaping the whirlwind of the future.

Having cut themselves off from their past they know not where to turn. The euphoria of affluence is now confined in the straitjacket of fear, greed and inaction. Dreams of the future have turned sour with the catalysts of synthetic and nuclear pollution in the slush money of oil, in the cauldron of violence and brutality. A commitment to the future meant a total break with the past. Chairman Mao said in a talk to Chinese workers in 1956:

> Every nation in the world has its own history and its own strengths and weaknesses—excellent things and rotten things have mingled together and mingled over long periods—but we must not reject history because of this difficulty. It is no good cutting ourselves off from history and abandoning our heritage. The common people would not approve.[5]

Developed affluent societies have a twin commitment to an entire range of imperatives of the post-war world: first, to the continued acceleration of techno-economic processes and the maximum use of resources and, second, to a politico-socio-economic framework within which such development must take place. Both in scope and objectives these two commitments are contradictory. As such, either the framework or the techno-economic processes are threatened from within. Protective reflex action, instead of increasing its inherent strength by removing some contradictions, by some strange logic threatens the system itself.

Thus the failure of the system to meet the challenges of poverty in the midst of affluence in an orderly manner is attributed to the evil designs of or intervention by external forces or outside power centres. This has added new contradictions of increasingly rising levels of investment in destructive weapons as a natural consequence of parity and arms limitations, leading up to expenditure in arms of more than $500 billion. A fraction of this amount would be adequate to initiate a world-wide attack on poverty and usher in a new era of plenty for all.

Leaders of many developing countries have allowed themselves to be manoeuvred into becoming, or have willingly chosen to become, part of a world-wide system of armament accumulation and defence preparedness. In the process they have forfeited their freedom to choose the system of development most suited to their needs, resources and genius of their peoples. This has led to destruction of the environment, major disparities in the economic system and quite often siphoning away of surpluses to the suctional power centres. Numerous international confrontations have, behind the scenes, had somebody's interests, resources, strategic location and trade routes at stake.

[5]Mao Zedong, *Unrehearsed Talks and Letters, 1956-71*, (ed.) Stuart Schram, London, Penguin Books, 1974, p. 85.

The commitments of the major power centres also often become commitments of satellites within their orbit. Thus defence and trade linkages also become linkages in technological orientation, capital intensity of production processes, pressures of unemployment, inflation and currency fluctuations. Such relationships have most often been found working to the detriment of the developing countries.

The brave new world of developing societies is the same old world with new relationships, largely depending upon the intensity of their commitment. Their abilities to carve out new strategies and forge new links in accordance with their needs have remained restricted. Any of these relationships, whether defence, political or techno-economic, tend to become all-embracing in course of time.

But the strategy of nonalignment had a much wider connotation than the desire for neutrality between power centres representing conflicting interests. It meant the freedom to choose socio-economic policies related to the compulsive needs of the developing system.

After the withdrawal of Russian technicians for about two decades, China remained the only country with relative freedom of action with regard to economic policies, and techno-economic relations with other countries. As Chairman Mao said, "A blank sheet of paper is good for writing on."[6] It could achieve this status largely because of its isolation from the international polity.

The countries of the European Economic Community did, to a certain extent, retain their freedom of action as a collective entity because of their combined economic strength but not as independent units. In spite of the great vulnerability of its resources Japan exercises a level of independence of action through bilateral arrangements such as the recent one with China. These two complementary economic systems have exercised the options the relative lack of commitment to either of the two major power centres provided.

At the other end of the spectrum are countries like Brazil, Poland, the German Democratic Republic, South Korea, Indonesia and many others which have developed intricate suctional and diffusional relations with major power centres. They have linked their developmental processes, polity and defence with one or the other power centre in such a manner that independent action on any of these fronts is restricted except at the risk of economic dislocation, political upheavals or even war.

---

[6]*Ibid.*, p. 83.

Between these extremes of relative freedom and complete subservience float the developing countries of Asia, Africa and Latin America. Their need for protection and for resources and technologies determine their dependency on these major centres or their constituents. Their ability to demand equity in such relations depends largely on political, defence and resource investment, markets or other purposes of the major centres these societies can serve.

The nature and extent of commitment varies not only from country to country but also from time to time, and from one power centre to the other. One sided relations have more often than not led to unfortunate consequences for recipient developing societies. Only those societies which can retain relative freedom of action with regard to the major politico-techno-economic parameters can qualify as uncommitted societies.

So, what are their options? After the Second World War many new relationships have emerged between developed and newly independent developing societies. The nature of such relationships depends largely on the security and resource interests of the big powers. For instance, the focal point of relations between the US and the South American and Central American republics was the national security objectives of the United States. In the case of Iran, it was the assurance of availability and movement of oil from the Persian Gulf to the United States and her allies. Similar considerations also determined relations between the US and Southeast Asia and the Middle East.

With minor variations, most such relationships between the big powers, their satellites and developing societies in the end reach a similar orientation, and in this process the interests of the big powers become paramount and those of recipient developing societies only peripheral to the main concern. In the ultimate analysis it often becomes difficult to discern who are the real beneficiaries in such relationships, the affluent or the needy.

A common feature of most relationships is the emergence of elites whose interests are served and promoted through such associations. Another important characteristic is the rapid growth of GNP, massive increases in incomes and accumulation of surpluses in the hands of upper one-third of the population and the simultaneous impoverishment of the two-thirds of the population below the poverty line.

Many such relationships commenced with the large-scale injection of investment in technologies, equipment and financial resources from the controlling power centres into developing societies. Within a period of three to five years, a reverse flow of resources, often at rates as large as 30-40 per cent a year of the initial investment, begins from the developing countries to the dominating power centres. There is also an outflow of basic resources such as energy and raw materials from the developing to the developed.

Because of the deteriorating balance of trade of many important industrial nations there is a growing trend towards the transfer of resources back to the investing country, either in the form of return on capital invested or through the sale of arms to the emerging power centres as in the case of Iran. This results in reduced investment in new productive units, increased unemployment, widening disparities of income and hardships never before experienced, leading directly to progressive alienation of the leaders from the people and often leading up to an international ideological confrontation.

The presence of large contingents of foreign nationals as defence advisers, academics, intelligence operators and businessmen hobnobbing with the political, defence and business leaders of the developing countries often becomes the symbol of a new form of colonialism and intervention in the affairs of these countries.

This is the starting point of new revolutionary movements, terrorism and retaliation by the local power centres, often in collusion with some international mentors. When the collaborating power centres sense the emerging trends a quick search for an alternative leadership begins. Here again there is close cooperation between international business interests, government and some sections of the neglected local elites of the concerned country, thus further widening the schism between the people and their government and providing an opportunity for intervention by opposing power centres. South Africa, Angola, Iran, Chile, South Vietnam and Afghanistan and some more recent examples of such intervention.

RELATIONS WITH THE COMMUNIST BLOC

Relations between the Soviet Union and other countries of the Eastern bloc have many common elements with similar relations between the countries of the Western bloc and developing societies, though there are also certain vital points of difference. Firstly, relations with the communist bloc are directly at a government-to-government level and there are no independent business linkages promoting their interests quite apart from the interests of their governments.

The communist countries usually rely on the local communist parties to provide political and ideological support for such relationships, thus curbing the acquisitive tendencies of local elites and total alienation of the leaders. Public-sector enterprises, through which economic relationships are usually effected, are under attack more for their inefficiency than for exploitation or siphoning of resources as profits or royalties. Generally speaking, relations with such countries as North Vietnam, North Korea and Cuba have been relatively more stable than similar relations of the Western world with Chile, South Vietnam, Pakistan and Iran.

There are no ideal situations in such relationships. All comparisons are therefore only relative. Another factor which tends to destabilise them is the fluctuating economic fortunes of the major power centres. When economies go into recession, when unemployment mounts, when foreign exchange reserves deteriorate, when the value of currencies nosedives, the glamour of high GNP and consumerism wears off, with consequent pressures to alter relations with the declining economic power centres. The recent political trends in France, Italy and other countries of western Europe are a pointer in this direction.

The communist bloc economies, though less glamourous in periods of expanding consumerism, become very attractive in periods of inflation, unemployment and recession, winning devotees even among conservatives. In periods of grave crisis and depression the controlled economies become the hope of the future and the rallying point for the down-trodden.

Precisely for this reason in the last six decades or more countries accounting for one-third of world population and possessing over half the world's resources have chosen controlled economies for their process of development. Though there have been many soured relationships within the communist monolith these have rarely won long-term adherents for the capitalist system. Changes have meant only certain variations in the controlled economies. China and Yugoslavia are classic examples of such a transformation. On the other hand, there are continuing pressures within the capitalist system for the expansion of the public sector of the economy, for greater planning at micro and macro level, and more meaningful liberalisation of trade relations in the affluent countries, and between such countries and developing societies and their elites.

The expanding technological level of developing societies, particularly of the larger economies like India, China and Brazil, has become a dual threat to the rich and the affluent. Firstly, they have become users of their own low-priced raw materials, thus putting considerable pressure on prices and the availability of such raw materials for the wasteful economies of the affluent world.

Secondly, products of high technologies originating in low-wage economies of developing societies have become a major contender for the markets of the affluent countries. They are attacking the most vulnerable parts of the system by accelerating the pace of unemployment and inflation, with major socio-techno-economic implications. With many technologies reaching the point of counter-productivity or outright technological reversal the available options to counteract these trends with better technologies are simultaneously receding. The temptation to bring the developing societies within their orbit with a view to achieving more favourable aid, trade and defence relationships therefore becomes overwhelming. All elements in nation states which question or resist such relations with so-called free enterprise economies and democratic societies are dubbed anti-democratic and communist. Similarly, when they seek cooperation with the affluent they are labelled as running dogs of imperialism by international communism.

Through a world-wide information network the developing societies are projected as enemies or friends as may suit the interests of the major power centres at a given moment. In this process they are forced into irrelevant choices in respect of their techno-economic relations without any consideration for their own needs and compulsions. Such strategies are now becoming counterproductive, and are at best effective for short durations and diffusional in character, thus contributing very little to the interests of affluent societies.

Another approach for the developed countries would be accelerated, but at the same time regulated, integration of their techno-economic systems in the advanced stages of consumerism with those of developing societies at early stages of development. While this may provide some respite to the turbulent economies of affluent societies it would simultaneously launch developing societies on the inexorable path of consumerism, resource depletion and ecological lunacy. This would confine large masses of people in the developing world in perpetual backwardness because of inflation and employment limitation, which is dangerous and totally unacceptable in the last quarter of the 20th Century.

THE MULTINATIONALS

Massive inputs of financial resources and technologies into small recipient countries like South Korea, Taiwan, Singapore and Hong Kong often lead to almost the entire population becoming in one manner or the other beneficiaries in the rapid expansion of productive processes. In the short term, it is usually possible to contain undue distortions in such small systems. But very soon, often within less than a decade, low-wage productive processes with large economies of scale begin to balance out and tend to become counterproductive.

The industrial infrastructure supported and maintained by international corporations as a competitive outlet for their farflung markets, including those of their home country, ceases to be attractive. This leads logically to a dual policy of restraint on new investment and planned withdrawals in favour of greener pastures. The recipient countries try to fend for themselves in a competitive world, but they have already been sold on a total and inexorable commitment to the processes of consumerism, to the wasteful use of resources and complete dependence on outside markets for their burgeoning products. Though a static condition is reached in a few decades, the multinational connections help, in the protection of their own interests, the small productive capacities of such countries to be relatively easily absorbed in the world trade system at the expense of other societies struggling for survival.

But such relations between developed societies and larger countries such as India, Brazil, Mexico and Indonesia tell a different tale. The immediate effects are that even with relatively large investments the benefits of such growth reach only a small fraction of the population. This leads to the emergence of a spate of politico-techno-economic elites. They remain the sole beneficiaries of the system, apart from the large-scale benefits which pass on to their international connections.

A sharp conflict of interests between maximising production and profit and employment and equitable distribution is precipitated.

Cost per workplace follows the same trends as in the investing countries. With initial advantages in wages and costs the developing countries seek markets for their products and become major low-cost contenders for the high-wage, high-cost markets of developed countries.

A solution is sought by raising insurmountable trade barriers in the developing countries as one industry after another becomes vulnerable and employment-restrictive in the donor as well as receiver countries. The only controllable element left, if at all, among the basic cost elements of material, labour, overheads and profits in the high-cost economies of developed societies is the cost of raw materials and energy imports from abroad. Many proxy wars in countries in Africa, Asia and Latin America could be linked with the protection of some such interests somewhere along the line. Ideologies are the smokescreen behind which wars of trade interests are fought. The Bismarckian dictum that ideology was foolish and policy was "the art of the possible" was being proved right.

As the depletion of world resources is moving much faster than the discovery of new or alternative resources, and as discontinuities in the techno-economic processes threaten the stability of systems, both the area and intensity of conflicts are increasing. These are the basic facts of life. Neither the camouflage of negotiations on restricting armaments nor verbal sympathy and glamorous promises of aid to the developing countries, nor even the apotheosis of one kind of political system or the other, can hide these basic facts despite the massive information offensive or tacit tactical acceptance by the elites. These developments often highlight the futility of both aid and free trade as meaningful instruments of cooperation between conflicting aspirations and the interests of developed and developing societies.

With the collapse of the colonial powers a new kind of techno-economic colonialism has emerged in the relations between the two groups. So long as traditional attitudes form the basis of such relations, whether through compulsion, design or ignorance, the search for solutions will be illusory and an environment of mistrust will prevail. Most international forums for cooperation are thus being converted into arenas of confrontation.

The prevalent strategies for optimising individual, organisational and national interests as against international or larger human interests have in many ways been responsible for the growing insecurities in most systems, working to the short-term advantage of some but the long-term disadvantages of all. Unemployment is increasing today, not just in a few systems but in all of them. Recessionary trends, unrest and terrorism are plaguing almost all countries in one form or another.

Economic prosperity, destruction of environment, human alienation, international conflict, confrontation and exploitation, all go together, each fattening on the other. We see it all and yet continue to promote the so-called national and international policies. These negate our human interests as advantages for one are always at the cost of another as the systems operate inequitably.

If this is not true of all relations between the affluent and the poor it is true for most of them. And this is not entirely due either to viciousness or lack of desire to promote more equitable arrangements. Most avenues of growth are leading to some or all the negative factors such as inflation, unemployment, resource and environmental crisis, international confrontation and internal unrest.

Even where the desire to collaborate is genuine and based on mutual interest avenues for action are barred as the issues of complementarity are settled not just by interests and desires but by the nature of compulsions which operate within the cooperating systems. And such compulsions are shaping the techno-economic systems of tomorrow's world.

The leaderships in political turmoil, assailed by techno-economic distortions, confusedly reach out for age-old solutions for the problems of the late 20th Century. None of these problems, born out of high-energy, high technology, techno-economic systems of consumerism, are reacting to the promises of a slow boat trip to utopia.

The future will depend on our ability to forge equitable, workable and complementary relationships among the various techno-economic systems at different stages of development with differing needs and priorities. After three decades of aid, trade and technology exchange, most developed countries with growing needs for energy resources and markets for their overcommitted techno-economic systems, instead of creating new frameworks for sustainable complementarity with developing societies, are reaching out for a kind of uniformity eminently suited to defence partners needing standardised equipment, techniques and strategies. But this is deadly in its effects on trading partners, with each society having its own techno-economic compulsions. The visual demise of the Trilateral Commission and the trends in North-South relationships are adequate pointers to the faulted intentions.

CHINA

A proper assessment of post-war Communist China, its turmoils, achievements, failures and the personalities which dominated its policies, will not be possible for many more decades. But it is becoming clear that China is not permitting the manipulation of its techno-economic policies by any superpower. It did not allow consumerist overtones in its first stage of development. It has also managed to neutralise most outside pressures, whether political, military or techno-economic, through all kinds of techniques, including bluff, determination and the sheer weight of its population of nearly 900 million.

Its industrial and agricultural development has not been spectacular, but its distribution of welfare among a broad section of a continental community surpasses that of other countries. With adequate energy resources, large reserves of manpower, relatively less ideological vulnerability through large-scale involvement of the people in the constructive processes, at least during the Maoist regime, it has been in a stronger position than many other countries to exercise a level of freedom of choice in its future course for techno-economic development.

But the ideological rigidities and economic restraints which were a hallmark of Maoist China now appear to be undergoing a big change. The new regime appears to be moving towards pragmatic strategies not only in techno-economic policy-making but also in techno-economic relations with other countries.

It is now increasingly realised that the techno-economic structure of China is much narrower than it was represented to be and needs to be considerably renovated and enlarged to receive, adopt and assimilate new technologies. And such technologies will create their own environment to succeed. China is going through traumatic experiences in its movement towards some kind of conformity with the imperatives of new technologies. The extent of available options will depend upon its ability to effect this transformation.

The Nixon-Kissinger efforts at detente with China were designed to outflank the Soviet position in Asia by taking advantage of the

Sino-Soviet ideological confrontation. It was also meant to fill the techno-economic vacuum caused by Soviet withdrawal from China and the Maoist regime's aggressive posture in relation to the rest of the world. It would appear that the United States is not likely to be the major beneficiary of China's new policy orientations. China is learning from the experience of Western Europe, Brazil and many other countries that the US connection inevitably leads to big-power domination, not only in techno-economic areas but also political domination in protecting these techno-economic interests. Such was their experience earlier with USSR.

It would therefore appear that, as in the case of many other countries, the Chinese have chosen to avoid intimate big-power connections and seek relations with others who can fill the technology gap either by training their technicians or by supplying equipment and knowhow. The recent techno-economic agreement with Japan, though still brittle, is therefore the logical culmination of the policy of four modernisations—agriculture, industry, defence and science and technology.

This would bring together two neighbours with complementary economies, China providing markets and raw materials and Japan equipment and technology, within easy reach of each other. Their trade exchanges could total $20 billion over the period of the agreement. While the agreement would help Japan overcome some short-term problems regarding raw materials availability and markets, China would be the major beneficiary of such an arrangement.

Japan is reaching points of counterproductivity in many of its endeavours and would be unable to maintain its rate of growth in terms of real advantages while China will for many decades be forging ahead into the future with rapid expansion of her technological capabilities, techno-economic infrastructure, productive and defence organisation. By the turn of the century, China could, in view of its minimal infrastructural commitments, be in absolute terms a far greater power than Japan, and the socio-techno-economic structure of this new superstate would have changed beyond recognition in the process. Both Maoist ideology and ideologues would fade away in the midst of the emerging techno-economic compulsions and interests.

Virtually every dimension of the four modernisation programmes goes against the key tenets of Mao Zedong's thought as propagated and applied in the final decade of the chairman's life. And this ideological legacy could certainly provide support for those who might prove unwilling to pay the cost of the modernisation programme.[7]

Nor is there an iron-clad assurance that before the end of this decade new movements for broad-spectrum convergence between the old separated allies, that is USSR and China, will not emerge. This new monolith could well be the world's most important power centre, engulfing in its fold the entire landmass on the north and south of the axis in the northern hemisphere from Berlin to Shanghai. In such an eventuality Japan and Western Europe could on the fringes of this landmass at best command the status of eastern and western service stations.

Over the long run the question is whether this unity will hold up when the modernising coalitions confront the dilemmas China will face in the early 1980s as a direct consequence of the new technological culture and penetration by consumerist passions. None of these actions are an assurance that China will be able to hold to a course of rapid modernisation, but they do reinforce the formal commitment of the current leaders and help keep China's ambitious goals on the leaders' agenda for many years to come.

INDIA

Nonalignment was born in post-independence India and Prime Minister Jawaharlal Nehru was its architect It became a significant factor in world affairs in less than a decade, with an axis supported at four points—Indonesia, India, Egypt and Yugoslavia—in three continents. It was inspired and propelled by four great leaders—Sukarno, Nehru, Nasser and Tito.

While nonalignment remained a political weapon in an international and regional balancing act in Indonesia and Egypt, it moved deeper down into the rearrangement of the techno-economic structures of India and Yugoslavia. From the vantage point of the 1950s nonalignment was at best an escape route from the obligations and commitments of the Cold War, the armaments race, regional

---

[7]Kenneth Liberthal, "A Second Revolution Begins in China," *Fortune*, 23 October 1978.

defence groupings, and the marginal neutralisation of major power centres.

India made rapid strides in organising the basic techno-economic structure. With effective neutralisation of both power centres and assistance from both power groups, the twin structure of basis technologies and scientific research on the one hand and private-sector consumer industries on the other took a quantum jump into the future.

India's march forward under a canopy of drawn swords representing the two power centres was an exhilarating experience for Indians, the envy of those who, under an illusion of large quantities of aid from one or other power centres, ended up paying protection money to maintain their political entity between the pressures of the opposing power centres. India could poise herself in the dead centre of the world power game.

The big-power answer to this display of independence or leaning towards opposing power centre was seen in Iran, Egypt, Indonesia, Bangladesh, Hungary and Czechoslovakia through the displacement of their regimes. India and Yugoslavia escaped to the extent that political independence had been translated into techno-economic independence. India's size helped her to swing back partially into a continuation of old policies even after the debacle in the Chinese War in 1962.

But the sporadic instigation of insurgencies in the Northeast Frontier, on the borders with Pakistan and China and in the Indian heartland has been an important instrument in the hands of international power centres to maintain a constant state of uncertainty. To this has now been added the manipulation of regional, religious and caste sentiments to achieve and defend political purposes and swing political sentiment, a kind of democratic free-for-all.

This is more to neutralise the influence of other power centres and to gain acceptance for one kind of techno-economic policy or other rather than a direct subversion of the country's policy. The local elites play an important role in these processes in terms of their interests and are often the torch-bearers of the oft-repeated slogans of imperialism and communism as against democracy and socialism—all empty words without meaning and content in the world of late 20th Century yet powerful instruments to exacerbate class and caste sentiments.

The lesson the elites are learning and the message reaching the masses is that to give a free run to vested interests and a free play of words to opinion merchants hundreds of millions of people, their lives and interests, are held to ransom. Major power centres have a great deal to contribute to this state of affairs.

Recent events in India have helped to make visible the distant hands, the play of personalities, the search for dead illusions in an attempt to recreate the institutions of the past instead of seeking solutions for the future. The ingredients of a welfare state for the common good and human and other resources and an infrastructure for development already exist. Even the nature of the problem has been fairly accurately defined. The turmoil of ideologies, battle of interests, conflict of personalities, confrontation of power centres all conspire to convert future hopes into current disasters.

All action appears directed towards perpetuating the past as against a search for the future. Even such basic considerations as the need for planning, the vital role of basic industries, strategies for rural transformation and welfare of the down-trodden, have become reasons for confrontation rather than action.

Everybody is fishing in the troubled waters of Indian polity. The vector of forces within the power structure is shifting from one position to another with such rapidity that it is hard to discern the direction of events or policies. But this can only be a passing phase in a pluralistic, democratic society. Amid all this turmoil, the nonemergence of a predominant trend would negate commitments, whether ideological, political or techno-economic, from taking shape, form or coherence.

India's techno-economic structure displays eminently positive factors of foreign exchange reserves, food surpluses and trained manpower. It provides many options for becoming a major power centre through the free choice of a strategy for integrated development. But will India be able to exercise such an option in the midst of the political neutralisation of all the forward thrust in the techno-economic processes? This question will remain unanswered till a positive convergence of political forces emerges. To achieve this, India will first have to neutralise the internally or externally manipulated negative forces. A new synthesis supporting the emergence of decentralised rural communities and highly centralised technology-based key industries, along with linkages to stabilise rural-urban relations through control of incentives, wage differentials and many other devices will have to be evolved.

To avoid commitment to superpower connections would mean rationalising relations with the European communities of the East and West. There is no one country which could satisfy the broad spectrum of trade and technology needs of India. It would need many new relationships to assure complementarity.

While nowhere outside USA and USSR is there a critical mass of trained manpower and enlightened individuals as in India, a small percentage of the population, with commitment to the continuity of the consumerist mode of development, cannot usher a population of more than 680 million into the 21st Century. Wherever it has been tried, even on a fractional scale, it has brought about the same distortions, enlarging the welfare of a few and pushing larger and larger sections of the population below the poverty line.

It has brought the dreams of contemporary youth in conflict with the visions of aged leaders, and local, sectional or regional leaders against pressures of universality. It has thwarted the emergence of new cultures in the midst of dreams and illusions of the past, and a new humanism against religious dogmatism. But the real danger is the growing dichotomy between aspirations and fulfilment.

Obsolescence and rigidity of institutional frame are among the causes of world-wide disorientation and emergence of autonomous technologies, and these are aided by instruments of unrelated, centralised planning systems. While capitalist societies are suffering from unplanned chaos, centrally planned societies are paying the price of planned containment of initiative.

India's synthesis of the two made extensive gains in the 1950s and 1960s, resulting in broad-spectrum strengthening of the infrastructural and technological base of society and increases in agricultural and industrial production. But more recently there has been an aggregation of negative trends from both systems.

With a public sector plagued by mismanagement, uncertainty and labour indiscipline and a private sector lost in bureaucratic blind alleys and infrastructural inadequacies and failures, the vector of forces providing a forward thrust is reaching the point of near zero. The government does not enjoy absolute political power, nor has the private sector absolute control over the economic institutions.

Uncommitted Societies: Pace-Setters for Tomorrow

The exercise of economic control by government through state-controlled financial institutions and basic industries is neutralised largely by the political influence exercised by many interest groups, the farm lobby, labour unions, recognised minorities and, lastly, powerful industrial and commercial interests. All this may not appear to add up to a very effective forward motion or accelerated development. Quite often it paralyses the political processes into total inaction.

Any factor like labour unions and technological counterproductivity in Britain and overproduction, overemphasis on armament production and technological reversal in the United States can lead to a stranglehold on the system and containment of manoeuvrability in developmental strategies. Yet, because of an overall positive resultant of a wide variety of favourable and negative factors, India retains many of her options for development.

ELEMENTS OF COMMITMENT

In terms of manoeuvrability in formulating and executing techno-economic policies most developing societies could be classified today as under:

Country	Elements of Commitment			Resources in relation to population	Political will of system	Ability to exercise techno-economic options
	History & culture or historical behaviour pattern	To a system of development	Collaborative relationship with major power centres			
Brazil	Low	High	High	Medium	High	Low
Chile	Low	High	High	Medium	High	Low
China	Medium to high	High	Low	Medium	High	High
Egypt	Medium	Low	High	Low	Medium	Low
India	High	Low	Low	Medium	Low	High
Indonesia	Low	High	High	Medium	Medium	Low
Mexico	Low to medium	High	High	Medium	Medium	Medium
Yugoslavia	High	High	Medium	Low	Medium	Medium

No developing nation can be entirely uncommitted, but some nations are more committed than others. Commitment usually implies containment of freedom to act in terms of a country's needs and compulsions, unencumbered by political, economic and defence arrangements which by their very nature impose restrictions beyond the obvious. Quite often the true purpose of development is lost and the forward thrust neutralised in the process of satisfying the imperatives of balance of trade and contingencies of balance of power.

The fundamental features of an uncommitted society are thus a well-ordered political organisation, adequate resources and infrastructure, the will to change, and sufficient inherent strength to chalk out independent courses of action. Favourable trade and technology relations also help accelerate the processes of development without subservience to the interests of the major power centres such as in the case of Japan.

> The more basic political question, as we shall see, is not who controls the last days of the industrial society but who shapes the new civilisation rapidly rising to replace it. While short-range political skirmishes exhaust our energy and attention, a far more profound battle is taking place beneath the surface. On one side are the partisans of the industrial past, on the other growing millions who recognise that the most urgent problems of the world—food, energy, arms control, population, poverty, resources, ecology, climate, the problems of the aged, the breakdown of the urban community, the need for productive rewarding work—can no longer be resolved within the framework of the industrial order.
>
> This conflict is the super-struggle for tomorrow.[8]

The higher the level of infrastructural and emotional commitment to the existing social and economic order the lower the level of flexibility in contributing to the future. The uncommitted societies may well become the pace-setters for this emerging new world.

---

[8] Alvin Toffler, *Third Wave*, New York, William Morris and Company Inc., 1980, p. 32.

PART THREE

6. India—An Uncommitted Society

In absolute terms, India today possesses the world's ninth largest techno-industrial infrastructure. It has the third largest managerial cadre and trained manpower, one of the world's largest markets, fairly comfortable food reserves, a stable economy and adequate fossil fuel resources. It also possesses the world's highest availability and concentration of solar power and livestock population, which can enable it to build a decentralised energy and techno-economic system for its over half a million villages.

Far from using these opportunities for a massive thrust forward, many Indians have ignored the alarm signals and the inherent compulsions within its socio-economic system. In this process they have not only managed to confuse its objectives but have shaken the faith of the people in the system and those who run it.

But much that distorted our visions of the future all these years may soon pass into history. Something entirely new will have of necessity to emerge to replace the consumerist culture. What this will be is the greatest question mark of our times. Will it be based on justice, power or vested interests? Who will provide the moral leadership and have the dimension to transmit an integrated human vision of a new kind of progress to a tired and sick humankind?

A Leap into the Future

At this juncture in time, India is among the few countries which stand at the threshold of a new kind of leap forward into the future. But she has first to extricate herself from the illusion that what is happening elsewhere is progress. She can neither go back to her past nor race towards a borrowed future. Her destiny will be determined by the continuity of her history and culture. Her wisdom will be just as important as knowledge. It will depend upon her traditional ability to synthesise material welfare with social obligations and psychic evolution. But before India can set out to provide such a leadership she has to disown the Caesars who have conditioned her thoughts over the recent centuries.

The usurpation or domination of every aspect of human endeavour and the forcible acquisition or transference of most of the fruits, privileges and patronage of all such activities by those who control the politico-economic processes is the greatest impediment in the path of organisation of a just and equitable society. When a minimum of discipline and qualifications permit acquiring maximum rewards, acquiring the qualities on which the foundation of a society rests declines.

Irrespective of how many people exercise their franchise, any system of social organisation wherein every segment of society cannot escape the dominant trends in consumption patterns, or wherein minorities are subjected to racial or religious hatred, ceases to be democratic.

Up to a point the consumerist modes of production broaden the base of welfare and professionalisation in a democratic structure, but when the last stage of consumerism, with inbuilt processes of waste and destruction of the environment, takes over these become contradictions in terms and a confrontation between the democratic processes and the imperatives of consumerism develop.

Also in these last stages of consumerism the controllers of the techno-economic processes determine the contours of a society, but for all others the will to life takes precedence over the will to power. The voice of those who think is drowned by that of those who do not. This leaves all classes alike at the mercy of unscrupulous political exploitation and covert operations, for all political effort lacking a philosophical basis becomes merely opportunistic.

We made a beginning when Mahatma Gandhi projected a vision of non-violent, self-contained rural republics in terms of his own reaction to the Indian ethos. This view is now accepted by many thinkers around the world as a possible framework for escape from the consumerist jungle. Nehru projected another vision of modern India as a society protected from the confrontations inherent in systems which through the acquisition of world-wide resources set out to achieve and sustain wide differentials between and within different techno-economic systems. But in the continuity that is India, Gandhi and Nehru, like many others before them, illumined the pathways in periods of discontinuity and change. And they, like the eras they represented, have passed into history.

We are today the ringside observers of receding civilisations built on greed, guilt and genocide. India is fortunate in that long before her irrevocable commitment to a way of life the paralysis of will of the consumerist society has begun, and its distorted face is there for all to see. Through constantly relating these visions to the changing realities of India and the world, through an unshakable commitment to the Indian ideal of the unity of all life, India could collect the scattered but still visible remnants of those ideals which from time to time her great thinkers endeavoured to relate to her problems and environment. This is the only hope to wean her away from the short-lived but blissfully mystifying influence of a dying culture.

In this lies India's opportunity and hope. The shattering dreams of a dying culture, the search for new visions of an integrated life, her infrastructure of modernity and unfulfilled Gandhian dream of rural republics, her roots in the past and, thanks to Nehru, over a half century of broad-based contact with the world of the late 20th Century. And above all her people, intelligent, sensitive.

Only a leadership that can conceptualise a new framework for India in the world environment and will in these trying times have the political support and the will and capacity for total renunciation, can launch India on the chosen path of stability and welfare. Otherwise, she will move from one crisis of confidence and egoism to another.

The statistical signs of hopelessness and despair of the Indian condition only signify her freedom to act and are becoming the rays of hope for tomorrow. Only if the elite could cast aside the veil from over its eyes and see that there is much more to life and to India than the statistic of poverty, and that there is much more to the world-wide crisis than energy.

In surveying the territory of her future, she has been looking at the distant mountain peaks of consumerism and has projected her helplessness, and now with the shifting sands they can see that this was all an illusion. But there are many who still have their eyes and minds set on the consumerist mirage and cannot see the urban dungheaps of the 20th Century the country is being swept into.

POTENTIAL OF SANITY

But in spite of all the negative factors India is one of the major countries with a potential to make a transformation to sanity.

She has many options still open, but will she have the strength of will and agility to develop, in the words of Kirkegaard, "passion of the possible" in the universal sense against the illusions of a civilisation in rapid decay and retreat? The stability of India arose from the unbroken chain of continuity. Born out of a concern for eternity and indifference to time kept her firmly wedded to major human concerns and relationships.

But to step out of a cooperative society in centuries of decay and to relate it to the symbols and values of a consumer society has been a painful and destabilising process. The voices of dreamers, thinkers and visionaries have been drowned by the purveyor of consumerist utopias. The chain of unbroken continuity is being corroded by the lack of total vision, long-term objective and a sense of direction. But as Coomaraswamy said: "He who knows not whither he saileth, knows not which is a fair or foul wind for him."

The task before India therefore is:

> ... to relate the continuity of centuries to orderly intensification of the developmental or modernisation processes. This would involve the integration of the basic human values, with the compulsions and the demands which the successful emergence of a techno-economic system impose on the human system. The maintenance of human identity in the midst of defacing and dehumanising pressures imposed by the concepts of duality will become a prerequisite for the emergence of a new social order.

With irreversible and aggregating pressures the consumerist techno-economic systems are in a state of rapid decline. This points towards new designs for living. The existing assumptions, goals, strategies and tools are not just becoming obsolete but are disintegrating so rapidly that everybody is becoming disoriented.

Many frameworks have been presented and promoted as a basis for Indian development. The models are as far apart as outright nationalisation to the handing over of the industrial economy to multinationals. There are promoters of Japanese, North Korean, Singapore, Brazilian, Chinese approaches, and an entire variety of others. There are many others who recommend the Gandhian, the world order and zero growth models.

Limitless other possibilities are thrown in from within India and friendly or unfriendly proponents abroad. Each of these models may have risen from zero to considerable merit, but in terms of the totality of the Indian problem, and the environment and the realities within which such development has to take place, there are many consequential questions which need to be raised and answered before a total and irreversible commitment can be made to any particular techniques of development.

ROLE OF MIXED ECONOMY

A mixed economy created a broad consensus within the system and for a time contributed considerably in enlarging the base of the basic as well as consumer industries and agriculture. When the system was laying its foundations and creating an infrastructure, there were relatively fewer contradictions to cope with. Even the low technology rural sector progressed because of the relatively lower level of cultural penetration in the rural areas.

As the effects of such development started penetrating the structure of society and communications improved, many contradictions became apparent and created widespread instabilities in the socio-politico-techno-economic system.

These were the instabilities of rising expectations, widening income differentials, fast increasing unemployment, massive urbanisation and cultural penetration by consumerist ideas, emergence of new power centre to cope with. In recent years, the changing balance of world power, big-power confrontation and the armaments race, technological imperatives and the energy and resources crises have added another dimension to world-wide and Indian insecurities. And this has also exposed the vulnerability and raised questions about the validity of most techniques of development, particularly those in a state of aggregating crisis.

With minor shifts in emphasis from time to time, the country has continued on this path since independence. Any attempt to bring about structural changes in any of the parameters to correct the imbalances, be it in the form of land reforms or population control, constitutional changes for minor political restructuring, protection of cottage or small-scale industries or limiting expansion of larger industries, devaluation of currency, holding the price line for agricultural produce or introduction of computers in inefficient services, disciplining of some sectors to achieve high-technology objectives, gave serious jolts to the system. The farther India moved on the path of development the more constrained became its ability to bring about radical changes in the patterns of development. It had to suffer the consequences of the path of development it had chosen and live with its limitation.

Conceptual Clarity

The system thus lost its forward thrust, and reached a state of chronic imbalance at the same time. It can no longer reorient itself with minor shifts in emphasis, and broad-ranging structural changes and a higher level of commitment are called for. But before the country can even begin to approach such issues and create a national consensus on its objectives and role in the new world it must attain conceptual clarity on the issues at stake such as:

India's position in the economic crisis and armed confrontation of the superpowers and other world powers. The widening cracks in the worldwide resource and energy infrastructure are leading to an armaments race, terrorism, covert operations and intervention in the affairs of others. How does India assure its safety and security in this environment?

Can India launch herself on the consumerist road, the root cause of such a crisis, when energywise and resourcewise it cannot even sustain the present levels of urbanisation and development? Are the needs of decentralisation compatible with the needs of modernity, growth and correct international posture?

All knowledge of sciences and techniques is the human heritage. It is as much a part of human culture as the arts, philosophy and religion. But the institutions the greed of man has created for their exploitation should be a cause of concern. Vested interests are now subconsciously manoeuvring these very institutions to a leap to death. Should we accept or bemoan those institutions or project our future towards new paths with new institutions?

In the concluding decades of the 20th Century can we disown all known techniques for the alleviation of human suffering and for human betterment and revert to less tried and less acceptable techniques in today's environment? Many such techniques are propagated as part of the Gandhian model, zero economic growth and return-to-the-village slogans. How do we relate India to the present environment and compulsions with such techniques?

In other words, can we survive as a low-energy, low-technology society? Can we aim at a high-energy, high-technology society for safety and security and meet the need for resources? Can India align herself or become a follower of declining power centres because a few people in this country advocate such a course?

Will it be in our interest to encourage the penetration of the multinationals at the structural levels of the economy? Can we contain the further acceleration of disparities and avoid political manipulation of the nation?

Can anybody see 60 to 80 percent of India's expected population of about 950 million people by the year 2000 living in the culturally uprooted environment of a megalopolis in various stages of decay? Is the cultural disorientation of India the price to be paid for such development and, if so, where are the resources even to conceptualise such a possibility?

How do we propose to provide welfare if two-thirds of this population live in rural communities? To design a new socio-techno-economic system of this magnitude within a compulsive time scale will be a problem of colossal magnitude.

Need for New Visions

It will be necessary to project new visions, seek new directions and assess our advantages in creating a new socio-techno-economic environment more harmoniously related to the emerging realities. Only those who can retain their sanity in a world fast denuded of its energy and resources, caught in the cobwebs of duality, of mindless violence and purposeless life, can hope to attain such transformation.

If the imperatives of new sources of energy, and the intricate web of Indian society are any indication, pressures towards decentralisation of the techno-economic infrastructure will mount. These will fit like hand and glove with the Indian ethos, with India's geographic and resource pattern and a strong chain of continuity in Indian society. In other words, the need is to build from the bottom, where the problems are, upward rather than export the problems to urban centres and try to solve them in reverse.

The new sources of energy—sun, wind, biomass and waste recycling—are all compulsively oriented towards decentralisation, which in terms of India and most other developing societies mean relating them to an adaptive and friendly environment with a minimum of dislocation and social reorganisation, yet at the same time enlarging the productive, economic and welfare base of the community. Society will have to evolve its own social mechanism to establish a synthesis with an age-old culture to protect it from the corruptive, hypnotising and destructive influences of unrestrained consumerism. India is among the few countries in this category which can answer such a call.

In every conceivable term—psychic, emotional, intellectual and material—this could be expected or asked for from India, which though unbelievably old yet at the same time is incredibly young. The chasm between age and youth, the hallmark of a decadent, acquisitive society, has hardly touched the shores of the real India. This integrated wisdom and energy, relatively less disabled by the process of duality, can still stem the declining vision towards a sane future.

USE VALUE AGAINST COMMODITY-CENTRED PRODUCTION

It is increasingly realised that the use-value production techniques Gandhi advocated, transformed in terms of today's realities, could make an important contribution to retreat from the final stages of consumerism. This would however only be possible if:

—Technical modernisation of use-value economies could take place involving creative decentralised energy and technology infrastructure for rural communities.
—Stable linkages to protect the use-value productive processes from being swamped by the aggressive postures of commodity-centred processes.

The consumerist, commodity-centred techniques of production build high wage incentives into the productive processes, thus starting an irreversible trend towards the enlargement of commodity-centred production at the cost of use-value-centred activity. This can only be reversed through the reversal of incentives and introduction of equitable linkages between the two systems, one largely rural-based and the other largely urban-based. This would perhaps be the most logical 21st Century approach to modernity.

Uncommitted societies like China and India, largely because of their social organisation, the rural concentration of their population and comparatively much lower level of commitment to the industrial or consumerist mode of production, and above all their size and over one-third of world population, can provide the obvious experimental ground for the success of such an endeavour.

The tragedy in the Indian context has been that Gandhi's followers did not translate Gandhian thought to cope with the challenges of the late 20th Century. They worked under the misconception that Gandhi represented a return to backwardness. But he was not averse to modern means so long as these did not destroy the content of use-value-centred productive processes and these were not merely a stepping stone towards consumerist modes of production, particularly as applicable to basic commodities.

According to Ivan Illich, one of the greatest hurdles in the stable organisation of use-value-productive processes is the growing influence of the specialists in the consumerist processes. "The specialists who now dominate the creation, adjudication and implementation of needs are a kind of cancer without a precedent. They are more deeply entrenched than a Byzantine bureaucracy, more international than a world church, more stable than any labour union, with a tighter hold than any Mafia. Professionals tell you what you need and claim the power to present it to you."

The use-value, non-consumerist technique of production can only take off when the consumer can exercise the autonomy to consume or not to consume and yet survive in socio-economic and psychic terms in the prevalent system of social organisation or else the change of the system will become a prerequisite for the organisation of a use-value-centred productive process. Identification of the thresholds beyond which tools become oriented towards consumerist production therefore becomes imperative.

India obviously requires many techno-economic processes, which by their very nature would need planning, centralisation and techniques of advanced management. Many individuals with a knowledge of special techniques are required to operate such a system. This does not mean that they should be placed on a high pedestal and given incentives quite out of proportion to the rest of the society, as if they are making a special sacrifice in acquiring new knowledge.

Massive profits to the owners of enterprises, inequitable incentives to managers and operators, and attaching special values and symbols to the processes of consumption, are important contributory factors in accelerating the processes of consumerism. One by one, the tools in use cross the point of social criticality and intervene in social arrangements within a community, thus affecting its culture and distribution of political power and always working and exerting pressures in favour of the industrial mode of production.

This is an important cut-off point, to be managed either through tools, new social arrangements or incentives. It has to be understood that when a society launches on accelerating the productive processes through new tools it is performing many functions:

—Investing in capital-incentive tools.
—Making obsolete existing skills and training operators to handle new tools.
—Possibly throwing many operators out of work.
—In all likelihood converting hard physical labour by many into machine-watching by a few.
—Destroying the crafts of the community and making craftsmen an unnecessary appendage of the social organisation.

When technologies cross the threshold of the use-value system of production in such an environment, if there is inadequate regulation of the incentives between the use-value and commodity-centred systems, regression of the use-value system and unrestrained growth of consumerism commences.

Parallel Streams of Development

India's techno-economic and social development will have to follow many parallel streams, including the enlargement of the techno-economic base of rural communities with new and renewable sources of energy supplemented with fossil fuels, medium-energy agriculture, and an infrastructure for employment in agriculture, horticulture, animal husbandry and craft-based industries.

An entire spectrum of technologies—high, medium and low in

terms of appropriateness—will have to be adopted. But the social organisation will have to restrict the diversion of incentives towards high-energy, high-technology processes. The level of energy and technology used in a productive endeavour should be a social decision, and the multipliers and surpluses created in such a system should, instead of disturbing the balance and starting a trend towards higher and higher technologies, as is the case in most consumerist societies, create incentives for the use of appropriate technologies.

This would help balance the techno-economic system and contain the relentless pressures towards acquiring continuously aggregating incentives within the system. This would also contain the trend towards socially irresponsible, economically counterproductive, ecologically disastrous, high-energy, high-technology system leading up to the points of outright reversal in terms of socio-economic costs. These modern, integrated, self-contained rural communities will be the hallmark of the world of the 21st Century. And India has most of her options open to develop such communities without an outright reversal of the present techno-economic trends.

Development also includes a high-energy, high-technology centralised infrastructure of basic metals, energy, construction, chemical and other industries and research effort to support the decentralised sector of the economy, as also defence, transport and communication. This sector will have largely to be socially controlled though not necessarily socially owned. The incentive for those operating this sector, would have of necessity to compensate economic risk, long years of training, living in a centralised, ecologically hazardous and alienated environment. But the outer limits of the incentives will have to be restricted to contain the exodus of talents to the centralised urban sector. There are few parallels for such development elsewhere, and its success would rest on India's ability to establish adequate and viable linkages to synthesise the two parallel techno-economic streams into a mutually supporting, as against mutually destructive, whole. And the farther we are from the realities of today's world the more relevant can we be to the new world taking birth.

Manpower Resources

India has vast manpower resources, both in numbers and quality.

The aggregating numbers have added to her problems, that is not permitting the processes of social welfare to overtake the demands made on the socio-economic system, thus creating an economy of shortages, inflation, preemption of the benefits or welfare by a new, increasing disparities and social tensions. It is reinforcing deep-seated impressions of helplessness in dealing with problems of colossal magnitude and encouraging trends of self above society, thus further aggregating the very same processes.

To cope with the growing disorientation brought about by uncontrolled growth of population and its consequences, the bureaucratic system, while proliferating faster than the population or the economy, has become increasingly rigid, inefficient, unsympathetic and corrupt. Largely taking advantage of the socio-political trends and the opportunities inherent in the situation, everybody has got into the act to get his share of the spoils. Salary and perquisites are only a retainership fee, the real benefits accruing in the exercise of political or economic authority, howsoever minuscule. Even the humblest job in the structure of power and bureaucracy therefore provides both security and opportunity, a combination unknown in most other professions or areas of opportunity.

To meet the rising demands of this inflating bureaucracy, direct and indirect taxation is being forced beyond the point of counter-productivity by transforming national resources into a fairly respectable parallel or untaxed money economy. This is bringing about profound changes in the socio-economic system. It is squeezing out the elements of idealism, honesty and integrity and thus any hope for orderly transformation within the framework of urban based centralised social organisations. It is eliminating the middle classes, usually the bastion of stability in societies, particularly hierarchical societies. A few instances of upward mobility in this group are enough to push the rest on the downward path by generating centrifugal forces within it.

It has also shifted the emphasis from investment in productive enterprises to generate employment and wealth to properties and speculative activities. Uncontrolled and blatant generation of fictitious wealth of such magnitude is striking at the very foundations of the economic system. Large percentage of the urban population is being manoeuvred out of its security through these processes of manipulation. The rural-urban shift is acting as a conduit to transfer many of these trends, instabilities and unrest into the rural areas.

While many of these trends may explode as a consequence of market pressures, they will bring about in their wake irreversible changes in the system and psyche of the people. The power centres seeking redress will proliferate to a point that it will become impossible to neutralise them through local, regional or national action. Decentralisation of the socio-economic system will become compulsive even to begin to approach such large multiplicity and variety of issues and problems.

In this world-wide ferment of the late 20th Century there is no valid system of authority here or elsewhere which can control, direct or create new social organisations. Destruction of existing systems is possible, but creation of new ones outside the inherent compulsions is not.

The negative aspects of large and proliferating population are obvious. The social frame within which we have been endeavouring to bring about radical changes on such a scale have proved totally inadequate, and have in fact compounded the problems manifold and increased the uncertainty and risks in the situation.

The decentralised polycultural population linked through the hidden bonds of the Indian psyche, is one great asset for continuity, stability and orderly change. The capacity to absorb shocks displayed at regular intervals all through history is one of the great sources of strength and a protective veneer. All peripheral social delinquency ultimately gets sucked into the ocean of the Indian reality and loses its structure, form and movement. The metropolis of today will become the Angkor Wat of tomorrow, lost in the cycles of Indian eternity. Because the strength to India has always been her total indifference to time and her undying concern for eternity. Her subconscious, intuitive links with reality have ever been the foundation of the Indian psyche, rarely understood but always present.

On the other hand, the structure of affluence has its foundation built on the physical sciences and the duality between physical and psychic. After centuries of experimentation, search and transfer of this knowledge to material advancement, the message reaching the highest forums of science is that the search for the next stage of advance must return to man himself, because he in fact is that reality—"Thou art that", the lesson every Indian learns even as a child. This vast manpower subconsciously imbued with what the fraternity of science learns at the frontiers of new knowledge could be a major factor in assuring the continuity of what the Indian elite was ready to trade off with decaying consumerism.

On the material plane a wide variety of attributes, talents, markets and resources can be harnessed to further the objectives of welfare in a new, integrated framework more related to the path of continuity and stability and less to dynamism and explosion. The containment of infant mortality through the use of new medicines and techniques has contributed greatly to the increase of population in developing countries such as India.

Survival of the fittest also means the body's immunity from disease and reduced use of drugs. This has now been altered to an increased dependence on drugs and the disturbance of the natural balance in the human system. However, no acceptable and reliable system of reduction of births has yet been devised, nor the social consequences of uncontrolled permissiveness ascertained. Can a permissive society and orderliness go together? Permissiveness is all engulfing, it cannot be contained in narrow boundaries.

The net ecological and developmental effect of population increase is marginal compared with the proliferation of consumerist products. The resources, energy and environmental costs of adding 30 million new automobiles is at least ten times greater than the same number of new births. This is not a justification for uncontrolled population growth, but population control alone is not enough. We need new lifestyles.

Trained manpower has drawn its sustenance from the fountainhead of consumerism. As the Indian imperatives will not permit the unrestrained growth of consumerist institutions, the search for new directions has become compulsive. India has enough material resources to create a society without want, a welfare society forever dedicated to seeking the meaning and purpose of life. This indeed appears to be the only answer to centuries of aimless drift to a decline of vision, destruction and chaos.

India is well endowed with resources essential to human survival, even those which are becoming a cause for concern in affluent societies.

Clean Air

In spite of heavy pollution in the major urban centres, the quality of air in most of India remains relatively clear of lethal wastes.

Water

The underdeveloped groundwater of the Indo-Gangetic plain is one of India's great resources. Her great rivers cover vast areas and have for millennniums brought prosperity to large sections of the country. But, above all, nature's great boon, the monsoon, which bestows on India a yearly blessing of hundreds of millions of cubic metres of water, washing her mountains, fields, deserts and shores, can be harnessed with known techniques.

Food

After centuries of neglect, India's soil is being transformed to achieve enhanced productivity. The efforts of the last three decades, supported by natural factors, are reflected in increased productivity and reduced dependence on others. Many future transformations would still be necessary to reduce the impact of soil destroying and polluting remedies and to rebuild the soil in neglected areas with ecologically non-destructive techniques. Here again our marginal commitment to such techniques gives hope for ecological sanity and increased productivity at the same time.

Energy

While the prospects of achieving high levels of self-sufficiency in the production of oil and other nonrenewable energy sources in the 1980s to sustain India's infrastructure of basic industries and to expand it to meet her projected requirements, appear to be bright, her greatest strength and hope lies in the new and renewable energy sources. With a minimum commitment to the high-energy infrastructure, with a decentralised population pattern, with the high intensity of solar radiation throughout the country most of the year makes, this is the most abundant and inexhaustible source of energy obvious for India.

There is no existing energy infrastructure in rural India of any consequence to scrap, and she can therefore innovate appropriate technologies to build a new infrastructure to exercise the solar option to its maximum advantage, at a minimum cost. In creating a new infrastructure for the solar age, we shall elevate the already decentralised rural communities to the new status of integrated, self-contained, humane communities of the future. An unfulfilled dream of the visionaries of the future, a new energy source, a new socio-techno-economic infrastructure, a new blood-stream in the arteries of age-old continuity awaiting to be rejuvenated by the sun it has worshipped for millenniums. In this process, the innovative capabilities of hundreds of million people for constructive action will be released.

Recycling of animal, plant and human waste through scientifically devised systems for generating energy in the form of methane gas and soil-sustaining effluents is another area of considerable potential. There are large untapped resources to be brought into service in a decentralised rural society while affluent societies in an energy straitjacket are concerned largely with salvaging their own highly centralised oil-based energy infrastructures. India can move right on towards creating new energy links between sun and soil.

For integrated development of this type, tools have to be placed in focus. Energy and tools are twins. Tools only optimise use of energy. The energy of coal was optimised through the steam engine, and that of oil through the internal combustion engine. Appropriate technologies cannot be innovated without first placing the dominant source or combination of sources of energy in the correct perspective. In an agricultural community with a high incidence of solar radiation, the role of this source of energy for cooking—constituting some 50 percent of the total energy used—and drying crops could be an important consideration. The availability of animal and plant waste will provide the basis for generating methane to operate machinery, lighting and some cooking and soil improvement with slurry from biogas plants.

Combination of the two sources could help meet a broad spectrum of needs of such a rural community. It would set energywise sustainable, technologically feasible limits on the entire socio-economic process and the extent and nature of the use of human and animal power and the range of extension of human capabilities.

It would help release the innovative capabilities of the entire community and give it ability and freedom to recognise the point beyond which tools would interfere with social arrangements and create compulsions for higher energy concentrations, thus disturbing the balance in the energy system and destroy the twin-sisterly relationship between the available sources of energy and tools in use. In the emerging societies of the future, choice of the dominant energy source and range of tools in use will become major social decisions, whether exercised at an individual, community, state or national level.

HIGH-ENERGY INFRASTRUCTURES

The areas of development requiring high energy concentrations will have to function under a different set of compulsions, a high level of social organisations and discipline. Apart from the complexities inherent in energy systems and matching technologies, the questions of international availability and social consequences, both intended and unintended, become an important factor in all such considerations. And if such a system is linked with the world trade and the defence system, which in other words means the consumerist orientation of the sector of the economy, the technological differentials and consequent disturbances between the international system and within the national system become difficult to contain. Realisation of a higher level of welfare, except within the framework of the existing institutions, now in rapid decline, becomes difficult even to conceptualise.

How to lay the foundations of the integrated rural communities of the future and save them from the approaching havoc brought about by the rapidly obsolescent energy, technology and human infrastructure, is perhaps the most important issue which should concern thinkers and leaders of uncommitted societies. Before we can even begin to approach this we must however build buffers between the international system and the national high-energy, high-technology infrastructures. At the same time we must retain objectivity in national terms, another important task facing the political processes.

Convergence of international corporate monopolies at the deep structural levels of the society without adequate and enforceable safeguards against their influence can be disastrous to attaining these objectives. To earn foreign exchange through international remittances, the floodgates of inflation have been opened and the orderly growth of the urban system barred. Once such intrusions take place there will be no retreat from the synthetic modernity of consumer societies. Any arrangement to achieve a balance between high-energy, high-technology centres and integrated rural communities will become unsustainable. And this will be to the detriment of the interests of the large mass of people and unplanned drift towards an uncertain and insecure future.

Whose future are we conjecturing? If only the elite would project an image of it and the power structure delivers it, the future would be like somebody else's, born out of somebody else's compulsions, transmitted through somebody else's instruments, geared for somebody's profit, and will project somebody else's insecurities. It may only meet goals of output and consumption.

The true future can however only emerge if people do not just consume but participate in the productive processes and develop capabilities to innovate improved tools and satisfy their creative urges. These decisions have moved away from the people in the rural areas in developing countries with the aggregation of concentrated high-energy, high-technology systems.

Wherever commitments to a dominant energy source reach a point of no return because of increasing pressures on the existing infrastructure, the regression of the socio-economic system begins. There will now emerge a trend towards the use of decentralised renewable energy sources. Whatever may happen in the short term, the long-term consequences of an energy shift cannot be escaped. Compulsion for such a shift will provide the necessary psychological environment for change The innovation of appropriate tools will be another consequence.

The highest socio-economic multipliers can only be achieved through:

—The optimisation of new decentralised energy systems through research and development. These new energy sources or combination of these sources may vary widely on a regional or even community basis between solar, wind, biomass—all manifestations of the central source, the energy of the sun.
—Employment intensive but human and animal energy amplifying technologies and tools for agricultural operations.
—Investment in non-agricultural rural sector for a symbiotic interaction between a labour-intensive sector and energy-optimised agriculture. This would help create stable and sustainable linkages with high-energy centres.
—Basic infrastructural support will provide the greatest potential for creating integrated communities.
—Balancing rural and urban earnings and relating them to relative purchasing power. With runaway inflationary food costs,

urban housing and industrial and social inputs, this balancing act is steadily moving into the realm of possibility.
— Sophisticated science and technologies can also be used in improving simple tools left in a state of neglect and disuse.
— The concept of equating high culture with high energy has reached the end of the road and is fast fading away because it has also meant graduating from coal smog to nuclear radiation, unemployment and alienation.
— The less privileged have been growing in numbers and the privileged in affluence. That is how compulsions for industrialisation and urbanisation begin. Only by placing tools in perspective will population regulation be possible.
— The cost of providing jobs with identical levels of welfare to the urban poor has been many times higher than in the rural areas, and these costs are escalating. Partial transfer of resources to integrated rural communities will provide much larger multipliers than in the urban metropolis.

In the context of India it will not be necessary to disrupt the present structure of basic industries but to integrate it in long-range plans for the future. Over a period of time a state of disequilibrium within the planned overall system will end, and it will reach a state of dynamic balance in terms of socio-techno-economic parameters. In the process not only could the foundations of high-energy, high-technology infrastructure be laid but an orderly and protected growth of integrated self-contained rural communities will become possible. Thus liberation will also be attained from the international consumerist, defence, foreign exchange and energy straitjacket. Compulsive and planned obsolescence of machines, materials and men, which in the name of progress and affluence have played havoc with world-wide human energy and material resources, can be avoided.

Through small communities, the choice of lifestyle and self-renewal would shift from the board rooms, the media-promoted value system, the psychology of envy and consumerist addiction, to the individual and the environment. The objective is to build a society, not a production system, establish norms of behaviour in harmony with the fundamental laws and not an externally promoted standard of living. Emphasis will have to shift to socially useful activities and not socially useless illusions of affluence. Housework, farming, handicrafts, home building, all subsistence related activities, will become noble professions and not symbols of backwardness.

A new post-industrial society will be born out of the crumbling structure of consumerism. The social organism, the people, energy resources and the will to live are all getting exhausted through physical, mental, aesthetic and spiritual excesses performed in the processes of assuring the continuity of a system in decline.

For about the last century the condition of social organisations have largely been determined by technological change around an established and dominant source of energy, that is oil. In recent decades there have been some minor, largely centralised, intrusions by nuclear and other sources of energy and matching technologies.

This is expected to change as the technological edifice becomes unsustainable. In the organisation of a new society we have to take care that we do not cross the threshold beyond which even new sources of energy, such as the sun, achieve social progress at the cost of equity. Beyond this point, social arrangement and the institution of participatory democracy begin to wither away.

7. Three-Tiered Development

The bulk of infrastructural investment for self-contained rural communities will have to be provided through cooperative action, the contribution of human labour and the provision of a catalyst by district, state or regional agencies. Emphasis should be on organisation, incentives and expansion through common effort and not through doles.

Externally imposed economic and technological structures seldom survive, and instead of building and expanding the welfare of the community, the surpluses are sucked through conduits provided by an army of middlemen into urban centres and accelerate the processes of consumerist production. Decisions concerning what should be provided rest with the urban elites, and in turn with international trends and distorted images of good life.

Thus the images of the future shift from green pastures and idyllic rural republics to tenements in urban slums listening to blaring film music, aimlessly moving with crowds, providing mass markets to promoters of consumerist utopias.

Community direction of energy resources, such as fuel wood on the village common, developing a pool of available animal and plant and other wastes to generate biogas, the equitable distribution of gas and effluent from the biogas plant at a fair price or as a proportion of at sight waste contribution.

Maintenance of community or individually owned services such as water supply for irrigation and domestic use, schools and on-the-job training, local dispensary, marketing assistance and transport linkages, if any, cultural revival and entertainment.

Important and effective incentives to ensure the stability and viability of such a rural system would be:

—Satisfaction of basic human needs in a pleasant agricultural and rural environment.
—Generation of adequate surpluses to provide facilities for health, education, entertainment and trading off with urban

and semi-urban centres for goods and services not available in the immediate environment.

— To provide adequate employment opportunities in agriculture and agriculture-based industries and services and in an infrastructure for social welfare. The cumulative economic and social benefits should be at par with those in semi-urban and urban centres.

— Widespread understanding that human aptitudes and longings are broadly diverse and expressed in a variety of ways. To try to contain these in the tightening straitjacket of uniformity and monocultural development tuned to the consumerist mode of production is the cause of broad-spectrum excesses, fragility and vulnerability of the entire social structure. The shift from rhythmic continuity and flow of life to irrelevant concerns about every aspect of human existence and satisfaction of ever-growing needs is a dangerous trade off with human sensitivities, diverse cultures and awareness.

Aggregating instabilities and risks in the world environment can provide the psychological frame for the reversal of the suicidal course and the integration of the new social organism with the processes of polycultural development, environmental harmony and larger welfare. This is not a retreat to backwardness but a projection of new and sustainable images of the future.

Semi-Urban Centres: Shock Absorbers

These semi-urban centres will provide buffers between rural communities and high-energy, high-technology concentrations in the metropolis. They will protect these communities from the cultural shocks which the urban centres continuously receive internationally and transmit to the environment. Population movement to these centres should be aptitudinal and not through flow of incentives.

These semi-urban areas will play an important role in providing employment to the surplus manpower from the widely dispersed but adjoining integrated rural communities. Apart from a higher level of services and maintenance organisation, employment opportunities should relate to satisfying basic needs, processing and distributing surplus agricultural produce, and rural-oriented ancillary industries.

Against the bulk of energy requirements of the integrated rural communities which will come from new and renewable sources of energy, part of the high-concentration energy needs of these communities till the year 2000 will be met through fossil fuels and existing technologies. The energy flow through the system, though not the incentives, may be 50-100 percent higher than in rural communities.

URBAN CENTRES AND METROPOLITAN CITIES

These centres symbolise human technological achievements, alienation and social decay at the same time. They represent the single-pointed concentration to achieve consumerist and power goals by satisfying the organisational needs for complex high-technology systems. As the schism between the needs of these systems and the social organisation widen, the system starts breaking down, or it follows the human breakdown. Most high-concentration systems have either arrived at or are in the process of arriving.

Ultimately, every technological process needs renewals which in terms of the consumerist societies means continued development and new markets. But if growth is stopped because of any cause, including the limitations physical phenomena impose, the social organisation pushes technologies in destructive directions, automobile industries towards tanks and other military vehicles, nuclear technology towards nuclear weaponry, space technology towards missiles and military aircraft, electronics towards surveillance and espionage, chemical industries towards chemical and germ warfare, and even psychological techniques serve an offensive purpose.

A system of high incentives and rewards sustains the last stages of consumerist production and increases risks to the world system. Urban metropolises transmit the inadequacies of the dominant international systems to the other world systems, and thus accentuate the processes of concentration and destabilisation at the same time. The per capita energy flow through these systems is of the order of 10-20 times that in the semi-urban or rural environment. A sizable proportion of this energy does not provide useful work and gets lost in the processes of aggregation and concentration.

As we move farther from the socially useful sectors of the economy largely satisfying basic human needs, we simultaneously move away from integrated rural communities. The content of socially useful production in these communities may be about 80-85 percent. In the urban metropolis at the other extreme we may be performing less than 20 percent of socially useful work at a relatively much higher cost.

In other words, the processes of consumerist development have of necessity to transfer surplus manpower and resources to increasingly less useful sectors of the economy to increase the viability of the system. In affluent societies, when the productive or socially useful systems start breaking down, the crisis reaches critical proportions because of the weight of socially less useful and service sectors. This is one of the major causes of crisis of industrial consumer societies.

In India, the wage structures, though out of line with per capita income, are still within adjustable limits and apply to only a fraction of the working population, thus giving the country the option to determine where to get off from the compulsive movements of technologies. This is no longer possible for economies with an exceedingly high rate of commitment to high-energy, high-technology, high-wage, low market-growth economies. This means that in terms of socio-economic needs India and other uncommitted developing societies are still in a position to evolve appropriate technological levels to balance techno-economic systems.

On the economic front the fog is lifting. The dark clouds which threaten consumerist societies with the triple danger of inflation, recession and unemployment may do relatively less damage to India, an economy of perpetual shortages and rising consumer demands. The country has a well-established techno-economic infrastructure though adequately modern, yet is not plagued by the technological rat race which is continuously making capital and consumer equipment and products obsolescent with hardly any peripheral economic or utility advantages.

India is a synergy society, where the behaviour of the whole is totally unpredictable and different from the behaviour of its separate parts. Many attempts to weaken the parts have quite often led to strengthening the whole. But the tragedy is that the business of the whole is left to those who neither understand the behaviour of the part nor of the whole. In the human cycle all man-made laws have a life span. Only physical and metaphysical laws are permanent and can form the basis of human organisation. India has a store-house of this knowledge to draw from.

While the cost of finding solutions to problems which create insecurity and wars is much less than the cost of wars in socio-economic, human and synergetic terms, wars and armaments have become the language of affluence. When all other base for the survival of the social order cease to exist, societies are compelled to resort to destructive techniques to create illusions of safety.

Utopias or near utopias do often emerge at turning points of history, only their life span varies with the wisdom of the community. All these centuries the black trinity of ownership, power and knowledge has led to dualism and oppression. It would therefore need an entirely new orientation to achieve:

—Continuity of our existing traditional institutions.
—Injection of new knowledge and to relate it to the national psyche. Change of structure only is not enough. A change of consciousness is also necessary.

Equity Through Energy Planning

The processes of development are in reality the conversion of low-energy societies into increasingly higher-energy societies through energy converters. When such converters are optimised the processes of development also accelerate. At this point, the minimum introduction of energy and matching technologies provide the highest multipliers to the economic system. In the early stages of development small energy inputs provide large benefits at minimum cost. In low enegry sectors such as agriculture and rural development in developing countries, every minor improvement in technology or increase in energy supply rapidly increases welfare, with widespread implications.

Improvement in tools, cooking equipment, provision of fertiliser and water to agriculture and maximisation of labour in peak periods can make an important contribution to the socio-economic welfare of the community. At this level both the use of energy and its benefits are maximised. Most of the energy of the community is directed towards socially useful activity and can be performed with locally available low-energy converters.

This kind of development is least destructive of the environment and sustainable energywise. It should be the cornerstone of India's developmental policies. But such development cannot be imposed;

it can only be innovated by the communities, themselves in terms of their needs, resources, cultural background.

Energy Relationships

The total per capita energy used in India at present is between 250 and 300 kilograms of oil equivalent. While urban centres consume over 500 kilograms per capita per year, the share of rural communities is less than 100 kilograms per capita.

To improve agricultural production, provide employment and increase the level of welfare, it would be necessary to increase the energy flow either directly or in the form or energy-related inputs to about 300 kilograms of oil equivalent.

By the year 2000 the potential to supply two-thirds of this requirement, equivalent to 70 million tons of oil, can be met through renewable sources such as animal, plant and human waste, firewood, sun, wind and water power. The balance third will come from outside inputs. This three-fold increase in energy flow can improve the level of welfare by a factor of five.

Semi-urban Centres

With the changing population pattern, size of the community, location of service organisations and some ancillarisation and linkages with the metropolitan areas would need a largerflow of energy, about 800 kilograms of oil equivalent of which 50 percent should be provided through new, renewable sources. Though the level of welfare in these communities will improve substantially compared with their present condition, it should not be such as to create a major migration of population from the adjoining rural communities.

Metropolitan Centres

With large concentrations of population larger energy flows are required. The need for high-energy converters to process basic metals and large energy transformations would need around 1500 kilograms per capita of oil equivalent and would have linkages with the international system and intermediate semi-urban areas.

At least 80 percent of the energy requirements for this development will have to be provided till the year 2000 through non-renewable energy sources. Through processes of energy conservation, using the most appropriate energy source for an application, improvement of the public transport system needing low per capita energy consumption, a high level of security, welfare and infrastructural support can be developed in countries like India.

If such a strategy is followed, the total annual energy need for India by the year 2000 will stabilise at minimum and sustainable energy levels (see enclosed table).

Such a strategy will achieve these objective among others:

—Reduce the pace of commitment to fossil fuels and start a trend towards new and renewable sources of energy based on an adequate mix that can be sustainable rationally.
—Rural areas are already using renewable sources such as firewood, animal and plant waste, human and animal labour. But the use is inefficient. The system can be optimised through adequate technological inputs as in the bioconversion improvement of energy converters, systematising of energy plantations, introducing wind and solar technologies. It may perhaps take more than 20 years to achieve the targeted energy use-level but the direction of change should be clear and commitments judiciously made.
—Wherever possible the bulk of energy requirements should be met through new sources. Strategic introduction of non-renewable sources can help the process of transformation to the new sources in a planned manner, but major infrastructural commitment to oil or other fossil fuels should be avoided.
—Metals and infrastructural inputs can be supplied from high-energy centres. Fabrication of energy converters depending upon complexity could be undertaken in semi-urban communities.
—The mode of transport in integrated communities should be a bicycle and between communities and semi-urban centres animal-driven and motorised public transport.
—For the next quarter century high-energy, high-technology centres will be compelled to follow international trends—not for equity but for survival. The process of regression of affluent consumer societies has already begun. Continuation of their lifestyle depends largely on their ability to widen the areas of complementarity with the resources and opportunity-rich developing world. In this lies both India's safety and oppor-

ESTIMATED RURAL-URBAN ENERGY RELATIONSHIPS IN INDIAN DEVELOPMENT IN THE YEAR 2000

	Population	Total energy (mil. tons of oil eq.)	New & renewable sources—solar biomass, hydro, wind geothermal agriculture, gaste, etc.		Oil & Gas (tons of oil eq.)	(percentage)	Other non-renewable sources such as coal (tons of oil eq.)	(percentage)
Per capita energy use			Energy units (tons of oil equivalent)	percentage				
Metropolitan high energy high technology centres	$1500 \text{ kg} \times 125 \times 10^6 = 1875 \times 10^6$ say 190×10^6		38	20	57	30	95	50
Semi-urban area	$800 \text{ kg} \times 125 \times 10^6 = 100 \times 10^6$		40	40	20	20	40	50
Rural areas	$300 \text{ kg} \times 700 \times 10^6 = 210 \times 10^6$		136	60	42	20	42	20
		500×10^6	214		119		117 = 500	

At an oil price of $40 a barrel the cost of oil energy used in the early 1980s will be of the order of US $12 billion (40 million tons at $300 per ton). This will increase to $36 billion by the year 2000 (that is if the prices remain stable at the present level). This means a per capita oil cost of $17.50 in 1980 and $36.00 in the year 2000. The total energy, including non-oil, is of order of $60 per capita.

The United States is spending $1000 per capita on energy alone and Western Europe $600.

tunity. We should not permit ourselves to be caught in the consumerist syndrome or deflect from the areas of our strength to serve the purposes of the affluent against the millions seeking hope.

—The areas of our opportunities are enlarging. There are hopeful signs that we have adequate oil and other energy resources to be self-sufficient sometime in the 1980s. But however large these resources, they will not carry a nation of 950 million people (by the turn of the century) for any length of time on the path of consumerist squandermania to which the affluent nations are committed. Addiction and envy will not be the route to stable sustainable societies of the future.

—All this will not be a process of retreat for the developing societies but a search for new directions and a moderate shift based on equity, justice, continuity and security. And through this approach we can begin to relate the processes of modernity with age-old continuity. Our guiding star will be the decentralised, integrated, self-contained communities.

—These can become the symbols of the future India, centres of human excellence against technological excellence. Many countries take pride in having moved all their population to major urban centres and megalopolises. By reversing this trend and by placing man and his instruments such as energy and technology in proper perspective India will be able to accomplish the loosening of the mental straitjacket so necessary to seek new directions.

—The key to the emergence of new directions would lie in our ability to create acceptable images of the future, a system of values, incentives, balances to protect the decentralised communities from the illusions as against realities of progress. There is also a compulsive need to establish linkages between the international system and the high-energy technology system in India and such a system and the rural system.

—The present world-wide crises, disorientation and insecurity of affluent societies, the destructive armaments race, all point towards new directions for those who dare. This may make all the difference for uncommitted countries like India.

—Most affluent societies are chained to the present and unable to seek solutions. A consumerist institutional framework can serve only material ends. This monocultural development knocks down all the supporting pillars of the social order, making it highly vulnerable.

The polycultural base of India is its greatest safeguard. We have our options open to decide how the social milieu relates itself to the institution that will emerge, largely as a result of our own efforts and partly because of the processes of modernisation which India set in motion in the post-independence period.

The institutions of affluence are disintegrating rapidly because of the illusion that these are being threatened from without, while in reality the paralysis is from within.

This is therefore not meant to be an invitation to poverty but a return to sustainable images of the future.

Index

Adams, Henry, 23
Agricultural-based, liquid fuels, 124-25
Agriculture, production trends in, 91-95
Akbar, 47
Ashoka, 47
Aurobindo, 47, 51, 59

Bell, Daniel, 175
Bhagawad Gita, 47
Britain, techno-economic system in, 84
Brown, William, 26
Buddha, 47
Bureaucracy, failure of, 37-39
Byzantine bureaucracy, 205

Carson, Rachel, 31
China, power centres of, 153; techno-economic infrastructure of, 171-72, 187-89
Club of Rome, reports of, 31-37
Coal resources, 140 43
Communist monolith, 171-72
Consciousness, Indian concept of, 45-49; and knowledge, 56; Western approach to, 42-45
Consumerism, development stages of, 15-18
Coomaraswamy, 51, 200
Copernicus, 21
Cosmic order, 60-62
Cottrell, W. Fred, 117

Counterproductivity, of agricultural products, 91-95; and atomic development, 95-96; and GNP, 87-88; grand finale of, 82-84; of human phenomenon, 98-99; as prime mover, 80-82; and productivity changes, 78-80; strategy for, 74-76; and techniques of medicare, 88-91; unpredictable elements in, 76-77

Dance of Shiva, 51
De Chardin, Teilhard, 31, 42-45, 52, 58
De Tocqueville, Alexis, 167
Development process, effect of energy planning on, 221-22; energy relationship of, 222-26; Gandhian approach, 71-74; and semi-urban centres in, 218-19, 222; and urban centres, 219-21
Developing societies, 172-86; classic examples of, 175-81; effect of multinational relations on, 184-86; relation with communists, 181-84
Dualism, Western thought on, 58
Dulles, John Foster, 172

Ecological system, and pollutants, 102-6
Education, impact of counterproductivity on, 96-97
Einstein, Albert, 49
Ellul, Jacques, 24, 44, 79
Energy, economy of livestock, 122-

23; future perspective for, 143-44; instruments of, 114-18; policy in agriculture, 118-21; policy planning for, 132-34; resources of, 123-29, 136-43; subsidy for, 134-35; use pattern for, 135; uses of, in urban community, 129-32

Fear psychosis, 13
Fishing, changing trends in, 93-94
Fuller, Buckminster, 27, 58
Future Shock, 31

Gallop, Frank, 78
Gandhi, M. K., 47, 152, 198-99, 204-5
Gross national product (GNP), 87-88
Goals for Mankind, 34-35

Human future, effect of continuous growth on, 13-14, 26-27; fundamental challenge for, 30-32; and industrial revolution, 23-26; one dimensional approach to, 19-23
Human life, disparities and discontinuities in, 40-42; Indian concept of, 47-48; stages of, 46-47
Human society, duality in, 51-52; Indian approach towards, 53-56
Humanology, 73-74

I Ching, 19
Illich, Ivan, 205
India, development strategy for, 217-26; energy relationship for development of, 222-26; energy sources in, 211-13; future perspectives of, 198-99; high-energy infrastructures in, 213-16; man-power resources in, 207-10; mixed economy of, 201-2; need for conceptual clarity for, 202-3; need for new visions, 203-4; power centres in, 152-54; sanity potential of, 199-201; techno-economic infrastructure in, 172-73, 189-93, 206-7, 213-16; use-value production techniques in, 204-5

India's energy requirements, for agricultural production, 120-21, 148-50, for food, 120, 123-25, 145-46; for rural community, 119, 148-50
Industrial revolution, 23-26
Intermediate technology, effect on craft culture of, 66-71; and Gandhian approach to development, 71-74
International power centres, 156-62
International system, need for modifications in, 34-35

Jorgenson, Dali, 78

Kahn, Herman, 26
Kalidasa, 47
Karma, Hindu philosophy of, 54
Kirkegaard, 200
Kissinger, Henry, 187

Laszlo, Ervin, 34
Life, limits to quality of, 88-91
Limits to Growth, 31-33
Livestock energy economy, 122-23, 125-26

Man, reality of, 54-56
Mankind at the Turning Point, 32
Mao Zedong, 153, 171, 177, 179, 188
Marshall Aid, 155
Marx, Karl, 27
Mead, Margaret, 97
Meadows, Dennis, 32
Medicare, techniques of, 88-91
Mesarovic, Mihajlo, 32
Metropolitan centres, flow of energy in, 222-26
More with Less, dictum of, 27-30, 58

Nasser, 189
Nehru, J.L., 154, 168, 172, 189, 198-99
Nietzsche, Friedrich, 59, 110
Nineteen Hundred and Eighty Four, 61
Nixon, Richard, 187

Index

Noise pollution, 106
Non-alignment, movement of, 189
Nuclear energy, 136-40; promise of, 95-96

One-dimensional approach, limitations, 19-23
Orwell, George, 61
Ouspensky, P.D., 19-20
Overcentralisation, problems of, 85-86

Patanjali, 47
Pestel, Eduard, 32
Physicist vs. mystic, 49-51
Pierre, 42
Pollution, control of, 106
Populism, politics of, 84-87
Power, *see*, energy
Power centres, assessment of, 164-65; in developed countries, 154-55; international, 156-62; suctional-diffusional elements of, 155-56
Productive process, growth and stability of, 74-75
Protective mechanism, 83

Ramakrishna, 47
Reagan, Ronald, 155
Reshaping the International Order, 33
Rhythmic energy, 59-60
Roosevelt, Franklin D., 155
Rural community, energy need of, 119-20, 123-25; incentives to stability of, 217-18; urban shift, 131-32
Russell, Bertrand, 52

Sanity, potential of, 199-201
Semi-urban centres, 218-19, 222

Sankaracharya, 47-48
The Silent Spring, 32
Solar energy, 127-29
Suctional-diffusional, force of, 155-56, 163
Sukarno, 189
Superindustrial revolution, challenges of, 37-39

Tao, 48-49
Tarot, 19
Taylor, Henry Osborne, 23
Technological reversal, escape routes to, 108-9; factors for, 106-8; impact on unemployment of, 111-13; process of, 96-106, 109-11
The Will to Power, 59
Tinbergen, Jan, 33
Tito, 189
Toffler, Alvin, 31, 36-38

Unemployment, impact of technological reversal on, 111-13
Uncommitted societies, 197-216
United States, power centres in, 154-55; techno-economic status of, 169-71
Uranium resources, 138-40
Urban community, centres, 219-21; energy perspectives for, 129-32; energy relationship within, 222-26
Urban elitist groups, 173-74
USSR, techno-economic activities in, 171-72

Vivekananda, 47

Western thought, dualism in, 51, 58
World order, models for, 39-40